Sea-Brothers

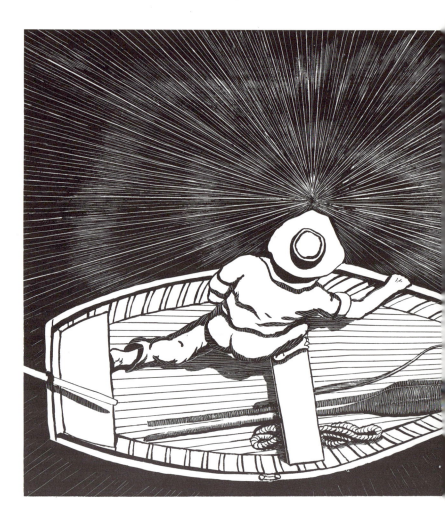

Sea-Brothers

The Tradition of
American Sea Fiction from
Moby-Dick to the Present

Bert Bender

Drawings by Tony Angell

upp

UNIVERSITY OF PENNSYLVANIA PRESS
Philadelphia

*(Frontispiece) It was only the great deep prisms
in the blue water that the old man saw now. . . .*
—Hemingway, *The Old Man and the Sea*

Drawings © 1987 by Tony Angell

Library of Congress Cataloging-in-Publication Data

Bender, Bert.
    Sea-brothers: the tradition of American sea
fiction from Moby-Dick to the present.

    Bibliography: p.
    Includes index.
    1. Sea stories, American—History and criticism.
I. Title.
PS374.S4B46   1988   813'.009'32162   88-17321
ISBN 0-8122-8124-1

For Charles
In Memory of Our Mother,
Fern Evelyn Stroud, 1913–1984

Contents

Preface: The Sea, and the Blue Water of It

One hundred years ago Herman Melville published *John Marr and Other Sailors*, reclaiming after half a lifetime his old identity as a sailor-writer. Then, continuing until his death to write of the sea as he had known it during "the time before steamships," he gave us *Billy Budd, Sailor*, the first masterpiece of American sea fiction since *Moby-Dick*. Melville's last two sea books provide a consoling sense of symmetry in his life and career. And they also mark a time in literary history when the tradition of American sea fiction that had preceded *Moby-Dick* was beginning to renew itself. Like Melville in his last years, a number of Americans who were born between the 1860s and 1890s knew that they were witnessing the last days of sailing ships; knowing also of the narrative tradition that had been established by James Fenimore Cooper, Richard Henry Dana, Jr., and Melville, they either wrote of the sea because they had been there or went to sea because they wanted to write. When their work began to appear in the late 1880s and 1890s, they could not have known that Melville was himself at work on his last sea books, but for some of them at this time, long before the Melville revival, *Moby-Dick* was as alive as it was for W. Clark Russell, the English sea-writer to whom Melville dedicated *John Marr and Other Sailors*. *Moby-Dick* contributed powerfully to a resurgence of American sea fiction that has developed over the last hundred years, first in the work of several writers who are now unknown, and then in the work of Stephen Crane, Jack London, Ernest Hemingway, and Peter Matthiessen. My aim in *Sea-Brothers* is to describe the literature of this tradition and to assess its contributions to American literature as a whole.

In his "Inscription Epistolary" to *John Marr and Other Sailors*, Melville referred to the traditional elements of sea fiction in a way that provides a clear sense of how he had given them new meaning and emphasis in *Moby-Dick* and how they would continue to figure in American sea fiction of the twentieth century. As Melville had been the first writer to give such profound emphasis to the sea itself, it is this that he most admired in Russell's work. Claiming for Russell the "naval crown in current literature," he wrote,

> What writer, so thoroughly as this one, knows the sea, and the blue water of it; the sailor and the heart of him; the ship, too, and the sailing and handling of a ship? And, withal, in his broader humane quality he shares the spirit of Richard Henry Dana, a true poet's son, our own admirable "*Man before the Mast.*" (*John Marr*, 5)

The "sea, and the blue water of it" is the essential element in *Moby-Dick*, the medium in which Melville could pursue "the ungraspable phantom of life" (*MD*, "Loomings"). Believing that all life is joined in the sea, from the "multitudinous, God-omnipresent, coral insects" (or brit) to the great whales and simple seamen, he projected his sea-vision of the Creation— the natural source of Christian and democratic values that he celebrated in a brotherhood of sailors before the mast (*MD*, "The Castaway"). The ship and the sailing and handling of it, the domain of mere officers, is clearly secondary in this formulation, as it is in Melville's own sea stories. Moreover, in the blue water Melville also found the compelling logic of his famous cetology. It was a revolutionary idea in the tradition of sea fiction that biological thought is not only relevant but indispensable in any effort to know the sea life. All writers in the tradition of American sea fiction after Melville have been guided by biological thought, but from the cataclysmic new point of view that was created by the *Origin of Species*. The kind of biology (i.e., "natural theology," as it is known to historians of science) from which Melville developed the cetological materials of *Moby-Dick* had collapsed, and no writer thereafter could depict the ocean reality without focusing on the mechanism of evolution by natural selection or, more important, attempting to interpret its implications for the human community. Like their precursors, Cooper, Dana, and Melville, the seamen-writers of this tradition have celebrated experience, but with their sense of the new biology. Determined to know this new life that was also an old life, they have embraced it actively, with a sense of adventure and courage, seeing the tradition through a dark transitional period beyond the ages of sail and steam on into the age of atomic-powered vessels. But they have retained the sense, as suggested in Hemingway's "On the Blue Water," that the sea *life* is still our essential subject, well worthy of Melville's old passion for "the sea, and the blue water of it."

As I have suggested in the foregoing paragraphs, *Sea-Brothers* presents a number of related theses: that the tradition of American sea fiction has not only survived the passing of the sailing ships, but has developed with renewed vitality late into the twentieth century; that the writers of this tradition have self-consciously followed Cooper and especially Dana and Melville in claiming the authority of their experience as seamen; that in its development over the last century, the tradition has been most influenced by the values and vision of Dana, Melville, and Darwin; that, despite the lamentable changes in maritime experience and the history of ideas which the tradition has recorded over the last century (particularly in the expiration of the sailing life and in the faith-testing development of Darwinian thought), it has found in the seaman's elemental existence a compelling basis for celebrating life, even with all the violence of its evolutionary thrust, and for affirming the democratic values that are inherent in a brotherhood of working seamen; and that the sea's influence on American literature has been more profound and continuous than is presently accepted, exceeding even that of the inland frontier.

Should *Sea-Brothers* prove successful in establishing this last, slightly heretical, proposition about the sea's role in American literature, one might still justifiably respond that even though the tradition of American sea fiction has endured for these 150 years, surely it cannot long survive. For if the expanding continental frontier temporarily overpowered the American imagination between 1850 and 1890, can we not expect that the developing frontiers of outer space will inevitably exert a dominant influence on our literature? Can the sea continue to speak to the modern imagination? Although such questions are beyond the scope of critical inquiries into literary history such as those I offer here, they are not irrelevant in this context. It is in keeping with the spirit of Melville to give at least brief consideration to such questions, as he did himself in asking, "Does the Whale's Magnitude Diminish?—Will He Perish?" (*MD*, chap. 105). He thought it fitting to raise such questions, "inasmuch . . . as this Leviathan comes floundering down upon us from the head-waters of the Eternities."

In claiming that the "eternal whale will survive," Melville expressed his faith in the Christian possibility. But the contemporary writer will be more inclined to pose other questions: Can the ocean itself survive the pollution by man? Can we avoid depleting the ocean resources? Can man himself, indeed, can *life* survive on earth? Perhaps such questions are more legitimately the concerns of oceanographers and ecologists, or of institutions like the Cousteau Society or Greenpeace. But they are very strongly implied in the most recent masterpiece of American sea fiction, Peter Matthiessen's *Far Tortuga* (1975). And surely some future writer's imagination will find in the ocean-discoveries of contemporary science some stimulus to his or her wonder, as Melville did in the biological thought of his own time. What might the contemporary studies in bioluminescence, for example, reveal about that phenomenon that has generated so much mystic speculation among writers of all time? Or, what might we discover about life in general in the ongoing studies involving the intelligence of dolphins and whales? What might an imagination like Melville's make of the recent discovery of life forms that exist at deep-sea vents in complete independence of light, using the process of chemosynthesis? The "only ecosystems on Earth supported by terrestrial instead of solar energy," these vent communities could be the only survivors on earth should some disaster cause the sunlight to be blocked (Jannasch 78). In a darker vein, what might a contemporary Melville make of the recent developments in naval warfare whereby dolphins and whales are trained to serve as living torpedoes? And what might we discover about the history of man through marine archaeology or, in more specific reference to the literary past in this tradition, as a result of such recent dives as those on the *Scourge* (of Cooper's *Ned Myers; or A Life Before the Mast*), the *Titanic*, the *Commodore* (of Crane's "The Open Boat"), or the *Somers*?

One is tempted to imagine, almost as Melville did in celebrating the whale's immortality, that man *will* find his way in the ocean world, whether through advances in oceanography and marine biology (as in the mining of the ocean floor or aquaculture) or through renewed achievements in the ancient mode of knowledge we treasure when a voyaging spirit goes to sea.

Acknowledgments

Several parts of this book were presented as papers at annual conferences of the American Culture Association, in its section on Literature of the Sea. The group of scholars who gather there each year—the only national forum for this subject—have contributed significantly to our knowledge of American literature, and for the support and helpful commentary I have received there I wish to thank in particular Haskell Springer, Dennis Berthold, Robert Madison, Donald Wharton, Gail Coffler, and Lee Werth. I also thank my friends and colleagues at Arizona State University who have read parts of the manuscript and offered suggestions and encouragement: Roger Murray, Willis Buckingham, Robert White, Paul Morris, and the late Leo Levy. And I am indebted to five other scholars who took time to read parts of my manuscript in its very early stages and, in their positive responses, helped me see it through: Edward Leuders, Jay Martin, Thomas Philbrick, Hennig Cohen, and James Millinger.

For permission to reprint parts of essays that have appeared previously I wish to thank the editors of *American Literature, The American Neptune, Studies in the Novel,* and *The Journal of Narrative Technique.* And for permission to reprint a number of photographs I am grateful to Harvard University, Yale University, the Massachusetts Historical Society, the Huntington Library, and, in particular, Ellen (Mrs. Archie) Binns, Mrs. Nancy Hallet Woods, and Donald Mortland.

A number of fellow commercial fishermen whom I have had the good fortune to know over the last twenty-five years on Cook Inlet, Alaska, have also contributed to *Sea-Brothers,* though unwittingly—by demonstrating in many ways that there is a brotherhood of the sea.

For her constant patience and encouragement, her questions and suggestions, and her shared love of literature, I am particularly grateful to my wife, Judith Darknall.

The College of Liberal Arts and Sciences at Arizona State University has provided financial assistance toward reproducing the accompanying drawings by Tony Angell. And for the drawings themselves I can scarcely begin to thank Tony Angell, my friend of many years. His contributions to this book began long ago, when he gave me his own copy of *Moby-Dick*. His dramatic illustrations of scenes and themes from the literature I have discussed in *Sea-Brothers* are a high form of criticism, in the tradition of Rockwell Kent's illustrations for *Moby-Dick*. Indeed, in his drawing of the leaping marlin we can see his tribute to Kent. But his renderings of the sea life and the biological themes that are so prominent in this literature derive from his own life's work and from the rare combination of his gifts as reader, author, naturalist, and artist.

Note on Texts

The texts I quote in *Sea-Brothers* are as indicated in the Bibliography. However, in my chapters on Melville and Stephen Crane, I have documented references to several of these texts in an unconventional manner and refer to chapters (by either title or number) or parts of a text rather than to pages. I use this method in consideration of the general reader who might be expected to have one of the many editions of *Moby-Dick*, *White-Jacket*, or "The Open Boat," for example, but not the authoritative text that is often available only in university libraries. This method is particularly helpful in discussions of Melville's novels, with their many short chapters. Thus, a reader with any edition of *White-Jacket*, *Moby-Dick*, or "The Open Boat" can easily locate passages cited as (*WJ*, "The Jacket Aloft"), (*MD*, chap. 102), or, in reference to "The Open Boat," (pt. 6). I have referred to particular chapters by title rather than by number when the title seems to echo the sense of the quoted material, as in "A Squeeze of the Hand" or "Faith and Knowledge." Finally, in my discussions of Melville's work I have used the following abbreviations: *CP* (*Collected Poems of Herman Melville*), *GSW* (*Great Short Works of Herman Melville*, my text for several of Melville's shorter pieces, including "Benito Cereno" and *Billy Budd, Sailor*), *IP* (*Israel Potter*), *M* (*Mardi*), *MD* (*Moby-Dick*), and *WJ* (*White-Jacket*).

Sea-Brothers

"Accept my best thanks for your kindness & believe me fraternally yours—a sea-brother—."
Excerpt of letter from Herman Melville to Richard Henry Dana, Jr., 6 October 1849.
Courtesy of the Massachusetts Historical Society.

1

The Voyage in American Sea Fiction after the *Pilgrim,* the *Acushnet,* and the *Beagle*

You got to have confidence steering.
—Ernest Hemingway, *To Have and Have Not*

Richard Henry Dana, Jr., "changed the face of maritime fiction" in America by publishing his "*voice from the forecastle*" in *Two Years Before the Mast.*[1] He influenced James Fenimore Cooper's last sea novels and prepared the way for many less significant books that immediately capitalized on the new value he had given to the actual experience of ordinary seamen (Nicholas Isaacs's *Twenty Years Before the Mast,* 1845, for example); he initiated "the genre of journey narratives that was to play a central role in the literature of the American Renaissance"; and, most significantly, he exerted a profound influence on the career of Herman Melville (Philbrick, Introduction, 22–23). On first reading *Two Years Before the Mast,* shortly after returning from his own first voyage, Melville had been filled with "strange, congenial feelings" of being "tied and welded to you by a sort of Siamese link of affectionate sympathy," as he wrote to Dana on 1 May 1850 (Leyda). At the time he confessed this "shock of recognition" (we might say) that he had felt ten years earlier, he thought that he was "half way in the work" of writing *Moby-Dick.* Four months later, he would feel and express the more famous "shock of recognition" that he knew in his relationship with Nathaniel Hawthorne and that would alter the course of his voyage and prolong it. But he had already made a career for himself as a sea-writer. And beginning in the 1890s, long before the Melville revival, his work would begin to exert a recognizable influence on the tradition of American sea fiction, as successive generations of writers looked not only to Dana as an example, but to Melville and, increasingly, to others, just as Melville had looked to Dana in 1849. Having completed two books, *Redburn* and *White-Jacket*, which were heavily influenced by *Two Years Before the Mast*, Melville acknowledged his debt to Dana, asked for his help in defending *White-Jacket* if its "aggressive" condemnation of "the usages to which a sailor is subjected" should offend the public, expressed his "thanks for your kindness," and signed himself, "fraternally yours—a sea-brother" (Leyda 1:317).

But in the beginning, before the existence of any sea-brotherhood, there was the sea itself. Long before man began to recognize that, as with all life, he had emerged from the sea, he was irresistibly drawn to the sea—as the biblical mind was drawn into the watery darkness that existed before there was light, when "the Spirit of God moved upon the face of the waters" (Genesis 1.2); or, not so long before the sea origin of our own species was scientifically established, as Melville was drawn to the water when he wrote that "meditation and water are wedded forever" (*MD*, "Loomings").[2] It is unimaginable that any individual of any culture or any time could ever see and think about "the all-contributed and all-receptive ocean" without yielding to wonder (*MD*, "The Blacksmith"). And certainly no one who has ever experienced or even imagined the experience of being alone *in* the "open ocean" can deny the "intolerable lonesomeness" that Melville describes: "The intense concentration of self in the middle of such a heartless immensity, my God! who can tell it?" (*MD*, "The Castaway"). I would begin this study by observing that no *one* person can tell it, finally, not even Melville himself. Most cultures of the world have a literature or at least a mythology of the sea, and these have developed over time as man's knowledge of himself and of the sea has evolved. The dimensions of this literature are determined in general by the ancient mythic appeal of the voyage and, no doubt, by something like the oceanic feeling that Freud discussed in *Civilization and Its Discontents*. Although he could not "discover this 'oceanic' feeling in [him]self," he contemplated his friend's description of it as "a sensation of 'eternity,' a feeling of something limitless, unbounded—as it were, 'oceanic.' . . . [It] is a purely subjective fact, not an article of faith; it brings with it no assurance of personal immortality, but it is," his friend thought, "the true source of religious sentiments" (11). The similarity between this feeling and that which Melville expressed about the actual ocean is clear: "In landlessness alone resides the highest truth, shoreless, indefinite as God" (*MD*, "The Lee Shore"). And without this sense we cannot appreciate the essential motive for all literary voyages: the desire for renewal, discovery, light. Just as in antiquity, troubled nations initiated voyages of exploration and discovery as part of their strategies for survival, the troubled mind finds its own natural strategy in the mythic or literary voyage. Moreover, as Melville suggested, the mythic voyage and the myth of Narcissus are as inseparable as are the concepts of self and other. The voyaging mind can never escape itself, and the myth of Narcissus is no less hauntingly relevant in twentieth-century sea fiction than it was when Melville cited it in his conclusion to the incomparable meditation on water that he gave us in "Loomings": "That image, we ourselves see in all rivers and oceans. It is the ungraspable phantom of life; and that is the key to it all." Melville wrote his great sea book at a time when the Western mind seemed more troubled than ever with the old problem "Know thyself." But if the voyagers of successive generations have envisioned the phantom of life from different perspectives and therefore in different forms from that which Melville saw reflected in the water, none can claim to have grasped it. In this study of American sea fiction from 1851 to the present I hope to describe what a series of American writers have seen of themselves—as individuals in life, as Americans, and as participants in our maritime heritage—as each has turned to the sea in his own time.

The larger story of the sea's influence on American literature has never been told.[3] It would be a monumental undertaking that would require contributing scholars working in poetry, fiction, nonfiction narrative, drama, history, and natural history. But the first chapters in the study of American sea fiction have already been told by Thomas Philbrick in *James Fenimore Cooper and the Development of American Sea Fiction* (1961). Sensing that "*Moby-Dick* is too often thought of as the first appearance of the sea in American literature," Philbrick demonstrated how Cooper's twelve sea novels justify our remembering him as the "originator of the sea novel," as well as the creator of the Leatherstocking tales (vii–viii). Moreover, Philbrick helped us to see that the national character as it is reflected in literature is more deeply influenced by maritime experience than many imagine it to be: "During the first half of the nineteenth century, the sea occupied much the same place in the imaginations of many Americans that the continental frontier was to fill after 1850" (1). Philbrick develops this general thesis in his chapters "The Sea in American Literature Before 1820," "The Work of Cooper's Contemporaries," and on Cooper's own sea fiction. He shows clearly that our early literature of the sea is characteristically romantic (in the manner of Byron) and nationalistic, and he explains how Cooper liberated "the fictional treatment of the sea from the satiric tone of Smollett." More important, he describes Cooper's three "essential services" to the tradition of sea fiction: he created "a tone which, by evoking a mood of high romance, lent the narrative the aura of legend"; he created, in the middle period of his sea fiction, a tone or "atmosphere of sober realism, an atmosphere that gave the seaman the full dignity of a human being and made him, as a man, the center of the reader's concern"; and in his last novels, particularly in *The Sea Lions* (1849), he transformed "the sea novel from a fiction in which the chief interest depends on the depiction of a special occupation and a special environment into a fiction in which that occupation and environment become the symbolic ground for the dramatic conflict of ideas and attitudes having universal significance" (264).

Philbrick's work laid the foundation for succeeding chapters in the history of American sea fiction such as those I offer here. But we must challenge Philbrick's conclusion that the tradition of American sea fiction virtually drew to a close in 1851 with the publication of *Moby-Dick*: "Melville's work, like the great clipper ships which were its contemporaries, was something of a historical anomaly, the last, magnificent flowering of a plant that was dying at the roots" (262). This conclusion mistakenly assumes a parallel between the intensity of American maritime industry and the production of sea literature; it distorts the significance of a single element among the three that are featured in traditional sea fiction, the sea, the sailor, and the ship; it suggests that only sailing ships can excite the writer's imagination; and it does not account for the very impressive quantity and quality of American sea fiction that has appeared during the last century and a quarter. There certainly was a "golden age" of American sea fiction in the 1840s, as Jeanne-Marie Santraud has called it (77). Far from ending in 1851, however, the tradition extends into the present and includes significant contributions to American literature by Stephen Crane, Jack London, Ernest Hemingway, Peter Matthiessen, and the several less famous—by now even forgotten—writers whom I discuss in Chapters 7 and 8: Thornton Jenkins Hains, James Brendan Connolly, Arthur Mason, Felix Riesenberg, Bill Adams, Lincoln Colcord, William McFee, Richard Matthews Hallet, and Archie Binns. The tradition continued intermittently after *Moby-Dick* in Melville's own work, in *Israel Potter*, "Benito Cereno," *John Marr and Other Sailors*, and *Billy Budd, Sailor*. Then, coinciding with Melville's return to writing sea fiction in the late 1880s, and partly in response to the careers of Dana and Melville as well as to the certain but prolonged expiration of the sailing life, the tradition began to renew itself in the 1890s. A series of writers who were born between the 1860s and the 1890s and who went to sea as working seamen—most of them as sailors before the mast who knew full well that they were, in effect, chasing ghosts: these men produced a considerable volume of serious and highly acclaimed sea fiction between the 1890s and the 1930s. And in the work of Ernest Hemingway and Peter Matthiessen the tradition has reasserted its vitality in the latter half of the twentieth century.

The tradition as it exists after *Moby-Dick* is greatly transformed, indeed, from what it had been in its golden age. This transformation, evident in Melville's career in the difference between *Moby-Dick* and *Billy Budd*, can be broadly attributed to the passing of the sailing ships, to the related developments in America as the western frontier advanced and then closed officially in 1890, and, by far the most important, to the repercussions of Darwinian thought. American sea fiction after 1890 reflects the revolutionary significance of biological thought by emphasizing the sea itself as the essential element of sea fiction. As I hope to explain in Chapter 2 on *Moby-Dick,* the tradition's emphasis on biology and the sea originated with Melville, particularly in the cetological materials in *Moby-Dick.* But Melville's cetology conforms to the kind of biological thought ("natural theology") whose foundations were destroyed by the *Origin of Species* in 1859. Thus, when the tradition began to renew itself late in the century, it would be shaped not only by what Dana and Melville had made of their voyages on the *Pilgrim* and the *Acushnet* but by what Charles Darwin had produced from his voyage on the *Beagle.* From the 1890s onward, the course of American sea fiction is determined largely by the writers' intent to explore the implications of our biological reality, or, as Hemingway suggested in his original title for *The Old Man and the Sea,* "The Sea in Being." Still, transformed as it was in responding to the eclipse of sail by steam and, more important, to the new biology, the tradition is continuous from Melville to the present in two major ways: first, in its return to Melville's sense that the "ungraspable phantom of life"—all life, "the same sort of life that lives in a dog or a horse"—is at least more nearly graspable in the watery world than it is ashore (*MD,* "Loomings," "Brit"); and second, in its tendency, as in Melville, to affirm and celebrate this life.

To suggest a two-stranded continuity in American sea fiction from Melville to the present is, more deeply, to suggest its essential Americanness. That is, the tradition has survived this enormously stressful period by finding in the sea experience a way of preserving, perhaps more fully than in any other discernible tradition in our literature, some of the essential values and qualities of our cultural heritage: a desire for simplicity that entrusts itself more to the faculty of wonder or the naive vision than to reason, analysis, or authority; a corresponding faith in the democratic individual and the validity of his "enormous sense of inner authority"; and, first in Melville and then with an increasing sense of desperation in many others toward and after the turn of the century, a willful commitment to something like "the Christian belief in equality and brotherhood" that had contributed so much to the "extraordinarily concentrated moment of expression" that F. O. Matthiessen described in *American Renaissance* (656, vii, xi).[4]

We can see a good deal of the essential Americanness of our tradition of sea fiction during these years by comparing its characteristic way of responding to Darwinian thought with that of Joseph Conrad. Conrad began his career as a sea writer during the years when our tradition renewed itself, and he knew, knew of, or influenced a number of writers in that tradition, including Morgan Robertson, Stephen Crane, Jack London, Lincoln

Colcord, and Peter Matthiessen. But his response to Darwin is as different from that of the typical American sea-writer as is his fictional point of view. Writing from the captain's point of view and exhibiting his sympathy with the captain's need to maintain his discipline and dignity, he could not sympathize with the simple seaman—particularly one like Ishmael, who could "marry" a cannibal like Queequeg, sit down with him "all the morning long" while squeezing spermacetti, and affirm, "let us all squeeze ourselves into each other; let us squeeze ourselves universally into the very milk and sperm of kindness" (*MD*, "A Squeeze of the Hand"). Rather, as Redmond O'Hanlon has remarked in *Joseph Conrad and Charles Darwin* (1984), "Conrad's quiet heroes . . . command the symbolic ship of society, guide their vessels safely through the worst that nature blindly can do either from within or from without, the brute or the storm, and they carry out their life's work upon the surface of the sea, and sail home, as Marlow says, to 'touch their reward with clean hands'" (121).[5]

By contrast, in their characteristic tendency to affirm the vitality of a simple, primitive existence, even when, after the *Origin of Species*, that requires an affirmation of our animal nature, writers in the American tradition have (with a certain willfulness) created heroes whose promise is identifiable with their primordially organic, even reptilian, power: Wolf Larsen, in whose flesh is embodied the "essence of life," that "which lingers in a shapeless lump of turtle meat and recoils and quivers from the prod of a finger" (London, *Sea-Wolf*, 14); the "old shell-back," Captain Crojack, in Thornton Jenkins Hains's *The Voyage of the Arrow* (1906); Captain Glade, "the old spouter," in Felix Riesenberg's *Mother Sea* (1933); Harry Morgan, in Hemingway's *To Have and Have Not* (1937), whose love-making is compared to that of a loggerhead turtle (112); or Captain Raib, the turtle fisherman in Peter Matthiessen's *Far Tortuga* (1975). Whereas such characters as these in the tradition of American sea fiction have a natural affinity with water and survive, often as fishermen, because they are successful participants in the elemental order, Conrad views water with a good deal of alarm, often associating it with "the unconscious depths [and] the speechless desires of the instinctive evolutionary past" (O'Hanlon 60–61). Thus it is only when he wishes to portray characters as evolutionary degenerates that he portrays them as reptilian—as when "the captain of the *Patna* oozes and secretes," or the chief engineer remembers "the sinking *Patna* as having been "full of reptiles" (59, 63). As O'Hanlon observes, these "reptiles" are the degenerate "old mankind" who had "flowed" aboard the *Patna*:

> Below the officers upon the bridge (ostensibly, at least, the seat of reason, discipline, and command) the old mankind, in search of the impossible fulfilment of wishes for immortality, "upheld by one desire," in a mystical dream of eternal self-preservation, "flowed forward and aft,

overflowed down the yawning hatchways, filled the inner recesses of the ship—like water filling a cistern, like water flowing into crevices and crannies, like water rising ever silently within the rim." (60–61)

American writers of this period were also interested in the idea of degeneration, but, expressing a democratic faith in the common man, they tended to construe it in a positive sense: the idea itself—degeneration as "progressive simplification of structure," as opposed to "progressive elaboration"—is inherently appealing to writers who wish to idealize the simple sailor (Chamberlin 266). Conrad, on the other hand, recoils from the degenerate Kurtz and the uncivilized darker races with a sense of horror that parallels Max Nordau's fear of those "who place pleasure above discipline, and impulse above self-restraint," for this is to wish "not for progress, but for retrogression to the most primitive animality" (O'Hanlon 49).[6] With his abhorence of mysticism (a characteristic tendency among American writers of the sea, as D. H. Lawrence noted with approval in his essays on Dana and Melville: "The Best Americans are mystics by instinct" [Lawrence 125]), and with his distrust of "democracy" and the idea of "universal brotherhood" (O'Hanlon 127), Conrad could not bear to read Melville.[7] Nor could he have agreed with Jack London's attitude toward degeneration as expressed in The Mutiny of the Elsinore (1914). The Elsinore's crew were a degenerate bunch of "gangsters," "broken men and lunatics" (51), but London suggests that they, along with the ugly new iron ships, were the products of a brutal industrial society, the price of "progress" according to the Social Darwinist captains of industry. Although the representatives of social order do put down the mutiny aboard the Elsinore, London mocks them, reserving his sympathy only for the deformed ordinary seaman, Mulligan Jacobs. London sees at least some hope in Jacobs's defiance and intellectual power; among other things, he expresses his very low opinion of Joseph Conrad's latest work (96). Similarly, Conrad would have been repulsed by Eugene O'Neill's suggestion that the degenerate seamen in The Hairy Ape might eventually enable them to reclaim their dignity as human beings from the higher but far less vital social order that had victimized them.

Despite the enormous changes in American life between the time of Melville's first sea books and London's Mutiny of the Elsinore—especially the disruptive new biological thought—there is an obvious continuity in their work that derives from their shared sympathy with the common seaman. Similarly, despite the years that separate Conrad from Darwin, one can see a good deal of Conrad in The Voyage of the Beagle (which appeared long before "Darwinian" thought had evolved)—in the naturalist's "astonishment" at first seeing a "barbarian" "in his native haunt": "One's mind hurries back over past centuries, and then asks, could our progenitors have been men like these? . . . I do not believe it is possible to describe or paint the difference between the savage and civilized man" (506–7). In view of "the march of improvement, consequent in the introduction of Christianity throughout the South Sea," evident in the recent rise of Australia "into a grand centre of civilization," Darwin confessed that it was "impossible for [himself as] an Englishman to behold these distant colonies, without a high pride and satisfaction. To hoist the British flag, seems to draw with it as a certain consequence, wealth, prosperity, and civilization" (508).

Still, however continuous the tradition of American sea fiction has been in its sympathy for the common seaman, the way has not been easy. Traditionally, the chief problem has been how to resolve the conflict between the ideal of brotherhood and the reality of discord necessitated by the Darwinian view of warring nature and the Spencerian idea of the survival of the fittest. As I have already suggested, in preserving this essential ideal, these writers from Melville to Peter Matthiessen have survived a long spiritual struggle only by exerting something like what William James would call the "will to believe": a kind of "faith"—even when "our evolutionary theories and our mechanical philosophies" make it impossible "to worship unreservedly any God of whose character [nature] can be an adequate expression"—"in an unseen order of some kind in which the riddles of the natural order may be found explained"; a "Belief that life *is* worth living" (James, *Will*, 43, 51, 62). Indeed, American sea fiction from Melville to the present dramatizes a long series of crises of belief that usually correspond to crises in navigation, and for this reason there could be no more fitting epigraph for a study of these voyages than the line spoken by Harry Morgan in Hemingway's *To Have and Have Not*: "You got to have confidence steering" (67). Moreover, in their choices to go to sea and to claim the authority of their sea experience, the sea-brothers of this tradition exemplify the optimistic tendency of many other American writers, as in Thoreau, to affirm life by actively embracing it. That is, as Thoreau's desire or will "to live deep and suck out the marrow of life" led inevitably to his sense that life *is* "sublime" and that he could "know it by experience," the sea-brothers of our tradition imply in their emphasis on actual sea experience that the will to believe and the will to live are perhaps indistinguishable, as James himself suggests in his "belief that life *is* worth living." This tendency to affirm life is particularly evident in our literature of the voyage, for the decision to embark upon any voyage, actual or literary, is an implicit act of faith. Invariably, as our sea-brothers from Dana to Matthiessen have looked back at their actual voyages or sea experiences (usually in their youth), they have affirmed and celebrated that life, realizing, as does Eugene O'Neill's autobiographical character Edmund, that the "high spots in [his] memories . . . [are] all connected with the sea" (*Long Day's Journey into Night*, IV).

The difficult but ultimately successful struggle for faith is clear in Melville's early work, but after 1850 it is first evident in the conflict between Ahab's doubt and Ishmael's faith in "the great God absolute, the centre and circumference of all democracy" (MD, "Knights and Squires"). By 1891 the struggle had become a much darker one for Melville, but, like many other late nineteenth and early twentieth-century writers, he could accept the apparent fact of evolution by natural selection and still deny that it should "exclude the hope," as he had written in the epilogue to Clarel: "If Luther's day expand to Darwin's year, / Shall that exclude the hope—foreclose the fear?" In Billy Budd, Sailor, comparing Claggart with "certain uncatalogued creatures of the deep," the "serpent" and the "torpedo fish," Melville suggests that the Darwinian interpretation of evolution need not exclude traditional Christian thought (GSW, 476). In the fallen world that he envisioned, "the envious marplot of Eden has more or less to do with every human consignment to this planet earth"; thus, as he links Claggart's satanic power to the dark evolutionary past, he sees that even Billy is flawed: this story "is no romance," Melville insists (439). But though Billy's illiteracy, his general simplicity, his feminine beauty, and his flawed speech would be conclusive proof of his degeneracy to Max Nordau and Conrad (who would see a resemblance between Billy's weaknesses and Lord Jim's), Melville proclaims Billy an innocent. Billy's "stigmata" (symptoms of degeneracy, as Nordau and his predecessors B. A. Morel and Cesare Lombroso would refer to them) may be taken as part of Melville's effort to portray him as "an angel of God!" (478).[8]

No major writer in the tradition after Melville was able to invoke a biblical reality, but all would regard life with a degree of wonder and mystery, often reflecting in their imagery of the natural world a lingering sense of Christian values. And each would sustain himself in his voyages by affirming his faith in the possibilities of brotherhood. Stephen Crane, who had written that "God lay dead in heaven," discovered the "subtle brotherhood of men" in "The Open Boat." Jack London, his faith in a possible brotherhood of American workers badly shaken, still envisioned a time when the common man might, by organized action, successfully engage in the social-biological struggle for power and justice; and in his last story he affirmed his faith that a primitive, simple fisherman could somehow save him from civilization. At a time when, to many, the world seemed hopelessly wasted, Hemingway could affirm the life force in a simple, brutal man, Harry Morgan in To Have and Have Not. Despite his despair over the "stench of comrades" (Green Hills, 145), he could, by an extreme act of will, affirm the bloody but biologically innocent or "saintly" brotherhood among his warring seamen in Islands in the Stream (362); and in his parable of a simple fisherman he could willfully accept his role in the brotherhood of all creatures, ritualistically affirming the voracious biological order. Finally, in Far Tortuga, a story that returns to the Caribbean waters where Columbus first found the New World, Peter Matthiessen envisions the island of Far Tortuga as "a shadow in the eastern distance, under a sunken sky, like a memory in the ocean distance" (336) and tells of half-brothers who make their separate ways on the spiritually and ecologically depleted "bleak ocean." Yet even in this "modern time" Matthiessen suggests through his strongest characters that the capacity for simple dignity, gentleness, and brotherhood among men can survive.

In addition to our democratic heritage, there is undoubtedly a simple psychological basis for the prominent theme of brotherhood in American sea fiction. That is, in the actual shipboard circumstances of men working together to survive, in their having to endure the mutual hardships of storm, shipwreck, and sometimes brutal authority, there is a powerful cohesive force, a natural bonding in actual experience. For this reason, and because of the typical forecastle point of view, there are surprisingly few mutinies in our sea fiction; when they do arise (as in "The Town Ho's Story" in *Moby-Dick*), they are usually understood to be natural outbreaks that lead to a natural and healthy resolution. If, after shipwreck, in the precarious confinement of an open boat, the conflict among individuals struggling to survive is intensified because of limited water, for example, the bonds of equality and brotherhood are correspondingly strengthened and sometimes justifiably enforced even by brute strength, as in the story "Thirst" by Lincoln Colcord, or in the conclusion of *Far Tortuga*. Once the dinghy in Crane's "The Open Boat" has pulled away from the sinking *Commodore* (thus escaping the absolute threat to brotherhood and equality posed by the desperate survivors who remained with the ship because there was no space in the dinghy), an ideal brotherhood exists. And even under the most desperate circumstances in our maritime experience, after the sinking of the *Essex*, the survivors willingly submitted to the final horror of cannibalism. In such stories and experiences there is surely a universal necessity that extends well beyond our national identity. Still, these are typically American stories that bespeak our democratic heritage and "a common faith," as John Dewey suggested in his book by that title. Writing about the "religious values inherent in natural experience," Dewey wrote that "whether or not we are, save in some metaphorical sense, all brothers, we are at least all in the same boat traversing the same turbulent ocean. The potential religious significance of this fact is infinite" (28, 85).

Moreover, the social and political possibilities are integral with the potential ideal or religious significance of brotherhood in American sea fiction. Larzer Ziff has explored the first of these in his chapters on Melville in *Literary Democracy*. Sensing that "Melville's sailors go to sea principally to find the community denied them on land," Ziff argues that "Melville's primary theme is that of social, not political, democracy, the inherent dignity of the common man and the way communities are shaped by this quality" (264–65). In choosing to go to sea as a common sailor, Melville consciously joined the "bottommost economic class," and from the forecastle he had the perspective of "a native-born outsider" that enabled him to express "America's deepest anxieties about savagery and civilization" (262–63). Dana had provided the example of serious literature written from a common sailor's point of view, but he expressed equally his fear of being imprisoned among that class of men, as Thomas Philbrick has emphasized in his discussion of *Two Years Before the Mast* as a "narrative of captivity and redemption" (Introduction, 28). Far more wholeheartedly than Dana, Melville overcame "the psychological distance between himself and those suffering fellow creatures"—"the most exploited segment of the American working class" (25, 9)—and in doing so, he more nearly realized the ideal of democratic expression than has any other writer; he established in the sea story from the common sailor's point of view a major (but too little recognized) contribution to the literature of the American labor movement.[9]

From another perspective, whereas Larzer Ziff develops his point about the social significance of Melville's forecastle experience—"a confinement so intense that an intimacy well beyond that of the tightest rural village was inescapable" (2)—Robert K. Martin develops the political significance of this situation. Examining the way in which Melville's work constitutes "a critique of power in the society [he] depicted," Martin begins by observing how "the fluidity of the sea itself, and the absence of social norms, serves as a constant reminder of the power of the natural world and of man's very small place in it" (3). But because of the captain's "extraordinary authority" (almost "an absolute monarchy"), there is a "violent clash" in Melville's sea fiction between "the claims of nature and its ultimate mysteries with those of man, incarnate in the captain, and his attempt to assert authority over the ever-changing" (3–4). Building on Leslie Fiedler's *Love and Death in the American Novel,* but arguing that what Fiedler sees as a "failure" in Melville's work is actually an "accomplishment," Martin explains the dynamics of Melville's critique of power. He focuses on "the conflict between two erotic forces: a democratic eros strikingly similar to that of Whitman, finding its highest expression in male friendship . . . reflecting the celebration of a generalized seminal power not directed toward control or production; and a hierarchical eros expressed in social forms of male power" (4).

Although many readers might prefer to ignore Martin's emphasis on the "institution of male friendship . . . [that Dana] called *aikane* and Melville called *tayo*" (Martin 19), to do so would be contrary to the essential spirit of openness, freedom, and discovery that is embodied in American literary voyages.[10] From its democratic center, our literature of "the all-contributed and all-receptive ocean" radiates in many directions—religious, biological, social, political—and in its desire to perpetuate the ideal of brotherhood, it ranges from the ethereal sense of Whitman's vision of the soul as shipmate—

> Joy, shipmate, joy!
> (Pleas'd to my soul at death I cry)—

to the erotic sense of Allen Ginsberg's image of "those human seraphim, the sailors" (Whitman, "Songs of Parting," *Leaves of Grass*; Ginsberg, "Howl"). There is no better way to grasp the full range of democratic possibilities and the full extent to which they inform the tradition of American sea fiction than to note how, in its towering masterwork, Melville brought so much together in the juxtaposed chapters "The Castaway" and "A Squeeze of the Hand" in *Moby-Dick*. Before Pip becomes a castaway, Stubb advises him on how important it is to "*Stick to the boat.*" Stubb could not "afford" to pick him up if he fell overboard, because "'a whale would sell for thirty times what you would, Pip, in Alabama. Bear that in mind and don't jump any more.' Hereby perhaps Stubb indirectly hinted, that though man loves his fellow, yet man is a money-making animal, which propensity too often interferes with his benevolence." Then it "happened," and Pip experienced "the intense concentration of self in the middle of [the] heartless immensity"; his "ringed horizon began to expand around him miserably." But when he was "carried down alive to wondrous depths, where strange shapes of the unwarped primal world glided to and fro before his passive eyes," Pip came to "the celestial thought": "Among the joyous, heartless, ever-juvenile eternities, Pip saw the multitudinous, God-omnipresent, coral insects, that out of the firmament of waters heaved the colossal orbs. He saw God's foot upon the treadle of the loom, and spoke it." Concluding this chapter, Melville indicates how much of his book is shaped by this vision. Pip's experience, says Ishmael, is "common in that fishery; and in the sequel of the narrative, it will be seen what like abandonment befell myself." In the next sentence, the first of "A Squeeze of the Hand," the story resumes, after Stubb's "so dearly purchased" whale is brought alongside, and Ishmael sits down with his shipmates:

> Squeeze! squeeze! squeeze! all the morning long; I squeezed that sperm till I myself almost melted into it; I squeezed that sperm till a strange sort of insanity came over me; and I found myself unwittingly squeezing my co-laborers' hands in it, mistaking their hands for the gentle globules. Such an abounding, affectionate, friendly, loving feeling did this avocation beget; that at last I was continually squeezing their hands, and looking up into their eyes sentimentally; as much as to say,—Oh! my dear fellow beings, why should we longer cherish any social acerbities, or know the slightest ill-humour or envy! Come; let us squeeze hands all round; nay, let us all squeeze ourselves into each other; let us squeeze ourselves universally into the very milk and sperm of kindness.

In these two chapters, Melville brought together the essential materials of *Moby-Dick* that gave him—in the sea life—so powerful a basis for affirming and celebrating his vision of a coherent universe. Viewed in a different light by successive generations of sea-brothers, as they would be viewed in a different, darker light by Melville himself after 1851, these materials have remained essential in the tradition of American sea fiction: the image of man immersed in the biological order of life, which, in *Moby-Dick*, Melville understood in terms of natural theology; of men in social, political, and—for the writers from the 1890s onward—biological conflict with themselves; and of men together as brothers "*in the boat.*" The coherence of existence that Melville celebrates in *Moby-Dick* is evident in these chapters in his extensive use of the imagery of circles: in "Pip's ringed horizon," the "colossal orbs" of creation, and the "squeeze [of] hands all round." As, in his view, the "mysterious, divine Pacific zones the world's whole bulk about; . . . seems the tide-beating heart of earth" (*MD*, "The Pacific") and as its waters seem to exert a magnetic attraction on crowds of men, causing them to "unite" at the water's edge with Ishmael ("Loomings"), so does he trace to the very center of existence the source of "democratic dignity": "on all hands, [it] radiates without end from God; Himself! The Great God absolute! The centre and circumference of all democracy! His omnipresence, our divine equality!" ("Knights and Squires"). Thus it is for Melville that the ideal sea experience is not available on "merchant ships" or "Men-of-War" and certainly not on "Slaveships," "pirate" ships or "privateers"; on such ships there cannot "be much right-down hearty good-will and brotherly love": "But look at the godly, honest, unostentatious, hospitable, sociable, free-and-easy whaler!" (*MD*, "The Gam"). And Melville can assert that, because of the Nantucketer's deeply intimate relationship with the sea, he "owns" the sea: he "lives on it" and draws his "living from the bottomless deep itself" (*MD*, "Nantucket").

In his playful exuberance for the sea life as whalers know it, Melville was in part developing Dana's "hint" that he write of his experiences on a whaler and a man-of-war, doing for those kinds of maritime experience what Dana "had done for the merchant marine in *Two Years Before the Mast*" (Lucid 244–45). But if we note also the vast difference between what he could make of the man-of-war and the whaling experiences, we can best account for the relative absence of fiction of naval warfare in the tradition of American sea fiction. In the considerable volume of American war fiction there are many great works, but among them are no great novels of naval war. Although a number of Americans have written about war from their position as experienced seamen—in recent years, Marcus Goodrich (*Delilah*, 1941), Herman Wouk (*The Caine Mutiny*, 1951), E. L. Beach (*Run Silent, Run Deep*, 1955)—none of them has earned a significant place in our tradition of sea fiction. For the very idea of war at sea runs contrary to the traditional writer's sense of wonder and mystery, his will to believe that in accepting our place in the natural order of ocean, bloody as it is, we may find our way. As Melville wrote in *White-Jacket*, the true sailor "expatriates [himself] to nationalize with the universe": "Life in a man-of-war . . . with its martial formalities and thousand vices, stabs to the heart the soul of all free-and-easy honourable rovers" (*WJ*, "The Jacket Aloft"); he reiterated this feeling in *Moby-Dick* in Father Mapple's admonition to be a patriot "only . . . to heaven," and in his remark that men-of-war are only "floating forts" ("The Sermon," "Nantucket"). He would later dramatize these feelings in the explicit context of naval warfare in *Israel Potter* and *Billy Budd, Sailor*. When later writers in the tradition do write about warfare at sea (for example, Morgan Robertson, Hemingway, and Peter Matthiessen), they are guided by biological considerations and an essentially Melvillian willingness to accept and affirm the simplest processes of life in our continued voyaging through time.

I conclude this introductory chapter by pointing out that the sea is a far more powerful presence in our literature and that American sea fiction has contributed a great deal more to our literature than is normally accepted. To press this point is, of course, to invite the objection that, as Frederick Jackson Turner, Henry Nash Smith, and many others have shown, the frontier, not the sea, has been the great shaping force in our cultural development. Setting out, more or less in Turner's footsteps, to trace "the impact of the West, the vacant continent beyond the frontier, on the consciousness of Americans and [to follow] the principal consequences of this impact in literature and social thought down to Turner's formulation of it," Smith came eventually to *Moby-Dick* (4). He had already shown that up until the middle of the nineteenth century "the Wild West considered as untouched nature proved to be unsuitable material for major literature" (84), but in his determination to show the frontier's "impact in [our] literature," he seems to have been compelled to emphasize how "metaphorical material derived from the Wild West plays such as important part in *Moby-Dick*" (85). His discussion of *Moby-Dick*, however, deals only with what he calls "the pivotal" chapter on the whiteness of the whale, and the only point he can make about it is that "the native wildness of the West [as in the White Steed] served him as *a* means of expressing *one* of his major intuitions"—that about the ambiguity of life (my emphases). If this were the end of critical interpretations of *Moby-Dick* as Western fiction, there would be no problem. But as later critics have developed the idea, one could almost forget that it is a *sea* novel. In Edwin Fussell's *Frontier: American Literature and the American West*, for example, *Moby-Dick* is presented as "basically . . . a hunting story" and, as "an American hunting story," therefore "inevitably a story about the West": "Everything [in *Moby-Dick*] follows from the initial interchangeability of sea and West" (257, 263).[11] Such sere formulations evaporate the very source of *Moby-Dick's* poetry and impoverish our sense of a national literary heritage with oceanic dimensions.

In his review of Jeanne-Marie Santraud's *La mer et le roman américain dans la première moitié du dix-neuvième siècle*, Thomas Philbrick wrote ironically that her book would comfort "subscribers to the heretical proposition that the sea was at least of equal importance to the inland wilderness" in shaping early nineteenth-century American literature (Review, 456). But if we can measure the relative influence of the frontier and the sea by the number of significant literary works that are centrally either *of* the frontier or *of* the sea, there is no basis for comparison. If to the group of sea novels that Philbrick has analyzed in *James Fenimore Cooper and the Development of American Sea Fiction,* we add the sea fiction that Melville wrote before and after 1850, as well as the sea fiction written by other Americans from 1890 to the present, such as *The Sea-Wolf,* "The Open Boat," *The Old Man and the Sea,* and *Far Tortuga,* the sea's enduring vital presence in American fiction is undeniable.

It is important to distinguish between what we can think of as the "American mind" (to use Henry Nash Smith's term) and the literary imagination: "the consciousness of Americans" as they felt and responded to "the magnetic attraction of [the] untouched" West, the attraction of "free land" that could yield either personal or national empires as America grasped its "manifest destiny"—as opposed to the writer's imagination that, in America, often envisioned another kind of empire (4, 6). In choosing "landlessness," the freeing vision, instead of free land, the American sea writer is free to envision the ideal American, a Bulkington, perhaps (as in "The Lee Shore"). He can find at sea the characteristically American perspective that Richard Poirier has described in *A World Elsewhere*—an environment created through language "in which the inner consciousness of the hero-poet can freely express itself, an environment in which he can sound publicly what he privately is" (232). Building his "world elsewhere" in terms of "the mystical experience to which William James alludes, an 'enormous sense of inner authority,'" the American writer (Poirier points to Melville as his example) differs from the characteristic Englishman (Defoe, for example). *Robinson Crusoe* is "a sort of idyllic parable of man's gaining merely economic control over an environment out of which he could try to make anything he chose. . . . [Defoe] has no interest whatever in merely visionary possession of landscape" (9). Similarly, I would add, drawn to landlessness, Melville's mind (like those of his later sea-brothers) is essentially at odds with the "American mind" that, in Smith's analysis, was drawn to free land in the West. A writer of Melville's sensibility was of course repelled by the thought of "progress and civilization," of building a personal or national empire on the "free" land of the American Indian. He had sailed (as many other American writers would) to and then away from such possibilities in the South Seas. In *Lightship* (1934)—the beautiful but forgotten novel by the last working seaman in our tradition who was born in the nineteenth century—Archie Binns tells this story from a few miles off the coast of Washington State, within sight of an Indian village. Like Melville, our ideal sea writer, he *could* imagine (as Smith suggests that Turner could not) "what was to become of democracy" once "the westward advance of civilization across the continent had caused free land to disappear" (Smith 301). And he chose the sea experience of the common sailor, preferring in Larzer Ziff's phrase, to "be a native-born outsider" (262). This tendency among the sea-brothers of our tradition is explicit not only in Melville's exuberant claim that "we [sailors] expatriate ourselves to nationalize with the universe," but in Lincoln Colcord's more matter-of-fact claim in reference to his birth at sea off Cape Horn that "I am a native of a latitude and a longitude" (*WJ*, "The Jacket Aloft"; *An Instrument of the Gods*, Preface).

From this perspective we are perhaps better able to see how the mythology of the American frontier and the inland wilderness forms only a small part of the "Western spirit," which, as Turner saw in his chapter "The West and American Ideals," is essentially the spirit of the voyaging mind. Thus Turner concluded his chapter by quoting "Tennyson's Ulysses [as its] symbol":

> . . . for my purpose holds
> To sail beyond the sunset, and the baths
> Of all the Western stars until I die"   (310).

A similar sense consoled Melville when in 1888 he wrote of his retired, now landlocked old sailor John Marr. Withdrawn into the "frontier-prairie," Marr could see "the remnant of Indians thereabout—all but exterminated" by the war they waged "for their native soil and natural rights" (*GSW*, 419). Seeing also the decaying remnants of white settlers, he was aware that "the unintermitting advance of the frontier" attested to "yet another successive overleaped limit of civilized life; a life which in America can to-day hardly be said to have any western bound but the ocean that washes Asia" (420). With this sense, Melville gives his old sailor John Marr a peaceful end, in a "visionary" "reunion" with his shipmates (421). In a similar visionary or metaphorical sense we might also see that, as the tradition of American sea fiction preceded the development of frontier literature and as it has survived even the passing of the sailing ships and the exhaustion of the continental frontier, American literature in English was itself born at sea, in the logs, journals, and sermons of Captain John Smith, William Bradford, and John Winthrop.[12]

2

Meditation
and the Life-Waters

That unsounded ocean you gasp in, is Life.
　　—Melville, *Moby-Dick*

Moby-Dick was the last great work, the "literary leviathan" in the tradition of American sea fiction, whose golden age coincided with that of the great clipper ships in the middle of the nineteenth century.[1] It was also a potent force in the tradition of American sea fiction when it began to renew itself late in the nineteenth century, as the sailing ships gave way to steam. And, as the tradition outlived the steamships, *Moby-Dick* has remained a vital force within it. My purpose in the following pages is to offer a reading of *Moby-Dick* that accounts for its integrity as the greatest of all American fictions and that at the same time describes the dynamics by which it helped to transform and perpetuate the tradition of American sea fiction. Briefly, my thesis is that by writing of the whaler's simple and natural pursuit of his livelihood, not only his proximity with the sea's life but, emphatically, his participation in its bloody processes, Melville gave to the tradition its sense that we might best grasp the mystery of our own lives by considering the biological wonders of the sea.

With Ishmael's assertion in "Loomings" that "meditation and water are wedded forever" and that the "key" to the "magic" we "see in all rivers and oceans" is "the image of the ungraspable phantom of life," Melville signaled that *Moby-Dick* would differ as profoundly from his two most recent popular sea novels as *Mardi* had differed from *Typee* and *Omoo*. He had written his "nursery tale" *Redburn* and the more ambitious *White-Jacket* within a single year, "almost entirely for 'lucre,'" as he confided to Dana (Leyda 1:374). Now, still possessed of the young man's exuberance and expansiveness that had contributed to his loss of control in *Mardi*, but with the writer's maturity he had gained from intense reading of Hawthorne and especially Shakespeare, he was at the height of his powers. Again, he had chosen a subject that might have led to another commercially successful book like *Typee* and that he might have developed rather easily through the reliable formula of a voyage narrated with autobiographical authenticity. And again, with "eternity . . . in his eye," he found himself embarked upon the kind of "chartless" voyage into "the world of mind" that he had described in the chapter, "Sailing On," in *Mardi*. The comparable chapter in *Moby-Dick*, "The Lee Shore," is less a tribute to the mysterious heroic mariner, Bulkington, than it is a "stoneless grave" of the popular literary figure Melville could have been had he lacked the faith and determination to accept the "mortally intolerable truth" "that all deep, earnest thinking is but the intrepid effort of the soul to keep the open independence of her sea." In "all the lashed sea's landlessness" he would search again for the "highest truth, shoreless, indefinite as God," and would willingly "perish in that howling infinite" before he would "crawl" "worm-like" to the "safety" of a merely authentic sea narrative ("The Lee Shore").[2]

In some respects, the way had been prepared for Melville's voyages "into the world of mind" by earlier writers in the tradition, as Thomas Philbrick has suggested. Edgar Allan Poe and James Fenimore Cooper had helped make "the sea novel serve as a vehicle for meanings of universal relevance" rather than simply as an occasion for presenting "the special realm of [the seaman's] experience." In *The Sea Lions*, especially, Cooper had changed the focus of his sea stories; rather than simply emphasizing "the uniqueness of the sailor, the ship, and the ocean," he made "the seaman . . . the representative of all men, and his environment . . . an analogue of the condition of all human existence" (*Cooper*, 258–59).

But in his radical de-emphasis of narrative development and plot in favor of his own "true method" of "careful disorderliness," Melville discovered the ideal form for the expression of his own meditative genius, even as he exceeded the bounds of both the conventional novel and the traditional sea novel (*MD*, chap. 82). In the earliest "prophecy of renown" for *Moby-Dick*, after its first thirty-three years of neglect, the English sea novelist W. Clark Russell wrote that "'Moby Dick' is not a sea-story—one could not read it as such." But despite its nautical improbabilities, he praised the book for its "medley of noble impassioned thoughts born of the deep": "It is like a drawing by William Blake . . . or the 'Ancient Mariner'" (reprinted in Parker, ed., *Recognition*, 118). And four decades later, as the Melville revival began, the American sea writer Lincoln Colcord was struck with what he knew would be a "malicious heresy" even in 1922, when he pointed out "how little of real nautical substance there is in 'Moby Dick'" (reprinted in Parker, ed., *Recognition*, 176). With the authority of an experienced seaman (he was actually born at sea in a gale off

Cape Horn in 1883), Colcord noted the lack of "nautical verisimilitude" in *Moby-Dick* and commented on Melville's relative disinterest in the ship itself ("the 'Pequod' . . . is a toy ship") and in "the psychology of handling a vessel"; and he wondered about the "mystery" of Melville's failure to create a convincing storm scene or to present "an understanding picture of a ship beset by a heavy circular storm" (176–79).[3] Colcord knew that traditionally, beginning with *The Pilot*, nautical realism had been an essential ingredient in American sea writing: Cooper, Dana, and Melville in his first books had capitalized on actually having been to sea. Yet despite his accurate observation that Melville was sometimes disappointing as a nautical realist, Colcord wished for no changes in *Moby-Dick*, for fear that this "would be to wish away the book's divinity" (186).

The key to *Moby-Dick*'s "divinity" in the tradition of American sea fiction (as well as in American literature in general) is that no novelist before Melville had exploited the first of the three elements of sea fiction—the sea, the ship, and the seaman—to the extent that he does there. No one had so creatively viewed the water itself as the essential unifying medium in which man and the natural world are one. Suggesting that we are all "Water-gazers," he imagines that we "unite" at the water's edge because we are drawn there by the "magic" force through which "meditation and water are wedded forever" ("Loomings"). This is the life-water that Ishmael sees in the "mysterious, divine Pacific"; it "zones the world's whole bulk about; makes all coasts one bay to it; seems the tide-beating heart of earth" ("The Pacific"). Eventually, Pip will descend into the wondrous depths of these waters and see "God's foot upon the treadle of the loom" ("The Castaway"). In these waters, in "Loomings," Ishmael sees "the image of the ungraspable phantom of life." And this image, as "the key to it all," is also in Melville's "monistic universe," the natural basis for a democratic brotherhood (Ward 172). Despite the merely official distinctions among men, as these are intensified in a ship's company, Ishmael has "the satisfaction of knowing that it is all right" to accept his humble position as a "simple sailor" before the mast, for in the "scales of the New Testament" we are all slaves in "either a physical or metaphysical point of view": "The universal thump is passed round, and all hands should rub each other's shoulder blades, and be content" ("Loomings").

Inevitably, the "Fates'" "springs and motives" that draw Ishmael to the water in "Loomings" lead him also to Nantucket. And in his tribute to the Nantucketers, we have one of our earliest concise and penetrating views of Melville's chief contribution to the tradition of American sea fiction. With repeated references to "the wide waters" and "the watery world,"[4] the chapter swells to its memorably lyric conclusion, which begins with the claim that "the sea is his [the Nantucketer's]; he owns it" by virtue of his effort "to draw [his] living from the bottomless deep itself"

. . . *while beneath his very pillow rush herds of walruses and whales.* —Melville, *Moby-Dick*

("Nantucket"). Drawing here on his own experience as a whaler and, no doubt, on the New Testament tradition of the fishermen-disciples (as when, in Luke, Jesus instructs them to "launch out into the deep, and let down your nets"), Melville suggested that the truest sea stories are those of fishermen, as opposed to the other kinds of seamen who had dominated traditional sea fiction: "Merchant ships are but extension bridges; armed ones but floating forts; even pirates and privateers . . . but plunder other ships, other fragments of the land like themselves."

> The Nantucketer, he alone resides and riots on the sea; he alone, in Bible language, goes down to it in ships; to and fro ploughing it as his own plantation. *There* is his home; *there* lies his business, which a Noah's flood would not interrupt, though it overwhelmed all the millions in China. He lives on the sea. . . . For years he knows not the land; so that when he comes to it at last, it smells like another world, more strangely than the moon would to an Earthsman. With the landless gull, that at sunset folds her wings and is rocked to sleep between billows; so at nightfall, the Nantucketer, out of sight of land, furls his sails, and lays him to his rest, while under his very pillow rush herds of walruses and whales.

Drawn to such "wild and distant seas," Ishmael concludes "Loomings" with his surmise that the Fates' "chief" motive for arranging this "whaling voyage by one Ishmael" "was the overwhelming idea of the great whale himself." If we would pursue with him this idea of the whale, we must voyage beyond "The Lee Shore" toward the open seas of chapter 32, where, already "boldly launched upon the deep," we are asked to follow further as he prepares us for these "unshored, harborless immensities" by instructing us in "Cetology." In this, as he developed it into the "cetological center" of *Moby-Dick; or The Whale*, Melville gave to the tradition of American sea fiction the sense that we might best approach the watery, "ungraspable phantom of life" through biology.

The biology from which Melville made the "cetological center" of *Moby-Dick* in 1851 was, of course, "pre-Darwinian," even though he had read Darwin's *Voyage of a Naturalist* and quoted from it in his "Extracts." But by 1876, *Clarel's* extensive imagery of the Dead Sea and its references in the "Epilogue" to Darwin and geology register the profound impact of the *Origin of Species* on Melville's view of life and the sea. He had lost the exuberance and wonder with which he had once contemplated the biological intricacies of life as embodied in the great whale—his sense, as in "Brit," that it is "very hard really to believe that such bulky masses . . . can possibly be instinct, in all parts, with the same sort of life that lives in a dog or a horse." Yet by the end of Melville's life, the tradition of American sea fiction would begin to renew itself—first through writers who are unknown today, whom I discuss in Chapters 7 and 8, then through Jack London, Hemingway, and Peter Matthiessen—by emphasizing, often from a fisherman's point of view, that if we would know ourselves, we must begin by recognizing that we, too, are creatures of the sea. But this would come only after our culture had struggled for several decades to come to terms with the revolution in biological thought that began in 1859, "the greatest of all scientific revolutions" (Mayr 501).

Among Melville's critics there is a general misunderstanding about the nature of his biological thought in *Moby-Dick*. Perhaps because his complexity and ambiguity so appealed to the academic critics who followed the Melville revival, he is sometimes construed as being more of a post–Waste Land modern than a man of his own time. Elizabeth Foster, for example, in "Melville and Geology," argued that "at some time between *Typee* and *Moby-Dick,* Melville's universe changed: the beneficient hand of a Father disappeared from the tiller of the world"; and she concluded that Babbalanja's "ominous" words in *Mardi,* "Thus nature works, at random warring" (in chap. 132, Babbalanja's essay on geology and evolution), mark the beginning of Melville's "long and agonizing search for a place for faith" (65). Addressing a related subject in "Melville as Amateur Zoologist," Tyrus Hillway suggested that in *Mardi* Melville was "definitely" an amateur "ichthyologist," as compared with "the real scientific awareness" he later displayed in his "masterful dissertation on the sperm whale" (164, 159). Both Hillway and Foster imply that by 1851 Melville was a more astute and systematic scientist than he had been in 1848; and Foster suggests that, because of his accurate knowledge of "precisely those discoveries of the new science which were proving most dangerous to religious faith in the nineteenth century" (65), he had lost his faith and more or less prepared himself in *Mardi* for the severe aftershocks from the publication of the *Origin of Species* in 1859.

Contrary to these opinions, Melville's understanding of science and his attitude toward it changed very little between 1848 and 1851. It is certainly clear in *Mardi* that he was aware of the new geological conclusions about the earth's age, that he discussed the growing evidence of evolution (in chaps. 132 and 155), that he saw clearly the war in nature, and even that he entertained the idea that "new species of beings" might eventually be produced by science (in chap. 98); but his purpose in expressing these ideas was to use the new scientific thought to heighten wonder and thereby defend his faith in a coherent, static universe. That is, wanting to "hold fast to all we have; and stop all leaks in our faith," he argued that "the higher the intelligence, the more faith, and the less credulity: Gabriel rejects more than we, but out-believes us all" (M, "Faith and Knowledge"). The difference between his understanding and use of zoology between 1848 and 1851 is mainly that, by placing the whale at the center of his

book, he had created a deeply relevant basis for his cetological meditations, and with the sheer volume of information he had at his disposal—in
Frederick Bennett, William Scoresby, and especially Thomas Beale—he
could prolong and intensify his "masterful dissertation" to a degree that
would have been impossible in *Mardi* (Hillway 159). In the whale he had a
single, vast, and mysterious subject for his meditative genius to dwell upon
and into which he could draw the whole universe.

In Melville's first use of zoological materials, in his chapter on sharks
in *Mardi* called "Of the Chondropterygii, and Other Uncouth Hordes In-
festing the South Seas," we can see the underlying logic of his interest in
the subject and where it would lead him in *Moby-Dick*. "I commend the
student of Ichthyology to an open boat . . . and the Pacific," he begins, for
there one can see "strange monsters" that do not appear "in the books of
the naturalists":

> Though America be discovered, the Cathays of the deep are unknown.
> And whoso crosses the Pacific might have read lessons to Buffon. . . .
> There are more wonders than the wonders rejected, and more sights un-
> revealed than you or I ever dreamt of. Moles and bats alone should be
> skeptics. . . . Be Sir Thomas Brown our ensample; who while explod-
> ing "Vulgar Errors," heartily hugged all the mysteries of the Penta-
> teuch. (M, chap. 13)

The first sharks he mentions, in a sort of prelude to his scientific classifications, are the "Devil Fish" ("Doctor Faust saw the devil; but you have seen
the 'Devil Fish'") and the "Bone Shark" ("large as a whale," this shark is
terrible to seamen, who well know that "the good craft Essex, and others,
have been sunk by sea-monsters"). Then, crediting the "German naturalists Müller and Hende" but commenting on "the most heathenish
names" they have used (such as 'Chondropterygii'), he lists and describes
the various sharks, using the common names and sometimes even the far
less scientific names by which sailors know them. Clearly, in this first brief
dissertation "there is little enough of a zoological nature," as Tyrus Hillway
has shown (161). But it is also clear that Melville's first essay into zoology
was in the same "spirit of godly gamesomeness" that he recommends in his
chapter on cetology in *Moby-Dick*. In both *Mardi* and *Moby-Dick*, Melville's attitude toward zoology is as it was toward the physiognomy he employed in examining the whale's head: "Physiognomy, like every other
human science, is but a passing fable" (*MD*, "The Prairie"). But he will
use physiognomy in his "endeavor" to understand the whale because, he
tells us, "I try all things: I achieve what I can." And at the end of his first
zoological essay on sharks in *Mardi*, we can see clearly that he had something larger in mind: "Oh, believe me, God's creatures fighting, fin for fin, a

thousand miles from land, and with the round horizon for an arena, is no ignoble subject for a masterpiece" (chap. 13). He would pursue this study of zoology at greater length in his masterpiece on the whale; but, scarcely more "scientific" than his first effort, it would remain essentially a study of "God's creatures," including sharkish man, in a watery universe whose unity and coherence are suggested by the "round horizon" (my emphasis). In *Moby-Dick* he would, as F. O. Matthiessen suggests, "draw a circle around his experience" in a way that he had been unable to do in *Mardi* (408).

Without representing the image of Melville as a scholarly biologist (for all his interest in it, he was certainly no less an amateur than Thoreau), it is important to see that his attitude toward biology was in accord with the view historians of science identify as "natural theology," the view that "dominated . . . British science up to the middle of the nineteenth century" (Mayr 103). According to this view—as suggested by the titles of John Ray's *Wisdom of God Manifested in the Works of the Creation* (1691) and William Paley's *Natural Theology: Or, Evidences of the Existence and Attributes of the Deity, Collected from the Appearances of Nature* (1802)— nature is comparable to a "book, a natural analogue to the revealed book of the Christian religion, the Bible" (Mayr 92). Despite David Hume's *Dialogues Concerning Natural Religion* (1779) and Immanuel Kant's *Critique of Judgment* (1790), "the leading English paleontologists and biologists [at mid-nineteenth century] were natural theologians, including Charles Lyell and other of Darwin's friends" (Mayr 105). Arguing from "design" (that is, that God's "original design" for the universe holds true), these naturalists could account in various ways for even the most troublesome new ideas. They accepted the increasingly apparent fierceness of the struggle for existence as essentially benign, a necessary part of the creation's balance and harmony, and they reconciled the idea of evolution "either with a stable, recently created world, or with a steady-state cyclical world, or with a series of catastrophes" such as the biblical flood (Mayr 322, 393). But the "cataclysmic event [in the development of biological thought] that would sweep the boards clean . . . was the publication . . . of the *Origin of Species*," the chief revolutionary principles of which were that "all organisms have descended from common ancestors" and, most dramatically, "the explanation of 'design' in the world by the purely materialistic process of natural selection, a process consisting of an interaction between nondirected variation and opportunistic reproductive success which was entirely outside the dogma of Christianity" (Mayr 507, 501).

Perhaps the clearest evidence that Melville's biological speculations remained well within the limits of natural theology is his sense that the "possible new species of beings" that Babbalanja imagines would not originate in nature but in the "jar" in which his friend was trying to "hatch a fairy" (M, chap. 98). Such fairies or monsters had long populated the

[The albatross] arched forth its vast archangel wings. . . . and
in those forever exiled waters, I had lost the
miserable warping memories of traditions and of towns.
                                    —Melville, *Moby-Dick*

laboratories of nineteenth-century gothic fiction. Clear examples of man's will to violate the natural garden, they project no sense that in nature herself resides the mechanism by which the static order is disrupted through the production of new species. But the cataclysm of Darwinian thought would inevitably influence Melville, and its effect on his attitude toward science is clear in the difference between his portraits of Babbalanja in 1849 and of the geologist Margoth in *Clarel* in 1876. Whereas he had entertained Babbalanja's speculations on geology, evolution, and zoology with a degree of patience and gentle comedy, he reviled Margoth, whose gothic villainy is evident in his name and in his explanation of the desolate landscape the pilgrims see at Siddim Plain. Was it brimstone and fire?

> 'Tut, tut—tut, tut. Of aqueous force,
> Vent igneous, a shake or so,
> . . . All's mere geology, you know.'   (II, xxxiii)

We can trace the essentially theological nature of Melville's geobiological meditations—his sense that the life-waters hold the key to our existence—from their beginnings in *Mardi* through *Redburn* and *White-Jacket* to their full development in *Moby-Dick*. Near the end of *Mardi*, Babbalanja attains a vision that had developed, in part, from his speculations on geological time and evolution, and the setting Melville devises for Babbalanja's dream-narrative is a seashore "laved" with phosphorescent waves: as "the fiery tide was ebbing . . . in the soft, moist sand, at every step, [Babbalanja] left a lustrous footprint" (chap. 188). His vision culminates when he "saw or heard" "soft, sad, and faint" things, "as, when, in sunny summer seas, down, down, you dive, starting at pensive phantoms, that you cannot fix." "'These,'" breathes his guide, "'are spirits in their essences,'" which are the sources of our souls. Then Mardi "glowed within a sphere, which seemed, in space, a bubble, rising from vast depths to the sea's surface." This vision of the soul's origin in the life-waters is an obvious version of the Creation as told in Genesis 1.2: "And darkness was upon the face of the deep. And the spirit of God moved upon the face of the waters. And God said, Let there be light." The failure of *Mardi* made it clear to Melville that he would need far more concrete and realistic materials for telling this kind of story—those of his own experience as a whaler which he had initially sought to exploit in *Mardi*, but with which he had lost touch as he voyaged more deeply into mind.

He kept the idea alive in *Redburn* in his brief references to whaling, particularly in "A Whaleman and a Man-of-War's-Man" (chap. 21), in which he wrote that "whalemen are far more familiar with the wonders of the deep than any other class of seamen." And for the first time he developed the idea successfully in his more memorable chapter in *White-Jacket*, "The Last of the Jacket" (chap. 92). His admirable description of a fall from the yardarm is so well known that it need not be quoted fully here. But to F. O. Matthiessen's remark that it demonstrates Melville's realization "that there should be no artificial separation between the life of the mind and of the body" (395), I would add that, largely because of the point Matthiessen made, the scene also demonstrates the key to what became Melville's chief contribution to the tradition of American sea fiction. That is, to the scene he had noticed in Nathanial Ames's *A Mariner's Sketches*, he added his own profoundly imaginative dive beneath the surface of the waters, where, touched by *life*, he could feel "the thrill of being alive again":

> As I gushed into the sea, a thunder-boom sounded in my ear; my soul seemed flying from my mouth. The feeling of death flooded over me with the billows. The blow from the sea must have turned me, so that I sank almost feet foremost through a soft, seething, foamy lull. Some current seemed hurrying me away; in a trance I yielded, and sank deeper down with a glide. Purple and pathless was the deep calm now around me, flecked by summer lightnings in an azure afar. The horrible nausea was gone; the bloody, blind film turned a pale green; I wondered whether I was yet dead, or still dying. But of a sudden some fashionless form brushed my side—some inert, coiled fish of the sea; the thrill of being alive again tingled in my nerves, and the strong shunning of death shocked me through.
>
> For one instant an agonizing revulsion came over me as I found myself utterly sinking. Next moment the force of my fall was expended; and there I hung, vibrating in the mid-deep. What wild sounds then rang in my ear! One was a soft moaning, as of low waves on the beach; the other wild and heartlessly jubilant, as of the sea in the height of a tempest. Oh soul! thou then heardest life and death.

Mind and body, life and death touch here and close the circle. From *Mardi* through *White-Jacket* and *Moby-Dick* (in the experiences of Jonah, Bulkington, and Pip); and then again (albeit with a far more desperate sense of hope) in *Clarel*; and finally in *John Marr and Other Sailors* and *Billy Budd, Sailor*, Melville's sailors survive their unwilling descents into the watery depths either by "apotheosis" or by keeping a "long watch-below."

Father Mapple dwells on Jonah's descent into the "living gulfs of doom . . . ten thousand fathoms down" ("The Sermon"), and his ascent into the light. But of those aboard the *Pequod*, only Pip descends beneath the surface of the waters, sees "God's foot upon the treadle of the loom," and returns with the "celestial thought" ("The Castaway"). Through Ishmael's diving imagination, however, we can peer with Melville into the "watery vaults" and see such wonders as nursing whales or other subtle "secrets of the seas," like "young Leviathan amours of the deep" ("The Grand Armada"). And we can share his meditation in "The Pacific":

> There is, one knows not what sweet mystery about this sea, whose gently awful stirrings seem to speak of some hidden soul beneath; like those fabled undulations of the Ephesian sod over the buried Evangelist St. John. And meet it is, that over these sea-pastures, wide-rolling watery prairies and Potters' Fields of all four continents, the waves should rise and fall, and ebb and flow unceasingly; for here, millions of mixed shades and shadows, drowned dreams, somnabulisms, reveries; all that we call lives and souls, lie dreaming, dreaming, still; tossing like slumberers in their beds; the ever-rolling waves but made so by their restlessness.

Perhaps the key source of Ishmael's meditation on the "hidden soul beneath" is his own "abandonment" at sea, which as he says, is like Pip's ("The Castaway"). And the deepest insight, the key bit of "Wisdom" that Pip saw there in the depths "among the joyous, heartless, ever-juvenile eternities" was the "multitudinous, God-Omnipresent, coral insects, that out of the firmament of waters heaved the colossal orbs" ("The Castaway"). These live "coral insects" are presumably bits of the same "minute, yellow substance," brit, "upon which the Right Whale largely feeds" and upon which Ishmael meditates in "Brit." Because this living substance literally gives life to the great Right Whales, Ishmael can refer to the sea itself as being alive. And he can insist that a biological fact is a metaphysical fact, despite the inability of "baby man['s]" "science and skill" to establish the link: "the full awfulness of the sea which aboriginally belongs to it" is that Old Testament awfulness by which the sea "whelmed a whole world" in "Noah's flood." "That same ocean rolls now"; every day "the live sea swallows up ships and crews." Thus the final "subtleness of the sea" that Ishmael considers in this meditation on the "live sea" is its "universal cannibalism." The biological fact that all sea "creatures prey upon each other, carrying on eternal war since the world began," is inevitably from Melville's point of view *the* awful metaphysical fact that should compel our faith: "Yea, foolish mortals, Noah's flood is not yet subsided; two thirds of the fair world it yet covers" ("Brit"). Or, as he puts it elsewhere, "That unsounded ocean you gasp in, is Life" (*MD*, "The Monkey-rope").

Writing to Hawthorne in June 1851 of the torment he experienced in struggling to finish his "Whale," Melville feared that it, too, would be a short-lived "modern book" and that "though [he] wrote the Gospels in this century, [he] should die in the gutter" (Leyda 1:410–11). This way of writing about himself and his work was more than hyperbole or "egotism," for

The thrill of being alive again tingled in my nerves,
and the strong shunning of death shocked me through.
—Melville, White-Jacket

he had undertaken to "produce a mighty book . . . [with] a mighty theme" (*MD*, "The Fossil Whale"), the Leviathan he would cite in his epigraph to "The Whale" from *Paradise Lost*. And knowing only that "I know him not and never will," he would nevertheless through his cetological meditations "mount that whale and leap the topmost skies, to see whether the fabled heavens with all their countless tents really lie encamped beyond my mortal sight!" (*MD*, chaps. 86 and 87).

In his essay "The Function of the Cetological Chapters in *Moby-Dick*" in 1956, J. A. Ward was able to assume on the basis of "recent criticism" that Melville's "unorthodox cetological chapters" were organically relevant and essential to the book's design (165). Howard P. Vincent had earlier described these chapters generally as the "cetological center" or "keel to Melville's artistic craft" and emphasized Melville's sources. But Ward's analysis remains the best guide to the cetological materials, for he shows how they all lead "to the center" of the book, which he sees as "symbolically and essentially a quest for a knowledge of the secrets of the universe" (183, 177).[5] To Ward's discussion I would add the emphasis that *Moby-Dick* is not so much "a quest for a knowledge of the universe" as a quest for the language that might most fully and beautifully *celebrate* the knowledge that Melville affirms at the outset of the voyage: his "Yes," that meditation and water are wedded in a monistic universe. This is the sense of Richard Chase's tribute to Melville's "incomparable discoveries of language" (61). As a quest for knowledge, *Moby-Dick* ends where, from Melville's point of view, any such voyage of mind must end: where it begins, in his belief that we can never "grasp" the mystery of life. Ishmael is aware of this hard truth as he glides down the Acushnet river toward Nantucket and the *Pequod*. Seeing the "world-wandering whale ships . . . safely moored at last," he realizes "that new cruises were on the start; that one most perilous and long voyage ended, only begins a second; and a second ended, only begins a third, and so on, for ever and for aye. Such is the endlessness, yea, the intolerableness of all earthly effort" ("Wheelbarrow"). But, "gaining the . . . open water" and snuffing the "Tartar air!" he is ready again to sail. Knowing that the "mingling threads of life are woven by warp and woof," Melville can weather the storms of doubt along with the "blessed calms" of faith, "a storm for every calm":

> There is no steady unretracing progress in this life; we do not advance through fixed gradations, and at the last one pause:—through infancy's unconscious spell, boyhood's thoughtless faith, adolescence' doubt (the common doom), then skepticism, then disbelief, resting at last in manhood's pondering repose of If. But once gone through, we trace the round again; and are infants, boys, and men, and Ifs eternally. In what rapt ether sails the world, of which the weariest may never weary? Where is the foundling's father hidden? (*MD*, "The Gilder")

Ultimately, for Melville, both the intolerableness and the exhilarating lure of the voyage derive from the single fact in his belief that we inhabit a static universe. That there can be no real change; that our fates are woven; that, since the world is not "an endless plain" on which we might sail ever "eastward," there is no real "promise in the voyage" (MD, chap. 52): this is precisely the paradoxical truth that enables him to buoy his spirits and sail again. Although less optimistic than he was at the end of White-Jacket, where he concluded, "Life is a voyage that's homeward bound"; still, in Moby-Dick he can proceed with the sense that life's voyage is set on course, however circular and inscrutable it may necessarily be. And he can affirm that, "Yes, the world's a ship on its passage out, and not a voyage complete, and the pulpit is its prow" (MD, "The Pulpit"). This image is not equivalent to that of a world-ship with a benevolent Father at the tiller (Foster 50), but it implies that our voyage is in a seaworthy craft and that we can endure.

With at least this degree of faith in his craft, even if he had not stopped all the "leaks," and imagining that "Death is only a launching into the region of the strange Untried . . . the immense Remote, the Wild, the Watery, the Unshored," Melville-Ishmael, like Perth the blacksmith, "went a-whaling" (MD, "The Blacksmith"). And as Ishmael was drawn to the water, he endures the voyage of the Pequod with a certain passiveness that is most evident in his willingness to accept the "universal thump" of authority when it "is passed round" ("Loomings"). More deeply, though, Ishmael's passiveness is his essential quality as the ultimate "water-gazer" and is reflected in his view of "the all-contributed and all-receptive ocean" ("The Blacksmith"). Finally, his survival—afloat at last on the "great shroud of the sea [that still rolls] as it rolled five thousand years ago" during the Flood—is an expression of Melville's confidence that in meditation he might achieve the ideal state of ocean-receptiveness that Ishmael first experiences at the end of "Loomings," when the "great flood-gates of the wonder-world swung open, and in . . . wild conceits . . . there floated into [his] inmost soul, endless processions of the whale." Illuminated by such "wild conceits" or, to quote Richard Chase once again, by Melville's "incomparable discoveries of language," Moby-Dick differs from traditional voyages to enlightenment in that it attains its end repeatedly—in its many meditations on the life-waters and the magnificent whale.

Although Melville's meditative method produced the unorthodox novel whose greatness went ungrasped for decades, the meditative path to literary expression was itself well established. Louis L. Martz has provided an excellent description of the method in his essay on Wallace Stevens's poem The World as Meditation: "Meditation is the essential exercise which, constantly practiced, brings the imagination into play, releases creative power, enables the human being to compose a sensitive, intelligent, and generous self" (134). Martz's analogs for this process are the meditative poems of John Donne's *Holy Sonnets* and the "rigorous meditative exercises commonly practiced by religious men of the seventeenth century." For example, François de Sales's definition of meditation describes Melville's method in *Moby-Dick:* "Meditation . . . is an attentive thought repeated or voluntarily maintained in the mind, to arouse the will to holy and wholesome affections and resolutions" (146). In *Moby-Dick* the wedding of meditation and water is also a wedding of meditation and cetology; that is, Melville's "cetology" and "poetry" alike originate in his urge to elucidate his single ancient "text," the "Leviathan" ("The Fossil Whale"). Wanting to produce a "mighty book" on this "mighty theme," he can only attempt the "outreaching comprehensiveness of sweep" that would "include the whole circle of the sciences, and all the generations of whales, and men, and mastodons, past, present, and to come, with all the revolving panoramas of empire on earth, and throughout the whole universe" ("The Fossil Whale"). If, in his meditations on the biological wonders of life, Melville "mocks" the "scientific approach," it is only to remind us that science is fully subservient to religious thought (Ward 176). That is, for Melville in 1851, zoology was as it was for the "natural theologian [who] studied the works of the creator for the sake of theology. Nature for him was convincing proof for the existence of a supreme being" (Mayr 103). In this view, the naturalist's task was "to complete the assignment of Adam: to name the plants and animals, to contemplate the handiwork of God, and to marvel at his creation" (Magner 348).

Melville's attitude toward such theological matters was resoundingly not like "the snug patronizing lee of churches" he refers to in *Moby-Dick* ("The Town Ho's Story"). But certainly "those lights of zoology and anatomy" (Frederick Cuvier, John Hunter, and Rene-Primiviere Lesson) whom he honors and pretends to have consulted in "Cetology" were "natural theologians," as was his chief source in cetological matters, Thomas Beale. The only trouble with Beale and Frederick Bennett, whose work Melville thought was "mostly confined to scientific descriptions," was that they tended to lose sight of the general truth—the "fearful thing," the "unspeakable foundations . . . of the world" ("Cetology"). Always with "eternity in his eye," Melville was most impatient with taxonomy in science, the "endless subdivisions based upon the most inconclusive differences" by which "some departments of natural history become so repellingly intricate" ("Cetology.") In his scientific method, Melville, like Joshua Slocum, is suspicious of seamen who are "a little too precise in [their] reckoning[s]"; both writers work "by intuition . . . more than by slavish calculations" and verify their positions, as Slocum puts it, by "reading the clock aloft made by the Great Architect" (Slocum 89, 158–59).

It is therefore both as burlesque and with a sense of the fearful foundations of natural theology that, as a preliminary to his own cetological classifications, Melville can correct Linnaeus, who "separated the whales from the fish": "I take the good old fashioned ground that the whale is a fish, and call upon holy Jonah to back me" ("Cetology").[6] Similarly, Melville's choice of a bibliographical method for classifying whales, according to size or "volume" (as falling into the *Folio, Octavo,* or *Duodecimo* classes), is more than just "arbitrary" or because "it would have been practically impossible for [him] to work out any other—a scientific—system" (Ward 176; Vincent 140). In the "spirit of godly gamesomeness," his playful method of classifying whales has a serious purpose: to study nature as though it were a "book, a natural analogue to . . . the Bible" (Mayr 92). For the same reason, in his speculations on evolution he spoke of the "first edition of mankind" (*M,* chap. 160); and in *Moby-Dick,* where the leviathan is his "text," he also refers to Queequeg as "a wondrous work in one volume" ("Queequeg in His Coffin").

To emphasize that Melville's classification of whales in "Cetology" is essentially—as science—in the spirit of natural theology is not to suggest that his "cetological center" serves only theological purposes. *Moby-Dick* is far too ungraspable and Melville's spirit far too exuberantly alive to permit the book's placement into this or any other category. But if we are assisted by Vincent's metaphorical sense that the cetological materials serve in general as the "keel" to Melville's craft, we should consider also Melville's idea that "the pulpit is its prow." Certainly when Melville enters into his meditations on cetological particulars in such chapters as "The Tail," "The Battering Ram," or "The Line," it is obvious that as a storyteller he wanted to prepare the skeptical reader for his wild ending—the *Pequod's* sudden destruction and Ahab's death in a "single, smoking minute" ("The Line"). But none of the short cetological chapters, even the apparently more mundane ones on whales and whaling, is motivated by Melville's need "to inject variety in his story" in recognition of "the obvious fact that on a long whaling voyage very little happens," as Ward thought (168). How much can happen on a whaling voyage, at least from Melville's point of view, must be clear to anyone who has considered his life and career, anyone who has felt the passion of his tribute to the Nantucket fishermen or his ascription of "all the honor and the glory" of his career to "whaling" (*MD,* "The Advocate").

It is worth emphasizing Vincent's observation that Melville's "general debt [to Thomas Beale] was his arrangement of Whaling materials in chapter groups" (129). This arrangement enabled both writers to analyze the complicated process of whaling and the enormous anatomical complexities of the creature in a clear, explanatory fashion. But Beale's part-by-part analysis is guided by his sense that "before long I shall be enabled, with the assistance of a celebrated naturalist, to produce from this interesting animal its entire and minute anatomy" (Beale 72). Always, Beale's "interesting animal" becomes Melville's wondrous "Leviathan, which God of all his works / Created hugest that swim the ocean stream" (as in the lines from *Paradise Lost* that Melville cites in his prefatory "Extracts" in *Moby-Dick*). Melville's short chapters are never "confined to scientific description" ("Cetology"), as Beale's are. If they begin in scientific description, they end in wonder. Never aspiring to present an "entire and minute anatomy" of the whale or the whaling process as Beale does, Melville nevertheless found in Beale's short chapters an ideal form, a logical sequence of occasions for his brief lyric meditations, each of which ends in wonder and affirmation of the essential fact that, "Dissect him how I may, then, I go but skin deep; I know him not, and never will" ("The Tail"). Melville's deepest motive in all the cetological passages of *Moby-Dick* is his desire to celebrate both the life and the way of life he discovered in his "whale-ship" education. And these passages—his "celebration" of the tail, for example, and his "singing" of the "romantic proceeding" of collecting the oil—are unified in his claim that as "the whaleman . . . seeks the food of light, so he lives in light" (chaps. 86, 98, 97).

In presenting *Moby-Dick* as a celebration of light, a celebration of universal coherence that flows from the wedding of mind and nature in water, I have avoided Ahab. But Ahab's power is of course both undeniable and indispensable in the dynamics of *Moby-Dick*. To the extent that *Moby-Dick* can be understood as a novel made of the conventions of narrative and plot, the story of Ahab is everything. In his own right Ahab is a towering character in literature, as well as the greatest of all sea captains. Only the full force of Melville's novel and the awful power of the white whale could drag him down. But to acknowledge the full Shakespearean grandeur of Ahab's language, his enormous pride, doubt, and diabolism, is to glorify the life-waters that overwhelm him and to amplify the celebration.

Melville was neither Ahab nor Ishmael, simply. And there is an element of truth in Charles Feidelson's conclusion that the "obvious dilemma" in *Moby-Dick* is not resolved because "Melville has not resolved it for himself": he "discovers that he is potentially an Ahab, the devil's partisan, the nihilist," as well as Ishmael, "the voyaging mind, the capacity for vision" (35). But in *Moby-Dick* Melville managed at least temporarily to resolve this conflict in a way similar to that by which John Donne could temporarily resolve his inner conflict in the *Holy Sonnets*—by dramatizing a colloquy between his conflicting selves within a single piece. Donne could, in "Death Be Not Proud," for example, address "Death" directly in order that it be defeated within the meditation, which ends, "Death, thou shalt die." Donne's victory over "Death" was possible only through the willfully sustained meditative act that brought his "imagination into play" and enabled him to "compose" a "generous" or victorious "self" (as Louis

Martz explains it). Similarly, the defeat of Ahab and the creation of Ish-mael's faith were possible through Melville's willfully sustained meditation on the leviathan and the life-waters.

Like the Holy Sonnets, Paradise Lost, or The Divine Comedy, Moby-Dick is one of literature's great defensive celebrations. But Melville's cele-bration of a coherent universe in the middle of the nineteenth century must have required a far more determined act of will than was required of Donne or Milton, and certainly than of Dante. Yet, separated as they are from William James's point of view in The Will to Believe (1897) by the biological revolution of 1859, Melville's meditations on the life-water flowed with an ease that would have been virtually impossible at the later date. And one clear measure of the enormous change in Melville's uni-verse during the last half of the century is that the sea captain of Ahab's diabolic grandeur would evolve with a vengeance into the merely human dimensions of Vere, whose involuted thought and devotion to legal tech-nicalities reveal his inner insecurity; he could never dare confront the uni-verse, and the satanic Claggart can claim only a minor role.

In Moby-Dick, much of what would come to overshadow Clarel in the figures of Darwin and Margoth had already swelled into the fiery doubt that Melville could embody and subdue in Ahab. Even Ishmael recognizes that the biological wonders of the life-waters have a dark underside. And in imagining (in the chapter "Moby Dick") that the white whale swims before Ahab as the incarnation "of all those malicious agencies which some men come to feel *eating* in them" (my emphasis), he seems to under-score Melville's point that Ahab is most tormented by the dark voracious-ness of life. It is true that when Ahab defies the light (in "The Candles") and rages, "There is some unsuffusing thing beyond thee, thou clear spirit, to whom all thy eternity is but time, all thy creativeness mechanical"— Melville expressed a vague fear of some mechanism in nature like that which Darwin would formulate in his theory of evolution through natural selection. But Ahab is most obsessed with the horror of life that he can see, that he has participated in with superb success as a killer of whales, and that he had known firsthand when "Moby Dick had reaped away [his] leg" with his "sickle-shaped lower jaw" ("Moby Dick"). Enraged at having been bloodied by the whale, and "gnawed within" by the "fangs of some incurable idea," he is all the "better qualified" for the "pursuit so full of rage and wildness as the bloody hunt of whales" ("Moby Dick"). So now, with his "barbaric white leg . . . fashioned from the polished bone from the sperm whale's jaw," he will challenge the voracious horror on its own terms and "dismember [his] dismemberer" ("Sunset"). In Ahab's view, the sea itself is "the insatiate maw" ("The Sphynx"). And near the end of his life, recalling how he had struck his first whale and contemplating his "forty years on the pitiless sea," making "war on the horrors of the deep," he wonders at himself—"cannibal old me" ("The Symphony"). It is one of his most human moments, and he might have relented and given in to Starbuck's pleas that they give up the hunt. But his "glance was averted" to the "smiling sky" and the "unsounded sea." Then, the final revealing outburst that "blanched" Starbuck "to a corpse's hue" and that gives way to the first of the three climactic chapters, "The Chase—First Day": "Look! see yon Albicore! who put it into him to chase and fang that flying-fish? Where do murderers go, man! Who's to doom, when the judge himself is dragged to the bar? ("The Symphony").

Considering "the full awfulness of the sea which aboriginally belongs to it" (in "Brit"), Ishmael, too, is troubled by "the universal cannibalism of the sea; all whose creatures prey upon each other, carrying on eternal war since the world began." Melville's desperation is undeniable at such moments. But in Ishmael's faith he imagines that this "universal cannibalism" is simply another aspect of "the same ocean" that "whelmed a whole world" in the Flood, the "same live sea" that every day "swallows up ships and crews." Remembering also the means of Jonah's chastisement and deliverance, he can, in the course of his cetological dissertation, examine the sperm whale's head and describe the inside of its mouth as "beautiful and chaste-looking . . . with a glistening white membrane, glossy as bridal satins" ("The Sperm Whale's Head"). Thus, seeing the essential innocence of nature's voracious order, Ishmael can accept and even "marry" the cannibal Queequeg. He can ask, "who is not a cannibal?" and report with apparent comic assent Queequeg's savage reverence: "Queequeg no care what god made him shark . . . wedder Fejee god or Nantucket god; but de god wat made shark must be one dam Ingin" ("The Shark Massacre").

Finally, Ishmael's meditations on the whale move him to affirmation and deep, if troubled, faith: like a whale whose vapory fountain is sometimes "glorified by a rainbow," he has "divine intuitions" that will sometimes enkindle his misty fogs of doubt "with a heavenly ray. And for this I thank God," he says. These "intuitions of some things heavenly" might not make a "believer" of him, but neither is he an "infidel" ("The Fountain"). Like the whales "surrounded by circle upon circle of consternation and affrights," he can, "amid the tornadoed Atlantic of [his] being . . . ever centrally disport in mute calm . . . [bathed] in eternal mildness of joy" ("The Grand Armada"). And, most significantly, perhaps, considering the end of *Moby-Dick* and Melville's sense of an Old Testament God, in "The Affidavit," Ishmael reports the sinking of the *Essex* and the case of the unbelieving Commodore J——, whose ship was damaged by an attacking whale: Ishmael considers this "providential. Was not Saul of Tarsus converted from unbelief by a similar fright?"

Fortunately, we are spared the thought of a surviving Ahab, converted, perhaps, from his grand defiance to a "pious Bildad." Without Ahab's full energies, expressed most concisely in his "Faith? What's that?" Ishmael's lyric meditations would not resound. And, certainly, we could never have known the magnificence of *Moby-Dick* itself had Melville already felt the full "whack" (profoundly more devastating than the "providential" one that shook Commodore J___) from the *Origin of Species.* It is tempting to think that in Ahab's doubt Melville saw it coming; he so appeals to the modern mind. But he did not, even if Ahab's sense that "eternity is but time, all . . . creativeness mechanical" ("The Candles") seems to foreshadow Darwin's theory of such a mechanism in natural selection. When this image of nature's mechanism grinding on through time became fixed in the *Origin of Species, design*—the eternal circle that literally washes over *Moby-Dick*—would break apart. *Moby-Dick's* thousand watery circles—from those Ishmael first imagines in "Loomings" (where he attempts to regulate his "circulation" and, "circumambulating" Manhattan, wonders whether it could be the magnetic compass attraction that unites us water-gazers at the water's edge), to his tribute to "the great God absolute! The centre and circumference of all democracy" ("Knights and Squires"), to the "slowly wheeling circle" into which he is drawn in the "Epilogue": these and the calms that prevail in the seas of *Mardi* and *Moby-Dick* would be forever disrupted. After the turn of the century, the seas would come alive again, but in a cataclysmic new sense; and they would storm in the tales of Jack London. But in 1851 Melville could encircle even science. Overpowering Ahab's abuse of science, as when he hypnotizes the crew into thinking he is "lord of the level loadstone" in "The Needle," and accepting it in the spirit of natural theology, he could dramatize and celebrate the forces that bring about the apocalyptic end of *Moby-Dick,* when Ahab's grand doubt and diabolism are snuffed in the life-waters on which Ishmael's lyric wonder floats forth.

Moby-Dick is above all our literature's greatest lyric celebration of a simple and coherent existence like that Thoreau had sought at Walden pond. But from his more sweeping and breathtaking point of view—at sea, "as a simple sailor, right before the mast, plumb down into the forecastle, aloft there to the royal masthead"—Melville could roll with "the inscrutable tides of God," sight and then mount the leviathan on which he would "leap the topmost skies," and dream that "in a charmed circle of everlasting December" he would "bid defiance to all pursuit from man" (chaps. 1, 35, 57, 105).

3

The Shipwrecked Soul

> He seemed alone, absolutely alone in the universe.
> A bit of wreck in the mid-Atlantic.
> —Melville, "Bartleby the Scrivener"

After *Moby-Dick* Melville returned again and again to the sea. Virtually everything he wrote would be touched with imagery of the sea, and two of his greatest literary creations, "Benito Cereno" (1855) and *Billy Budd, Sailor* (1891), would earn their places among the great sea stories of all time. Others, "The Encantadas" (1854) and *Israel Potter* (1855), would be heavily influenced by the sea. *Clarel* (1876) would contain four sea tales in verse by the seamen-pilgrims Rolfe and Agath. And in *John Marr and Other Sailors* (1888) he would produce yet another unconventional treatment of the sea in prose and verse. He also went to sea again on four occasions after 1851—first on a brief excursion to Nantucket in 1852, his first visit there; then on his voyage across the Atlantic and through the Mediterranean to the Holy Land and the Dead Sea in 1856 and 1857; then on his sailing voyage around Cape Horn to San Francisco and the return voyage by steamer in 1860; and, finally, on his last sea journey, to Bermuda and back, in 1888.

But for all his actual sea experience and all of his writing about the sea after 1851, his great whaling story would always remain the "prime thing" in his life's work. As he foresaw in writing "The Advocate" in *Moby-Dick*, there *would* be a "precious MSS. in [his] desk" when he died; but though we might "ascribe all the honor and the glory" of *Billy Budd, Sailor* "to whaling," its remarkable qualities, as well as those of his intervening sea pieces, are profoundly different from those of *Moby-Dick*. The intensifying darkness and complexity in Melville's writing after 1851 are attributable to a range of causes that is beyond the scope of this book, from the heartbreaking reception of *Moby-Dick* to his estrangement from Hawthorne. But, from the point of view of the tradition of American sea fiction, it is important to emphasize that both the darkness that would prevail in Melville's last forty years' work and the means by which he could subdue it momentarily in *Moby-Dick* are most clearly and essentially defined in the theological terms he developed in the opening pages of *Moby-Dick*—as Ishmael "by instinct followed the streets that took [him] waterward" ("The Carpet-Bag").

Having missed the packet that would take him from New Bedford to Nantucket, Ishmael is forced to spend a weekend that will seal his fate: not only will he meet and "marry" the cannibal Queequeg, but he will hear two sermons, the first preached by "a black angel of Doom" on Saturday night at "The Trap," and the second, on Sunday, by Father Mapple at the Whaleman's Chapel. He hears the first sermon after wandering through dreary "blocks of blackness," stumbling over "an ash box" that calls to his mind "the destroyed city, Gomorrah" and accidentally entering "a negro church." It is a sermon about "the blackness of darkness and the weeping and wailing and teeth-gnashing there." He flees this "trap" and concludes "The Carpet Bag" with a meditation on mortality, "poor [Saint] Paul's tossed craft," and the "tempestuous," God-sent "wind called Euroclydon." Now he can see the night as "fine" and "frosty," fix on glittering "Orion" and the "northern lights," and affirm his intention to go "a-whaling." The following morning, having "felt a shock" (of recognition, we might say) that ran "through all [his] frame" when "a supernatural hand seemed placed in [his]," and having felt the "very similar" sensations caused by Queequeg's "bridegroom clasp," he finds his way to the Whaleman's Chapel. There, contemplating the marble tablets commemorating lost whalemen, he concludes that "faith, like a jackal, feeds among the tombs, and even from these dead doubts she gathers her most vital hope." On his own, now, he seems ready to face death, the "speechlessly quick chaotic bundling of a man into Eternity" that he accepts as part of the whaling business. But as "instinct" had led Ishmael "waterward," Melville directs his attention to the pulpit and then to Father Mapple's sermon. When Ishmael contemplates the pulpit, he wonders, "what could be more full of meaning?" and concludes that "the pulpit is the earth's foremost part," that "Yes, the world's a ship on its passage out, and not a voyage complete; and the pulpit is its prow" ("The Pulpit"). Then he hears the sermon in which the voyage of the *Pequod* is charted.

It is fitting that Father Mapple kneels in the "pulpit's bows" in a posture "so deeply devout that he seemed kneeling and praying at the bottom of the sea," for his sermon will dwell on Jonah's feelings as he lay "beneath the ship's waterline," still an unchastened fugitive, and on his later experience in "the shuddering cold and blackness of the sea." But as Father Mapple's sermon soars to its conclusion from this underwater darkness—

celebrating Jonah's deliverance when "the whale came breeching up towards the warm and pleasant sun, and all the delights of air and earth"—the aesthetic dimensions of *Moby-Dick* are first fully displayed. Envisioning and celebrating the static order of a world balanced between darkness and light, *Moby-Dick* proceeds as does the *Pequod* itself, on an "even keel," when she counterpoises the hoisted head of a sperm whale with that of a right whale ("Stubb & Flask Kill a Right Whale"). The aesthetics of balance are projected everywhere in the book—in the "marriage" of Ishmael and Queequeg (in "A Bosom Friend") and in their "wedding" (in "The Monkey-rope"); in the contrasting but complementary personalities of Ishmael and Ahab; in Ishmael's saving sense of balance when he sways on the masthead with "the inscrutable tides of God"; and in the image of the Catskill Eagle who dives "into the blackest gorges" and soars out and up, "invisible in the sunny spaces."

Father Mapple, "a sailor and harpooneer in his youth," projects Jonah's ascent into light in terms that would be familiar to any simple sailor like Ishmael:

> But oh! shipmates! on the starboard side of every woe, there is a sure delight; and higher the top of that delight, than the bottom of the woe is deep. Is not the main truck higher than the kelson is low? Delight is to him—a far, far upward, and inward delight—who against the proud gods and commodores of this earth, ever stands forth his own inexorable self. Delight is to him whose strong arms yet support him, when the ship of this base treacherous world has gone down beneath him. Delight . . . Delight,—top-gallant delight is to him who acknowledges no law or lord, but the Lord his God, and is only a patriot to heaven. ("The Sermon")

The *Pequod's* voyage into the life-waters will follow a course set between the theological poles of light and dark that Father Mapple establishes in "The Sermon." Like Father Mapple, Ishmael will sail "before the mast, right down into the forecastle, aloft there to the royal-masthead," and he will survive his voyage with one of "the proud gods and commodores of this earth." But having been moved by the "damp, drizzly November" of his soul "to see the watery part of the world," he must wait until the even darker days of early December before the *Pequod* gets under weigh on a "cold Christmas" day. Finally, as a "cold, damp night breeze" blew and "a screaming gull flew overhead," the *Pequod* "blindly plunged like fate into the lone Atlantic," embarked on a voyage—like nothing even Melville could envision again—into the season of light ("Merry Christmas").

"The Encantadas": "Abased" Sea Stories

In his series of sea stories after 1851, Melville could envision neither the scenes of underwater wonder nor those of "top-gallant delight" that we know in *Moby-Dick*. Lacking both a simple sailor's lofty point of view and the magnificent whale to illuminate his meditations, these stories constitute a distinct withdrawal from the wild life-waters into memorable but somewhat shallower analyses of particular minds like Captain Delano's or, finally, Vere's. In November of 1853 Melville had accepted a $300 advance from Harper and Brothers for a book on "Tortoises and Tortoise Hunting," a subject he must have hoped would feed his imagination as *The Whale* had. But in February of 1854 he sent his regrets that for "a variety of causes," the book (then a month overdue) required "additional work" (Leyda 1:482). The "book" became a mere part of another, *The Piazza Tales*. But "The Encantadas or Enchanted Islands" (published serially under the name Salvator R. Tarnmoor, a name that suggests Melville's darkening and unsealike frame of mind) is a small achievement only in relation to something like *Moby-Dick*. The various sketches in "The Encantadas" offered Melville a number of attractive opportunities: to draw again on his own whaling experience, to pursue the zoological interests he had successfully embodied in *Moby-Dick*, and even to work in with them a story he had run across on his excursion to Nantucket in 1852, the "Agatha" story he tried to give Hawthorne and which became the story of the Chola widow Hunilla ("Sketch Eighth" of "The Encantadas"). But he could not bring these possibilities to life as a sustained organic tale.

Over a century later in the tradition of American sea fiction, Peter Matthiessen would produce the most worthy successor to *Moby-Dick* in his story of the sea turtle fishery, *Far Tortuga* (1975). But Melville's tortoises were land creatures, and his zoological meditations on them, as well as on the other inhabitants of the Enchanted Isles, including man, are far less "scientific" or systematic than were his previous meditations on the whale. In Darwin's earlier work from the Galapagos, he might have had another Bennett or Beale to guide him in zoological matters, but he was in no mood to follow. As H. Bruce Franklin has shown in "The Island Worlds of Darwin and Melville," Melville not only avoided mentioning Darwin's name (even though he had earlier quoted from *Voyage of a Naturalist*, a copy of which he had owned for seven years) but "questioned Darwin's individual observations" and parodied his methods (363–65). But Franklin's conclusion about the differences between Darwin and Melville obscure the historical developments in biological thought between the time of Darwin's visit to the Galapagos in 1835 and Melville's sketches of them in 1854. Referring to Darwin, Franklin says, "it is one thing to be told that one is only a higher form of animal, struggling for existence, surviving only if fit, part of a teleological scheme of things"; and, in reference to Melville, "it is quite something else to look into a mirror and see some kind of inanimate object like a skull" (370). There are two problems with this assessment of Darwin and Melville. First, since Darwin had not yet formulated and published the *Origin of Species* in 1854, we cannot conclude that Melville had considered the theory of natural selection implied in Franklin's remarks. Second, to emphasize that Melville's vision of "The Encantadas" can be represented by the image of an "inanimate object like a skull" is to obscure the fact that his biological observations, such as they are, are a kind of natural theology.

The main idea in Melville's view of the Encantadas in 1854 (and in 1876, when they appear again in *Clarel*) is that they demonstrate what he took to be the theological truth that we live in a fallen world: "In no world but a fallen one could such lands exist" (*GSW*, 100). Depressing as this thought may be, it merely presents the dark underside of a timeless, coherent universe, in which light ultimately prevails. Melville would always know a "paradise" midway across the Pacific that corresponds to the Encantadas' hell. He was reminded of this in the Mediterranean on his way to the Holy Land in 1856: "Such weather as one might have in Paradise. Pacific. November too!" (Leyda 2:532). Accordingly, his description of the tortoises in their Galapagos hell scarcely considers their anatomical particulars or their patterns of life. Rather, they are "victims of a penal, a malignant, or perhaps a downright diabolical, enchanter," and "their crowning curse is their drudging impulse to straightforwardness in a belittered world" (*GSW*, 105). This view of the tortoises grows out of a shipboard experience that recalls the rushing "herds of walruses and whales" beneath the Nantucketer's pillow in *Moby-Dick,* but the lyric exuberance and watery wonder of *Moby-Dick* are gone: "As I lay in my hammock that night, overhead I heard the slow weary draggings of the three ponderous strangers along the encumbered deck. Their stupidity or their resolution was so great that they never went aside for any impediment" (105). Similarly, his single imaginative plunge beneath the surface of the water after 1851 (until the "Epilogue" in *Clarel*, and then later in *John Marr and Other Sailors* and the ballad of "Billy in the Darbies") reveals how profoundly he had lost the sense of balance he had maintained in *Moby-Dick.* Whereas his earlier dives had ended in visions of darkness yielding to light, death to the wondrous life-waters, now, in the "abased sea-story of Redondo" he sees "labyrinthine lurking places," deception, and victimization (109–10)—qualities not so much of life as of the confidence-*man* in a fallen world.

Below the waterline, the rock seemed one honeycomb of grottoes, affording labyrinthine lurking places for swarms of fairy fish. All were strange, many exceedingly beautiful, and would have well graced the costliest glass globes in which goldfish are kept for a show. Nothing was more striking than the complete novelty of many individuals in this multitude. Here hues were seen as yet unpainted, and figures which are unengraved.

To show the multitude, avidity, and nameless fearlessness and tameness of these fish, let me say that often, marking through the clear spaces of water—temporarily made so by the concentric dartings of the fish above the surface—certain larger and less unwary wights which swam slow and deep, our anglers would cautiously essay to drop their lines down to these last. But in vain; there was no passing the uppermost zone. No sooner did the hook touch the sea, than a hundred infatuates contended for the honor of capture. Poor fish of Redondo! in your victimized confidence, you are of the number of those who inconsiderately trust, while they do not understand, human nature. (110)

In his story of the Chola widow ("Sketch Eighth"), Melville dramatizes his view that "the special curse . . . of the Encantadas, that which exalts them in desolation above Idumea [the desert wasteland near the Dead Sea] and the Pole, is that to them change never comes; neither the change of seasons nor of sorrows" (99). When Hunilla tells her tragic story, "the mariners [draw into] a voiceless circle round her," and, warning the reader who fails to feel, Melville offers his own tribute to her suffering: "Humanity, thou strong thing, I worship thee, not in the laureled victor, but in this vanquished one" (134, 132). But he cannot enter her mind and give voice to her suffering, as he had projected his diving and soaring meditations through Ishmael's voyaging mind. Yet Hunilla is definitely a projection of his own feelings about life and the sea, not as he had celebrated the wedding of mind with the life-waters in *Moby-Dick*, but as he had come to view them. Like Bartleby, whom the lawyer saw as "a bit of wreck in the mid-Atlantic," Hunilla is a "lone shipwrecked soul, out of treachery invoking trust" (132). Through this image of the shipwrecked soul we can grasp the essential impulse of Melville's sea fiction as it developed from 1849 in *Mardi* to 1876 in *Clarel*. In *Mardi* he had advised that we "hold fast to all we have; and stop all leaks in our faith; lest an opening, but of a hand's breadth, should sink our seventy-fours" ("Faith and Knowledge"). In *Moby-Dick* Ahab's defiant, "Faith? What's that?" had its inevitable consequences, but Ishmael could float to safety ("The Deck"). And the image of Bartleby and Hunilla as shipwrecked souls will culminate for Melville in the four tales of sea disasters in *Clarel*, most dramatically when the seaman-pilgrim Agath first sights Jerusalem:

> . . . the salt one sent his gaze
> As from the mast-head o'er the pale
> Expanse. But what may eyes avail?
> Land lone as seas without a sail.
> "Wreck, ho—the wreck! . . .
> . . . .
> "Wreck, ho! the wreck—Jerusalem!"   (IV, i)

Israel Potter

Israel Potter is not purely a sea story, nor does its considerable merit as a work of art elevate it to the distinction of "Benito Cereno" or *Billy Budd, Sailor*. Still, it is deservedly, if only gradually, finding a higher place in critical estimates of the Melville canon than it has previously enjoyed. And in the tradition of American sea fiction, it is a crucial book in Melville's long "story of ocean" (*IP*, chap. 19). Melville's description of Israel's early years as a seaman provides us with our best view of the transitional period between 1851 and 1856, when Melville fell from his mood of "top-gallant delight" into his long period of silence as a writer of fiction. Israel's "youthful adventures," like Melville's, culminated when, "entering on board a Nantucket ship," he embarked upon successive whaling voyages around the world. "Promoted to be harpooner" on his last voyage, Israel "unwittingly prepared himself for the Bunker Hill rifle" by "darting the whale-lance" (chap. 2). On "this last voyage, our adventurer experienced to the extreme all the hardships and privations of the whaleman's life on a long voyage to distant and barbarous waters; hardships and privations unknown at the present day [1854–55], when science has so greatly contributed, in manifold ways, to lessen the sufferings, and add to the comforts of seafaring men" (chap. 2). These long voyages made him "heartily sick of the ocean," but the falseness he finds at home, and his long series of experiences as a farmer, a soldier, a man-of-war's man, and an exploited wanderer in the deserts of London, never stifle his capacity for wonder. At last, he finds "time to linger, and loiter, and lounge—slowly absorb what he saw—meditate himself into boundless amazement" (chap. 24). And on his last sea voyage home he will see the "white-haired old ocean . . . as a brother" (chap. 25). Here we can see reflected not only Melville's sense of the crucial role his own "whaleship" education continued to play in his life, but one of his earliest backward glances to "the time before steamships" (as he would put it at the beginning of *Billy Budd, Sailor*). Melville is not only literature's greatest celebrant but the first great elegist of the sailor's existence.

Even before he conceived of *Moby-Dick,* Melville had felt firsthand the steamship's threat to the sailor's life he had known and in which he had recently delighted during his passage across the Atlantic.[1] On 27 November 1849, aboard the steamer *Emerald* in the English Channel, he recorded in his journal "a shocking accident [that] occurred to one of the hands of the boat. His foot was ruined in the machinery" (Leyda 1:340). By December, however, he wished that he "could go home in a steamer—but it would take an extra $100 out of my pocket" (349). In subsequent voyages by steamer he would descend with the engineer to "the fearful scene" of the furnaces, "a hell in the hull," and register the sense of loss that would haunt Jack London, Eugene O'Neill, and many others (Leyda 2:540, 550). The modern forces that impinge upon Israel Potter's life necessarily predate the steamship: the "modern" methods of naval warfare during the revolutionary war, the "polluted" Thames with its "coal-scows" drifting along like "awaiting hearses." But these reflect the increasingly complex modern forces in Melville's own time that made him look again upon the ocean in his last years (in *John Marr and Other Sailors,* especially) as Israel does at the end of his "forty years' wanderings," when, with "locks besnowed as [the ocean's] foam," he recognizes his "Ocean . . . brother" (chap. 25). Like the last old sailor Melville gave us in his "Daniel Orme," Israel is "the bescarred bearer of a cross" on his chest, the cross slash having come from "a cutlass wound" in sea battle. Near his death, Israel dedicates "a little book," as Melville would dedicate *John Marr and Other Sailors* to W. Clark Russell, but "long ago it faded out of print" (chap. 26). Both Israel and Daniel Orme are given peaceful deaths. But, having suffered even more than Israel had (across the tattooed "cross of the Passion" on his chest "and on the side of the heart" ran "a whitish scar . . . from the slash of a cutlass"), Orme is allowed to die on Easter. Recalling scenes "of the wide world's beauty dreamily suggested by the hazy waters before him," Orme sleeps into death and is "buried among other sailors" (*GSW,* 428). With Orme's death and the ballad of "Billy in the Darbies," Melville ended his nearly forty-year elegy for the simple sailor's existence.

In addition to the elegiac treatment of the sailor's existence that he began in *Israel Potter,* Melville made two other contributions to the tradition of American sea fiction in this book: his description of the sea battle between the *Bon Homme Richard* and the *Serapis* and, more important, his unique portrait of a sea captain in John Paul Jones. The sea battle, cited by Frank Jewett Mather in 1919 as "the best account of a sea fight in American fiction," is Melville's only naval war scene.[2] But, rousing as it may be, it is important to recognize that such battles are totally contrary to Melville's feelings for the ocean and to see that his purpose in treating it at length is to undermine the glory surrounding such accounts in traditional sea fiction. The true sailor, as he wrote in *White-Jacket,* "expatriate[s himself] to nationalize with the universe": "Life in a man-of-war . . . with its martial formalities and thousand vices, stabs to the heart the soul of all free-and-easy honourable rovers" ("The Jacket Aloft"). Some four years after *White-Jacket*, Melville pursued the same idea by describing the famous battle as a "Miltonic contest of Archangels" that ends with the *Richard's* sinking: "Gorged with slaughter, [it] wallowed heavily, gave a long roll, and blasted by tornadoes of sulphur, slowly sank, like Gomorrah, out of sight" (chap. 19).

The *Richard's* apocalyptic end is like Ahab's, but the essential difference between these whelmings of doubt and evil is that by late 1854 Melville could no longer sustain the lyric meditations that had buoyed his spirits in *Moby-Dick*. Israel is allowed but a brief return to something like the "top-gallant delight" he seems to have known in his youth; he can, at last, "meditate himself into boundless amazement" (chap. 24), but Melville can find no language to express it. By now his own wanderings in fiction had intensified his view of a diffusely ambiguous fallen world in which man's capacity for evil can no longer be concentrated in a heroic Ahab. Nor could he image life's awful, protean vitality in the elusive white whale. The poles of light and dark that gave clarity to *Moby-Dick* are now dissolved in the obscuring fogs and grey seas that will set the stage in "Benito Cereno." In *Israel Potter*, Melville can only question, "in view of [the sea] battle . . . what separates the enlightened man from the savage? Is civilization a thing distinct; or is it an advanced stage of barbarism? . . . Why cannot men be peaceable on that great common? Or does nature in those fierce night-brawlers, the billows, set mankind but a sorry example?" (chaps. 19 and 20).

The only conclusion Melville seems to have reached in answer to these questions in 1854–55 is that, "sorry" as nature's example might be, it is at least vital and therefore by far preferable to the weary, Waste Land view of life he envisions at last in chapter 24, "In the City of Dis." There, on a foggy, doleful November day in grimy London, Israel watches the "hereditary crowd—gulf stream of humanity—which, for continuous centuries, has never ceased pouring, like an endless shoal of herring, over London Bridge. . . . As ant-hills, the bridge arches crawled with processions of carts, coaches." Industrial smoke hides the sun from this scene, and the laborers' "sorrowful tramping" suggests to Melville the crawling "convict tortoises" of the "cursed Gallipagos." This much of life's sadness, at least, Israel is allowed to escape; for, a fated wanderer, he can return to the New World and, on the way, recognize his old brother Ocean.

No character in Melville's remaining sea stories will retain Israel's capacity to "meditate himself into boundless amazement," and no sea captain in Melville's fiction either before or after *Israel Potter* has John Paul Jones's potential for establishing a healing, democratic bond between himself and his seamen. Jones is a fantastic creation whose promising attributes derive from Melville's effort to embody in him some of the vital qualities he had brought to life in the bond between Ishmael and Queequeg. But in the confusion of battle and with sails suddenly filling with the chance winds, Israel and Jones are separated. The promising sea captain disappears from the book, never to reappear in Melville's later stories—a fleeting image of democratic authority under which America, which "is, or may yet be, the Paul Jones of nations," might have been truly united (chap. 19).

Sadly, Melville's next two sea captains, Delano and Vere, will either blindly support the institution of slavery or sacrifice a simple sailor to the institution of martial law. But John Paul Jones's fantastic qualities, as Melville renders them in *Israel Potter*, allow him to commit without censure even the traditionally unforgivable act of flogging a sailor (chap. 14). Jones is "an untrammelled citizen and sailor of the universe," or "a democratic sort of sea-king" (chaps. 10, 14). And the sources of his democratic spirit are, first, that he had sailed "before the mast" as a common sailor, and, second, that he had a heart: he was a man of "poignant feelings," who was subject to "sudden incitements of passion" (chap. 14). These feelings sometimes overcome and even embarrass him, as when he expresses "his sympathy with Israel" in "momentary ebullition," or when Israel first glimpses Jones in "a little bit of by-play [with a] pretty chambermaid" at the residence of Benjamin Franklin (chaps. 14, 10). Like Franklin, who is as "labyrinth-minded" and "sly, sly, sly" as Melville's confidence-man, Jones is a shape-shifting character (chaps. 8, 9). But his essential qualities of simplicity (as a common sailor) and passion clearly distinguish him from Franklin and reveal his similarity to Ishmael the poet. As distinct from Franklin, whom Melville views here as "the type and genius of his land" and who is "everything but a poet," Jones has "a bit of the poet as well as the outlaw in him" (chaps. 8, 10). His promise as a sea captain derives largely from his capacity to lose himself in passionate intuitiveness, as when Israel sees him "wrapped in Indian meditations" (chap. 11).

Working with Jones' essential qualities of simplicity and passion, Melville creates the promising but fantastic sea captain by attempting to revive the unifying force that gave coherence to *Moby-Dick*—the principle of marriage. Captain Jones and Israel will establish a bond that clearly resembles the "marriage" between Ishmael and Queequeg. But because *Israel Potter* is not a pure sea story that originated, like *Moby-Dick,* in a magic wedding of meditation and water, Jones could become no more than a minor character in Melville's fiction and his relationship with Israel could be only a passing episode in Israel's life. In *Israel Potter,* everything that the sea had represented in Melville's earlier mood of exuberant affirmation—his sense, as in "The Symphony," that the "feminine air" and "the masculine sea . . . seemed one . . . even as bride and groom"—is violated by "the martial bustle of a great man-of-war." This martial bustle was "indescribably jarring to [Israel's] present mood. Those sounds of the human multitude disturbing the solemn natural solitudes of the sea, mysteriously afflicted him" (chap. 14).

The bond between Israel and Captain Jones is not consummated as was the one between Ishmael and Queequeg in "The Counterpane," with Queequeg's "bridegroom clasp." When Potter offers to share his bed with the Captain ("why not sleep together," he asks, chap. 11), Jones declines, not because he is "notional," but because he does not presently "care to." Later, he gives up his own bed and stateroom to Israel, reminding him that "you offered me your bed in Paris." When Israel responds, "But you begged off, Captain, and so must I," Jones very reasonably declines, and in a way that preserves the positive potential of this union: "Lad, I don't sleep half a night out of three." Then, as a loving father and responsible captain, he sends Israel to his bed alone: "To hammock, to hammock! while I go on deck to clap on more sail to your cradle" (chap. 14). As a sea captain, Jones is unique in his willingness to share his bed with an ordinary seaman; and Melville emphasizes that the source of this promising attribute in his "democratic . . . sea-king" was in his sea experience "before the mast." As Jones tells Israel, he had for a "hammock-mate a full-blooded Congo. We had a white blanket spread in our hammock. Every time I turned in I found the Congo's black wool worked in with the white worsted. By the end of the voyage the blanket was of a pepper-and-salt look, like an old man's turning head" (chap. 11). This clear suggestion of Jones's wisdom in accepting his fellow man in the spirit of natural democracy places him in stark contrast with Melville's next sea captain. Amasa Delano is so blinded by his sunny vacuity that he cannot comprehend blackness. He can understand neither the blacks who confront him nor, emphatically, the reality of slavery; thus he bids to purchase a man: "'Tell me, Don Benito,' he added with a smile—'I should like to have your man here, myself—what will you take for him? Would fifty doubloons be any object?'" (GSW, 254).

By emphasizing a long series of matings in which seemingly contradictory elements are brought together in Jones (the "democratic . . . sea-king"), Melville develops his fantastic captain's capacity for creating unity. After we are told of his bedding with the Congo, we see, when Israel gets a "glimpse" of Jones's body, the "mysterious tattooings" on his arms—the "sort of tattooing such as is seen only on thorough-bred savages—deep blue, elaborate, labyrinthine, cabalistic" (chap. 11). Like any reader of Moby-Dick, Israel "remembered having beheld" such markings on an earlier voyage. The marriage of civilization and savagery is always in Melville's thought potentially saving, especially when the savagery partakes of Queequeg's cannibal vitality, or of this fantastic captain's, who is proud of being a "sort of bloody cannibal" (chap. 13). This is the source of Jones's "regicidal daring," which is "strangely coupled with octogenarian prudence" (chap. 16). And these "apparent incompatibilities" are merely one aspect of the fantastic unity that Melville would establish both *within* his individual seamen (Israel and Jones) and *between* them: "Give me your hand, my lion," Jones says to Israel as they seal the bond between them in opposition to the British: "By Heaven, you hate so well, I love ye" (chap. 14).

In Melville's view, the wedding of hate and love is a true reflection of the eternal war between light and dark. And in projecting this eternal conflict as a natural marriage, he can at least tentatively accept even the horror of ocean warfare: Jones tells Israel that he is "engaged to marry her [the ship-of-war *Drake*] tonight. The bride's friends won't like the match; and so, this very night, the bride must be carried away. She has a nice tapering waist, hasn't she? . . . Ah! I will clasp her to my heart" (chap. 16). Thus Melville's much-admired description of the battle between the *Bon Homme Richard* and the *Serapis* (clearly derived from Cooper's description in *History of the Navy*[3]) is insinuated with such images as these: in hatred, the *Serapis* is like "a wheeling cock about a hen, when stirred by the contrary passion" (chap. 19); or, "thus far the *Serapis* and the *Richard* had been manoeuvering and chasseing to each other like partners in a cotillon, all the time indulging in rapid repartee" (chap. 19).

From the point of view of American sea fiction, the most interesting product of Captain Jones's power and willingness to couple in so many ways is that it accounts for his superiority in seamanship among all Melville's sea captains. He has the wisdom to sail with the wind and yield to its superior force when it opposes "his purpose" (chap. 16). Once he demonstrates his sailing skills to Israel: "Paul stood lightly, swaying his body over the sea, by holding on to the mizzen-shrouds, an attitude not inexpressive of his easy audacity" (chap. 15). Another time, "when the wind turned against him again in hard squalls," he "abandoned the project." "Thus, seeming as much to bear the elemental commission of Nature, as the military warrant of Congress, swarthy Paul" darts "hither and thither" to his heroic achievements (chap. 15). In this way, John Paul Jones is diametrically opposed to Captain Vere, who is no seaman at all. In total contrast to Vere (who professes his "allegiance" not "to Nature," but only "to the King" [chap. 21]), "Captain Paul" even in the direst crisis is the image of mystic nature itself: "Paul flew hither and thither like the meteoric corposant-ball, which shiftingly dances on the tips and verges of ships' rigging in storms" (chap. 19). But in Melville's career as a sea-writer, the light shed by this fantastic sea captain ("he casts a pale light on all faces") can flicker only very briefly. The mystic weddings that made him, like those that had given life to *Moby-Dick*, had become virtually ungraspable phantoms in Melville's fiction.[4] As he wrote in 1856, in a passage called "The River," which he originally intended for *The Confidence-Man*, "Wood & wave wed, man is remote" (Leyda 2:518). More than the passing of the great sailing ships, the greatest loss in the history of American sea fiction was Melville's certainty that "meditation and water are wedded forever."

"Benito Cereno"

The sea . . . seemed fixed.
—Melville, "Benito Cereno"

Melville's last great sea stories, "Benito Cereno" and *Billy Budd, Sailor*, are scarcely touched by the waters that had given life to *Moby-Dick*. The "water" toward which Amasa Delano has been drawn in the opening paragraph of "Benito Cereno," unlike that in "Loomings," is the fresh water he seeks ashore on the southern coast of Chile. And the setting Melville establishes for this sea story is on a "sea," which "though undulated into long roods of swells, seemed fixed, and was sleeked at the surface like waved lead that has cooled and set in the smelter's mold" (GSW, 239). By contrast, eight years earlier, in *Mardi*, Babbalanja imagined diving into "sunny summer seas, down, down . . . starting at passive phantoms that you cannot fix." Moreover, it is appropriate that the *Bachelor's Delight*, Captain Delano's ship, remains at anchor for the duration of the story. Both the captain and his ship seem inherently unsuited for the kind of voyage Ishmael had welcomed in his affirmation that "meditation and water are wedded forever."

Melville's ironic design in "Benito Cereno" (as in "Bartleby" and *Billy Budd*) is to portray a mind constitutionally incapable of either meditation or "wedding." Delano cannot grasp the idea of unity because he has no sense of disunity: like his bachelor brothers Captain Vere and the lawyer in "Bartleby," he cannot conceive of the other realm of existence he is made to confront in the title character's life. An effective, fortunate man, Delano (unlike Ahab or the neglected creator of *Moby-Dick*) is a hero precisely because his fated mind is forever shielded from doubt. The sense of blackness that destroys the Spanish sea captain can never touch the American, whose last words emphasize his enduring blindness: "What has cast such a shadow upon you?" (314).

In this sea story in which there is no voyage, Melville uses sea imagery only to emphasize his sea captain's ironic ignorance of the ocean reality. When Delano boards the Spanish vessel he is immediately enchanted by the "living spectacle" he sees there, "in contrast with the blank ocean which zones it" (242). Melville associates Delano's blindness to the reality he now enters with his equally blind sense of the ocean's blankness, as though it had no life itself. Aboard the *San Dominick,* Delano will hear and accept as truth the fiction of her trials in a Cape Horn passage. The traditional sea story of the hazardous voyage is here a mere ruse, impenetrable to Captain Delano despite his estimable sea experience. Melville's point is that Delano is a man who cannot learn from experience; furthermore, as he unwittingly suggests himself, he is more suited to life ashore than at sea. "What, I, Amasa Delano—Jack of the Beach, as they called me when a lad . . . I, little Jack of the Beach . . . to be murdered here at the ends of the earth?" His limited mind cannot grasp such a possibility. With his "conscience . . . clean," and with his certainty that "there is some one above," he chides himself: "Fie, fie, Jack of the Beach, you are a child indeed" (272). He concludes that the ugly signs of slavery he had glimpsed resulted only from "a sort of love-quarrel, after all" (283); and later he welcomes "the sound of the parted waters [that] came more and more gurglingly and merrily in at the windows" as the *San Dominick* approaches the *Bachelor's Delight* (290).

But Melville's crucial stroke in emphasizing Delano's instinctive ignorance and even fear of the sea is the captain's confession of his own anxiety in regard to burial at sea. Mistakenly thinking that he "divined the cause of such unusual emotion" in Benito Cereno (his "quivering" at the mere mention of his dead friend, the slaveowner Alexandro Aranda), Delano attempts to console him:

> "By a sympathetic experience, I conjecture, Don Benito, what it is that gives the keener edge to your grief. It was once my hard fortune to lose, at sea, a dear friend, my own brother, then supercargo. Assured of the welfare of his spirit, its departure I could have borne like a man: but that honest eye, that honest hand—both of which had so often met mine—and that warm heart; all, all—like scraps to the dogs—to throw all to the sharks! It was then I vowed never to have for fellow-voyager a man I loved, unless, unbeknown to him, I had provided every requisite, in case of a fatality, for embalming his mortal part for interment on shore. Were your friend's remains now on board this ship, Don Benito, not thus strangely would the mention of his name affect you." (254)

Melville intensifies the irony at such moments, but his point here is not only that Delano is blind to the situation aboard the *San Dominick* (where Aranda's skeleton remains enshrouded at the ship's beak, "death for the figure-head, in a human skeleton"), but more deeply, that in his willful blindness to death and darkness, Captain Delano dramatizes his complete ineptitude as a sea captain with true authority. Unlike Ahab (or Ishmael), Delano has no sense that "the ocean . . . is the dark side of this earth, and . . . is two thirds of this earth" (*MD*, "The Try-Works"). In performing the sea captain's duty to preside meaningfully over the sacred ceremonial of sea burial, Delano would in effect walk "fast crossing graveyards," thereby demonstrating his unfitness to "sit down on tomb-stones and break the green damp mould with unfathomably wondrous Solomon" ("The Try-Works").

We can assume that to Melville, a captain with true credentials as a seaman would perform the ceremony with quiet strength and dignity, as his own brother did off Cape Horn on 9 August 1860. During a gale that day, a Nantucket sailor was killed in a fall "from the Main topsail yard to the deck." As Melville described the incident in his journal, "the body bled incessantly up to the moment of burying; which was about one o'clock, from the poop, in the interval between blinding squalls of sharp sleet." The body had been sewn up in a piece of sail cloth, with cannon balls at the foot; "and, when all was ready, the body was put on a plank, and carried to the ship's side in the presence of all hands." The ceremony was "made still the more trying for being under the lee of the reefed spanker where the wind eddies so." Then, while "all stood covered with Sou-Westers or Russia caps & comforters, except [the dead sailor's friend] Macy—who stood bareheaded," Melville's brother "Tom, as Captain, read a prayer out of the prayer book, and at a given word, the sailors who held the plank tipped it up, and immediately the body slipped into the stormy ocean, and we saw it no more" (Leyda 2:622–23).[5]

Ironically gifted with "enchanted" vision, Melville emphasizes repeatedly, Delano imagines that "naked nature" is "pure tenderness and love" (268). And Benito Cereno's sense that "God charmed [Delano's] life" (313) is underscored when circumstances prevent Delano from having to witness the decisive battle when the Americans board the *San Dominick*. Melville's brief description of the battle clearly specifies the underlying reality of life and the sea which Delano's charmed vision can never penetrate: "For a few breath's space, there was a vague, muffled, inner sound, as of submerged sword-fish rushing hither and thither through shoals of blackfish" (298). Had Delano viewed this scene, he would have transformed it into another sunny vision of "blue sea . . . blue sky . . . [and] mild trades . . . [that are] warm . . . steadfast friends" (314). And because Delano can neither change nor help himself, Melville can temper his exasperation with him by presenting him as a child, "Jack of the Beach." But if, recognizing Delano's fated existence, Melville hesitates to judge him harshly, he is relentless in emphasizing the treachery that lurks unconsciously beneath the surface of the captain's "good-nature." His vision of "suffering" as being "more apparent than real" will always "happily interweave" his "good-nature, compassion, and charity" and make him incapable of grasping the underlying tragedy of Christian thought or, most painfully from Melville's perspective in 1855, the institution of slavery (314). Finally, from the point of view of American sea fiction, it is important to note that Captain Delano's fated vision—his complacent, sunny vacuity—excludes him from the brotherhood of true seamen. That the *Bachelor's Delight* remains at anchor in "Benito Cereno" signals Delano's fatal incapacity: the impossibility of his embarking on the traditional quest or voyage that necessarily begins in darkness or doubt.

4

The Jonah Feeling

I am emphatically alone & begin to feel like Jonah.
—Melville's journal

During the year and a half after he completed "Benito Cereno," Melville produced the last fiction he would write for over thirty
years, "The Piazza" and *The Confidence-Man*. These accounts of inland
voyages took him more and more deeply into the dark mood from which
he sought relief in October of 1856 by embarking on his own actual voyage—a traditional voyage toward light, eastward to the Holy Land. These
were "times of failing faith," as he wrote in "The Piazza," where his narrator, "removed into the country," could recall his earlier days at sea,
when he had felt the "oceanic" "vastness and lonesomeness" and had
weathered cape Horn (*GSW*, 384, 386). Now, from the outset, the narrator knows that on his "inland voyage" he can aspire only to a "fairyland"
enlightenment. Inevitably, this voyage will lead to the sense that "truth
comes in with darkness. No light shows from the mountains" (395). Finally realizing that "to reach fairyland it must be voyaged to, and with
faith," the narrator can affirm only his own "failing faith" and resolve to
launch his "yawl no more for fairyland" (388, 395). Instead, in *The Confidence-Man*, Melville launched his Mississippi steamer *Fidele* ("Faithful")
on an even more intensely ironic voyage into darkness. Its fated course
downstream tested his own faith and virtually shattered his faith in the
vessel of fiction, which he abandoned here in desperation, when "the
waning light expired": "Something more may follow of this Masquerade,"
he wrote at the end of the book. And on 7 October he wrote to Peter
Gansevoort that "I think of sailing for the other side of the ocean on Saturday next, to be gone an uncertain time" (Leyda 2:523).

By the eleventh, having left to his brother Allan the task of complet-
ing contractual arrangements for the publication of *The Confidence-Man*,
he was at sea again. If he was far less confident than he had been seven
years earlier, when he had advised in *Mardi* that "we hold fast to all we

have; and stop all leaks in our faith," he was still the quintessential voyager, a man who could "neither believe, nor be comfortable in his unbelief," as Hawthorne described him at this time (Leyda 2 : 529). Traveling
alone on the steamer *Egyptian* toward the Middle East, Melville experienced a brief sense of having returned to the "Paradise" he had known in
the South Pacific, but inevitably, his pilgrimage would fill him with the
sense of desolation he reproduced later in the Waste Land imagery of
Clarel. The details of this desert landscape he acquired there, but he took
with him the general sense of it as a cindery landscape that he had already
projected briefly in "The Carpet Bag" (in *Moby-Dick*), "The Encantadas,"
and *Israel Potter*. On the first leg of this voyage, he recorded conversations
of "fixed fate &c."; he told Hawthorne in England that "he 'had pretty
much made up his mind to be annihilated'"; and in Hawthorne's description of him with his single "carpet-bag to hold all his travelling gear . . .
the next thing to going naked," he was the very image of his earlier fated
wanderers, the simple sailors Ishmael and Israel (531). The essential point
here is that in his image of himself as a fated, lone wanderer lay the saving
sense that would sustain him both on this actual pilgrimage and in his re-
creation of it in *Clarel*. Seeing himself as Jonah, more desperately alone
than even Ishmael or Israel, he could endure the extreme bitterness he
recorded in his visit to the Dead Sea: "The water, carried bitter in my
mouth all day—bitterness of life—thought of all bitter things—Bitter it is
to be poor & bitter, to be reviled, & Oh bitter are these waters of Death,
thought I" (546).

Jerusalem, as he viewed it from the hills on his way to Bethlehem,
was unrecognizable, "exactly like arid rocks"; and bathing in the Mediterranean at Jaffa he was struck by the sight of "some old ruins of walls by &
in, the sea" (547). The old image of walls that had tormented Ahab and
overshadowed Bartleby now intruded into the sea. "I am the only traveller
sojourning in Joppa," he wrote. "I am emphatically alone, & begin to feel
like Jonah. The wind is rising, the swell of the sea increasing" (547). But
he could affirm, after a sleepless night there, that "the genuine Jonah feeling, in Joppa too, is worth experiencing. . . . I have been to the alleged
house of Simon the Tanner—'by the sea' & with a wall." He can endure
this loss and loneliness "only by stern self-control & grim defiance" (548).
Still, in the depths of his despair, there is a muffled hope in his identification with Jonah, whose shipboard imprisonment in the "contracted
hold, sunk beneath the ship's waterline," as Father Mapple described it,
was a "presentiment" of his imprisonment within the whale and, ultimately, his deliverance. In his hotel at Jaffa, Melville's "genuine Jonah
feeling" was heightened by his observation that "the main beam crossing
my chamber overhead, is evidently taken from a wreck—the trenail holes
proving it" (548).

In a later moment of loneliness and despair on this pilgrimage, he sought relief by imagining himself at sea. He recorded how, having been lost in "the intricacy of the streets" in Constantinople, he thought of a pocket-compass. The streets were a "perfect labyrinth. Narrow. Close, shut in. If one could get *up* aloft, it would be easy to see one's way out" (Leyda 2:536). Perhaps he had in mind the kind of "top-gallant delight" that Father Mapple had promised in "The Sermon," a delight higher "than the woe is deep." But there in Constantinople he could ascend only to the watch tower; and if from there he had a glorious view, his descent into the grimy streets was inevitable. Finally, his pilgrimage left him mainly with the images of shipwreck and desolation that he later reproduced in *Clarel*—the kind, for example, that he recorded in Cairo, of "Ruined mosques, domes knocked in like stoven boats" (541). Repeatedly, he was "afflicted with the great curse of modern travel—skepticism." But even in this despair, his "spirit partook of the barrenness," giving him strength to "heartily wish Neibuhr & Strauss to the dogs.—The deuce take their penetration & acumen" (551). He was unaware at this moment that a far deadlier threat to his faith than either Barthold Niebuhr or David Friedrich Strauss was on the horizon in Darwin, whose *Origin of Species* appeared two years later. The cataclysmic revolution in biological thought crumbled the foundation of natural theology, and a greater darkness would descend upon Melville than he had envisioned and accepted as the sharkishness of life in *Moby-Dick*, darker even than the horror he had glimpsed in Cairo—the "multitudes of blind men"; "Flies on the eyes at noon. Nature feeding on man" (541). But by the end of the next two decades, which took him to the conclusion of *Clarel*—having portrayed the desolation and despair science had wrought in the lives of his pilgrims, including the shipwrecked sailors Rolf and Agath—he could deny that even "Darwin's year, / Shall . . . exclude the hope—foreclose the fear" ("Epilogue"). The narrator's final hopeful advice to Clarel draws on Melville's constant sense that hope is born in the deep, even as it had been for such a "pilot of the living God" as Father Mapple, whose prayer before the sermon was "so deeply devout that he seemed kneeling and praying at the bottom of the sea":

> Then keep thy heart, though yet but ill-resigned—
> Clarel, thy heart the issues there but mind;
>
> .   .   .   .
> That like a swimmer rising from the deep—
> That like a burning secret which doth go
> Even from the bosom that would hoard and keep;
> Emerge thou mayst from the last whelming sea,
> And prove that death but routs life into victory.   ("Epilogue")

John Marr and Other Sailors:
Phantom Shipmates on the "Long Watch-Below"

In 1860, having failed as a lecturer on the gleanings from his earlier voyages, Melville embarked again, and with high hopes. He wrote to Evert Duyckinck: "I go under very happy auspices so far as ship and captain is concerned. A noble ship and a nobler captain—& he my brother. We have the breadth of tropics before us, to sail over twice; & shall round the world" (Leyda 2:617). But the voyage around Cape Horn began for him in seasickness, developed into homesickness, and ended in the depressing assessment of his life's work that he saw reflected in these lines that he checked and underscored in books he carried with him: "The sea had soak'd his heart through" (from Chapman's Homer) and "The work that I was born to do is done!" (626–27). He had seen a collision at sea and passed through storms and calms, calms during which he meditated "darkly on the mysteries of Providence"; again he had seen the Southern cross and a "glorious view of the ship" from the "flying-jib-boom-end"; he had seen "the horrid sight of Cape Horn" and witnessed a sailor's death and sea burial; he had enjoyed his brother's companionship and even boarded a whale-ship (619–26). But he would not "round the world." Within a week of his arrival at San Francisco, he boarded the steamer *Cortes,* bound for Panama, and from there the *North Star,* for New York. There he would endure another quarter-century of even darker times, but twenty-eight years after his Cape Horn voyage he would go to sea again, to Bermuda; and by this time he realized that the work he was born to do was *not* yet done. He would return to "the time before steamships" and dream a fitting end for the aging sailors John Marr and Daniel Orme, and he would "recall the fresh young image of the Handsome Sailor" and enshrine him in *Billy Budd, Sailor* (GSW, 504).

Through the voice of John Marr, an old sailor who retired from the sea in the 1830s, Melville gave us our most memorable elegy for the sailor's life that he had briefly known in the last golden years of sailing. In the prose sketch of John Marr's life, he acknowledges the historical forces that wrecked the old sailor's life and left him stranded with unsympathetic inland companions for whom "the ocean, but a hearsay to their fathers, had now through yet deeper inland removal become to themselves little more than a rumor traditional and vague" (418). But Melville acknowledges these historical developments—the "unintermitting advance of the frontier"—in order to defeat them. He remarks that even the "prairie" is "now everywhere intersected with wire and rail," and he suggests that all this constitutes "yet another successive overleaped limit of civilized life" that in America can be bounded only by "the ocean that washes Asia" (420). In this way he can create for John Marr the consoling sense that the ocean

he had known is the reality in which all things past and future are subsumed. Melville's description of the prairie emphasizes its sealike qualities:
the encircling horizon ("hooped round by a level rim"); the "prairie-
schooner . . . voyaging across the vast champaign," steering "by the sun"
as in ocean "navigation"; the "enriched depressions between the long,
green, graduated swells, smooth as those of ocean becalmed receiving and
subduing to its own tranquility the voluminous surge raised by some far-off
hurricane" (420). The old sailor realizes that "it is the bed of a dried-up
sea." But Melville adds, emphatically, that Marr was "no geologist," no
mere scientific doubter like the villainous Margoth in *Clarel* (419). Through
"meditation," John Marr can reclaim a spiritual, watery reality like that
once envisioned by Ishmael (421). The "phantoms" of his parted "shipmates" with those of his dead "wife and child, become [his] spiritual companions" (421). Here again, in Melville's last years, "meditation and
water" were at least briefly wedded. The "ungraspable phantom of life" in
Ishmael's meditations is still ungraspable for the old sailor; but the "phantom" ship-mates do "come," "like tides that enter creek or stream" to
"visit" him. And they are "present" (422). The "heart-beat" (in the closing lines of "John Marr") with which Melville "musters" his dead shipmates from their "long watch-below" should not be mistaken for an old
seaman's lapsing into sentiment and nostalgia. Rather, it is an act of willed
belief comparable in its power to that by means of which Ishmael had prevailed over Ahab's fiery doubt and asserted, as he did in "The Pacific," that
the ocean is alive with dreaming souls:

> And meet it is, that over these sea-pastures, wide-rolling watery prairies
> and Potters' Fields of all four continents, the waves should rise and fall,
> and ebb and flow unceasingly; for here, millions of mixed shades and
> shadows, drowned dreams, somnambulisms, reveries; all that we call
> lives and souls, lie dreaming, dreaming, still; tossing like slumberers in
> their beds; the ever-rolling waves but made so by their restlessness.

If, in his last years, Melville could not celebrate the watery, biological
mysteries of life as he had embodied them in the whale, still he could
quietly invoke them in John Marr's recollection of "the stir that, to alert
eyes and ears, animates at all times the apparent solitudes of the deep"
(420). And in his last old sailor, Daniel Orme, he could welcome the
"animal decay" that befriended Orme in the end and left him on Easter
Sunday "with open eyes, still continuing in death the vital glance fixed on
the hazy waters" (428). In this closing emphasis, we can sense his final
triumph over the modern force ("Darwin's year") that had most severely
tested his faith in *Clarel*: "No, let us believe that the animal decay before
mentioned still befriended [Orme] to the close, and that he fell asleep re-

calling through the haze of memory many a far off scene of the wide world's beauty dreamily suggested by the hazy waters before him" (428).

In Daniel Orme's death and in the elegy for John Marr's shipmates of an irretrievable time, Melville expressed once again not only his fear but, resoundingly, his overriding hope that life would emerge "from the last whelming sea." But whereas he had extended this hope to Clarel in 1876 on the condition that he "keep [his] heart," he claimed it for himself in 1888 with the affirmation that a "heart-beat" does muster the lost seamen from their "long watch-below":

> Whither, whither, merchant-sailors,
> Whitherward now in roaring gales?
> Competing still, ye huntsman-whalers,
> In leviathan's wake what boat prevails?
> And man-of-war's men, whereaway?
> If now no dinned drum beat to quarters
> On the wilds of midnight waters—
> Foemen looming through the spray;
> Do yet your gangway lanterns, streaming,
> Vainly strive to pierce below,
> When, tilted from the slant plank gleaming,
> A brother you see to darkness go?   (422)

Billy Budd, Sailor

> If, at my death, my executors, or more properly my
> creditors, find any precious MSS. in my desk, then
> here I prospectively ascribe all the honor and glory
> to whaling, for a whale-ship was my Yale College
> and my Harvard.
>   —Melville, *Moby-Dick*

In *Billy Budd, Sailor* Melville returned to the "time before steamships," recalled "the fresh young image of the Handsome Sailor" of those times, and reaffirmed the values that had guided him on his literary voyages of the 1840s and 1850s. In effect, he had done this in his excursion to Bermuda in 1888 when, on his return voyage aboard the steamship *Trinidad*, he listed his age as thirty-seven instead of sixty-eight. He was beginning to receive a measure of recognition and praise for his sea books, most gratifyingly from W. Clark Russell, the English sea novelist and critic to whom he dedicated *John Marr and Other Sailors*. Finally, he prepared the "precious MSS." that he had imagined forty years earlier when he wrote

"The Advocate." It is his requiem for the simple sailor—for the sailor's life and values he had found in his "whale-ship" Yale and Harvard—and for the time in his life and in history when that simple existence was possible. As he began to work on *Billy Budd* late in 1888, he referred to Robert Southey's *Life of Nelson,* and he scored and underscored a reference to "perpetual fluctuation": Sir William Hamilton's remark that his "study of antiquities . . . [had kept him] in constant thought of the perpetual fluctuation of everything" (Leyda 2:810). Melville consoled himself with this sense as he looked back to the time before steamships. He could accept the ships' passing and the sailors', and above all he had come to accept as passed the view of nature he had celebrated in *Moby-Dick*—the natural theology with which he had buoyed his spirits in his meditations on the biological mysteries of the life-waters. But if he had been compelled to give up his earlier sense that in the wedding of meditation and water he might glimpse the "ungraspable phantom of life," he found that he could now turn again to the ocean and see reflected in its constant movements a higher principle of "perpetual fluctuation" whereby even "Darwin's year," like "Luther's day," would pass from view (*Clarel,* "Epilogue"). The mood of peace and acceptance that prevails in *Billy Budd, Sailor* does not derive from Melville's acceptance of the events over which Captain Vere presided, or of Vere's motives, but from his assertion, as in traditional elegy, that a higher justice would arrange for Vere's death, even as the elements join in sympathetic response to Billy's.

From Melville's point of view as he wrote *Billy Budd, Sailor,* the spirit of modern war constituted the chief threat to man. He had always recognized and resisted the spirit of war when it intruded upon his sense of ocean. He had written in *White-Jacket,* for example, that "life in a man-of-war . . . with its martial formalities and thousand vices stabs to the heart the soul of all free-and-easy rovers" ("The Jacket Aloft"). And he had emphasized how "the martial bustle of a great man-of-war . . . was indescribably jarring" to Israel Potter: it disturbed "the solemn natural solitudes of the sea" and "mysteriously afflicted him" (chap. 14). Now, in 1891, the spirit of war, as embodied in Captain Vere, literally destroys the innocent sailor. In his complete subservience to the Articles of War, Vere is a mere instrument of war, as Melville emphasizes in his image of the captain at the moment of Billy's death: he "stood rigidly erect as a musket in the ship armorer's rack" (*GSW,* 497). As a character in Melville's long story of ocean, Captain Vere exhibits the fatal flaw of being no voyager. He is in this way a more frightening development of what Melville had created in Captain Delano, who could not voyage because he could not question: Vere cannot voyage because he will not "proceed" beyond the "formulated . . . code" of the Mutiny Act (487).

Melville had learned a good deal about modern naval warfare from the Civil War, and he had expressed it memorably in what Newton Arvin described as "the metrics of an age of ironclads" (264). This modern warfare was far worse than the apocalyptic scenes he had created in *Israel Potter*; it was

> Beyond the strife of fleets heroic;
> Deadlier, closer, calm 'mid storm;
> No passion; all went by on crank,
> Pivot, and screw,
> And calculations of caloric.   (CP, 38)

Certainly Melville had felt the nation's pulse during the Civil War, but his diagnosis differs profoundly from that of another American seaman who also contemplated "the Navy in the War of Secession": as a result of his thoughts on the Civil War, Captain Alfred Thayer Mahan (1840–1914), the prophet of political Darwinism, produced the first book in his influential series on "Sea Power," *The Gulf and Inland Waters* (1883). His more famous *Influence of Sea Power upon History, 1660–1783* followed in 1890. Mahan envisioned a world of "struggle and vicissitude," as he wrote in his essay "The United States Looking Outward" (*Atlantic Monthly*, December 1890): "All around us now is strife; 'the struggle of life,' 'The race of life,' are phrases so familiar that we do not feel their significance till we stop to think about them. Everywhere nation is arrayed against nation; our own no less than others. What is our protective system but an organized warfare?" (18). Melville might have read this piece as he worked to finish *Billy Budd, Sailor*; if he did, we can only wonder at what he must have felt in seeing that both the Paradise and the Hell that he had known in the Pacific had now become mere way stations for war. "An inviolable resolution of our national policy," Mahan argued, should be "that no foreign state should henceforth acquire a coaling position within three thousand miles of San Francisco,—a distance which includes the Hawaiian and Galapagos islands and the coast of Central America" (26).

But Melville did not need Captain Mahan to tell him which way the world had turned since he had gone whaling. After having written his poems about naval battle in the Civil War, he had come to "dream"—as in his poem "The Berg"—that he

> saw a ship of martial build . . .
> Directed as by madness mere
> Against a stolid iceberg steer.   (CP, 203)

And in "The Haglets," he retold the story he had heard on his voyage to the Holy Land in 1856 of a warship's voyage to self-destruction. Unaware that the ship's compass was thrown off by the magnetic influence of arms stacked too near it, the admiral felt but ignored "the touch of ocean lone." In his confidence that "Discipline, curbing nature, rules— / Heroic makes who duty know," he crowds sail until the wreck. Then his men "cast about in blind amaze." And above the "gurgling grave," with "shrill screams" the circling haglets once again perform their "wheeling rites" (203–4), just as at the end of *Moby-Dick* the sea fowls "flew screaming over the yet yawning gulf" of the sinking *Pequod.*

Captain Vere inhabits the fictional "time before steamships," but he is the product of Melville's late nineteenth-century sense of time and bears a certain resemblance to Captain Mahan. As Vere gazes in his "absent fits" at the "monotonous blank of the twilight sea" (485), he has no sense of ocean like that which Melville had celebrated in 1850–51. Nor has he any of the legitimate heroism that Melville had depicted in Captain Paul—no sense of seamanship, none of the natural authority that had derived from Jones's experience before the mast. And most damningly, Vere does not bear "the elemental commission of nature" as much as "the military warrant of congress," as did Captain Paul in *Israel Potter* (chap. 15). Instead, in his complete devotion to the Articles of War, and therefore his explicit opposition to "the ocean, which is inviolate Nature primeval" (486), Vere breathes the steam of sea power and imperialism no less than Captain Mahan, whose strategic point was that "fuel is the life of modern naval war; it is the food of the ship; without it the modern monsters of the deep die of inanition" (26). That Vere possesses this kind of power; indeed, that he is possessed by it, is clear from Melville's analysis of the trial. Questioning whether Vere's sense of "urgency" in forcing the judgment was "well-warranted," he compares it with a modern "emergency" in navigation: "'The greater the fog the more it imperils the steamer, and speed is put on though at the hazard of running somebody down'" (489). This is Melville's most explicit comment on Vere's headlong incompetence. Of course, Vere does run down the idealized sailor. And in presenting Vere as the mad captain of a modern steamship, or as a man "thoroughly versed in the science of his profession" (444), Melville expressed an entirely different view of the time from sail to steam from that which Captain Mahan presented in his book by that title, published in 1907. Looking back on his career, Mahan (born four months before Melville set sail on the *Acushnet*) was "pleased" to have seen his "prophecy" of sea power fulfilled (326).

Captain Vere "steadfastly drive[s]" (488) toward a twisted justice in his manipulations of the court because he is in all respects the modern sea captain whom Melville viewed as antagonistic to the natural order of ocean. Melville details Vere's complete antagonism toward a natural order when, in the courtroom, the captain stands "unconsciously with his back toward" his junior officers, one of them the sailing master (485). Vere's attitude toward Billy and the junior officers is essentially the same as that which he exhibits in this scene when he paces "the cabin athwart, in [his] returning ascent to windward climbing the slant deck in the ship's lee roll": he "symboliz[es] thus . . . a mind resolute to surmount difficulties even if against primitive instincts strong as the wind and the sea" (485). In this way Vere exhibits something of Captain Ahab's monomania but nothing of his grandeur. Over a period during which the idea of evolution had undercut the possibility of a godlike captain in epic struggle with the Creation itself, Vere has descended to the dimensions of a mere officer whose "pedantic streak" (447) does not equip him for the kind of intellectual struggle Ahab knew in his "Forehead to Forehead" meeting with the whale. No sea-king of mythic proportions, Vere is "only allied to the higher [English] nobility," to whom he is indebted for his position and whom he represents in his explicit opposition to "The Rights of Man" (444).

Inevitably, Vere acts out his inherent opposition to the democratic values Melville always idealized in his simple seamen, from Jack Chase to Israel Potter and Billy. In centering his last sea story on this old conflict, from which, following Dana, he had wrestled his own identity as a sailor before the mast, Melville measures the extent to which the modern captain's separation from nature precludes a natural resolution to the natural conflict of mutiny. Whereas Melville himself was never frightened by the thought of mutiny, Vere is driven by his excited fear of it. Melville had felt the chafe of incompetent authority as a young sailor. In *White-Jacket* he emphasized how Jack Chase's refusal to obey Captain Claret's order had saved the ship. And in *Moby-Dick* he presented mutiny as a natural upheaval that brought about a natural justice. In "The Town Ho's Story," Steelkilt defies Radney's authority and breaks his jaw, but in resolving this dispute, the *Town Ho's* captain is wise enough to yield to Steelkilt in their two confrontations. Ultimately, a natural justice prevails in this incident when Radney is destroyed by Moby Dick in an act of "mysterious fatality, Heaven itself" seeming to step in. Indeed, in Melville's work, the essential mutineer is the great captain, Ahab himself, whose fiery rebellion is drowned in the mystic waters. By contrast, Steelkilt (the lakeman) survives because he has a natural affinity for water; after his last confrontation with the captain, he leaps "into the sea," swims to his boat, and sails to Tahiti and then on to France. Finally, in *Billy Budd* there is no actual mutiny, and Melville's point in referring to the mutiny of the Nore is that even in that mutiny, the seamen had justifiable grievances in the corrupt practices of war contractors and in the institution of impressment. Thus he regards "the Nore Mutiny . . . as analogous to the distempering irruption of contagious fever in a frame constitutionally sound, and which anon throws it off" (440). His proof of the analogy, and of Vere's incompetence, is that the legitimate naval hero, Nelson, did not "terrorize the crew into base subjection, but [won] them, by force of his mere presence, back to an allegiance" that was "as true" as his own (444). In this way Nelson resembles Melville's portrait of John Paul Jones and his Captain Turret in "Bridegroom Dick." Turret, a tower of a captain had the humanity to release a "true *sailor-man*" who could have been flogged according to the Articles of War, but realizing that "submission is enough," he refuses to "degrade [the] tall fellow" (CP, 177–78). Turret outlives the war, and, Melville observes, Nelson's crew of former mutineers won "plenary absolution and a grand one" in their service at the Nile and Trafalgar (441).

By the time he brought his career and virtually his life to an end with *Billy Budd, Sailor,* Melville had endured the darkest time our literature has known. After the actual voyages of his youth and his narratives of them, he "sailed on," as in *Mardi,* with "eternity . . . in his eye" and with the determination "to sink in boundless deeps" rather than "float on vulgar shoals." And he knew from the outset that such "chartless voyages" require "that we hold fast to all we have; and stop all leaks in our faith." At the end of *White-Jacket* he imagined that we might, through the example of Jack Chase, "save" ourselves and "never train our murderous guns inboard" ("The End"). But the succeeding decades of personal loss, war, and, resoundingly, the scientific revolution that would displace the vision of "eternity" with that of nature at war with herself in evolutionary time— these led to his conclusion in the "inside narrative" of *Billy Budd* that we *had* come to train our "murderous guns inboard."

Still, with an overpowering will to believe, which would be the legacy of American seamen who followed him, Melville could accept the losses of his dark time. In "Pebbles," his old sailor Orm could walk from the "stale schools" to the beach, where, with "reverent . . . ear," he hears the unswerving, undeviating "Truth" in a "conch hoar with time." And in other verses from "Pebbles," imaging the sea as "Elemental mad ramping of ravening waters— / Yet Christ on the Mount, and the dove in the nest!"—he wrote, "Healed of my hurt, I laud the inhuman Sea" (CP, 205–6). After the time of the sailing ships, American writers would voyage into new seas of meaning, with an increasingly desperate sense that "you got to have confidence steering," as Hemingway would express it (*To Have and Have Not,* 67). But in *Billy Budd, Sailor,* Melville returned to the time before steamships and to the essential values that had guided him in *Moby-Dick.* Dedicated to Jack Chase, *Billy Budd, Sailor* is his elegy for the life and sense of ocean he had found "as a simple sailor, right before the mast, plumb down into the forecastle, aloft there to the royal mast-head" (MD, "Loomings"). He could not revive the sense of wonder he had once expressed in his cetological probings of life beneath the surface, nor could he revive the moments of "top-gallant delight" he had felt aloft. But he could lay his simple sailor to rest in the "sea, whose gently awful stirrings"—still, in his last years—seemed "to speak of some hidden soul beneath" (MD, "The Pacific"). He held firm to the hope he had expressed in White-Jacket that his sea-buried messmates (like Shenly) would be swept by "the everlasting undertow" "toward our own destination" ("The End"). Like Shenly, John Marr's sea-buried "brother" will keep a "long watch-below" until "a heartbeat musters all." Surely this was Melville's hope for Billy, as in portraying nature's response to Billy's death and in concluding his tale with "Billy in the Darbies," he echoed Milton's elegiac vision of Lycidas "sunk . . . beneath the watery floor" yet "mounted high" in "kingdoms meek of joy and love."

Melville ended his long story of ocean, a voyage that had proceeded as he had known it must when he wrote "The Albatross" in Moby-Dick: "Around the world! There is much in that sound to inspire proud feelings; but whereto does all that circumnavigation conduct? Only through numberless perils to the very point whence we started." Thus he concluded Billy Budd, Sailor, by returning self-consciously to the imagery of the Whaleman's Chapel and wondering again with Father Mapple, "what depths of the soul does Jonah's deep sealine sound!" Father Mapple had warned "the captains of the earth" that ships "made by men" cannot take them "into countries where God does not reign." And by his own example—"so deeply devout that he seemed to be kneeling and praying at the bottom of the sea"—he showed the way: to be "swallowed . . . down to the living gulfs of doom . . . where the eddying depths sucked [Jonah] ten thousand fathoms down, and 'the weeds were wrapped about his head,' and all the watery world of woe bowled him over" ("The Sermon"). In an act of willed belief like that he had reserved for Clarel in hoping that he would emerge "from the last whelming sea," Melville arranged for Captain Vere to die "ashore"; and, after providing a messmate's simple communion and a shipmate's last shake of the hand, he sent his handsome sailor "fathoms down" into the "watery world":

> Fathoms down, fathoms down, how I'll dream fast asleep.
> I feel it stealing now. Sentry are you there?
> Just ease this darbies at the wrist, and roll me over fair,
> I am sleepy, and the oozy weeds about me twist.   (GSW, 505)

With Babbalanja, White Jacket, Shenly, Father Mapple, Jonah, Bulkington, Pip, Clarel, and John Marr's shipmates, Billy will keep a long watch-below.

5

The Experience
of Brotherhood
in "The Open Boat"

> In a ten-foot dinghy one can get an idea . . . of the
> sea . . . that is not probable to the average
> experience, which is never at sea in a dinghy.
> —Crane, "The Open Boat"

Stephen Crane was never a working seaman and so cannot be placed squarely within the tradition of American writers who were "sea-brothers." But on the basis of his very brief experience at sea he wrote one of the greatest sea stories of all time and centered it on the idea of brotherhood at sea. Few short stories in any language have won as high a place in world literature as has "The Open Boat." Its universal appeal is that it illustrates, simply and profoundly, "the essentials of life, like a symbolic tale," as Joseph Conrad assessed it (Beer 13). There can be no question that the experience Crane re-created in his story brought home to him what was essential in his own life. The ordeal in the dinghy was "the best experience of his life" because it brought him to feel "the subtle brotherhood of men that was [there] established on the sea" ("The Open Boat," pt. 3). A year after the incident, he dedicated *The Open Boat and Other Stories* to his three comrades in the dinghy. And in Cora Crane's report of his last hours, three and a half years after the incident, the profound personal significance of his experience resounds: "My husband's brain is never at rest. He lives over everything in dreams and talks aloud constantly. It is too awful to hear him try to change places in the 'Open Boat'" (Stallman 515).

Crane certainly idealized the working seaman in his portrayal of William Higgins. Billie the oiler "had worked a double watch in the engine room of the ship" before it sank, and then, in the dinghy, his tireless labor and his expertise as a seaman were instrumental in his comrades' survival. "A wily surfman," Billie saves them twice. First, when the dinghy had been caught "in a turmoil of foam" too far out for them to have swum ashore, he advised the captain to put to sea again: then "this oiler, by a series of quick miracles and fast and steady oarsmanship, turned the boat in the middle of the surf, and took her safely to sea" (pt. 4). And he saves them a second time, in the final crisis, by swinging the boat about so as to "keep her head-on to the seas and back her in" (pt. 7). In his presentation of Billie's actions and through such devices as the refrain "the oiler rowed, and then the correspondent rowed, and then the oiler rowed," Crane emphasizes that Billie's steady, simple labor is the tangible basis for his role here as a savior, whose "miracles" of seamanship complement Crane's idealized imagery of him as "the weary-faced oiler smil[ing] in full sympathy" and asking "meekly," "will you spell me for a while?" (pts. 3, 4, 5).

Crane's portrayal of Billie, the simple, working seaman, clearly expresses his sympathy with the democratic ideal of the sailor before the mast that figures so crucially in the tradition of American sea fiction. And to judge from the famous photograph of Crane aboard the *Three Friends* (barefoot and spread-legged, the image of a swashbuckling sailor) or from his signing himself, "Stephen Crane, able seaman S.S. *Commodore*" (Gilkes 62), one might even entertain, for an instant, the idea that Crane might have been a sailor had his life's circumstances been different. But it is impossible to imagine Stephen Crane in another time, the brilliant nervous energies of his life and style at rest for the duration of a sailing voyage of even modest length. Although he was born just two years after the *Flying Cloud* was launched, he would not pursue the dream of a simpler past like that suggested in the image of sail. Nor would he, after dashing out West and back, seek to perpetuate our myth of the western frontier: he grasped the collapse of all that in the imagery of the "Weary Gentleman saloon" and Scratchy Wilson's "funnel-shaped tracks in the heavy sand" at Yellow Sky. In his great war book, he returned to the past, but the new psychological realism that he achieved in *The Red Badge of Courage* was confusing to many, and it certainly violated the tenets of genteel realism. William Dean Howells thought it lacked "repose," and Charles Dudley Warner complained similarly that "great literature [unlike *The Red Badge*] is always calm" (Stallman 183).

There was little calm or repose in Crane's life and writings. Like many others of his generation, such as Ralph Delahaye Paine, Richard Harding Davis, and Frank Norris, all of whom were war correspondents with Crane in the Spanish-American War, Crane was fully absorbed in the excitements of his day. As an energetic journalist he was driven to witness, record, and comment on the most incandescent events, not the Klondike sort of thing (though he considered it), but the Greco-Turkish War and the Spanish-American War. In these outbursts he could see the world as it was being transformed and literally compressed under the pressure of steam. Less than four months after the *Commodore* incident, he was in Crete to cover the Greco-Turkish conflict, dispatching from aboard the French steamer *Guardiana* his memorable response to the age of sea power. As the *Guardiana* entered Suda Bay, the Concert of Powers' combined fleet came into view.

> Finally there were some faint etchings on the distances. They might have been masts, but they were more like twigs. And before the steady ploughing advance of the steamer these twigs grew into top-gear of war ships, stacks of tan, of white, of black, and fighting masts and the blaze of signal flags.
>
> It was the fleet of the Powers; the Concert—the Concert—mind you, this most terrible creature which the world has known, constructed out of the air and perhaps in a night. This fleet was the living arm and the mailed hand of the Concert. It was a limb of Europe displayed, actual, animate. The babe who disliked the motion of the steamer continued to cry in the cabin. (*War Dispatches*, 13–14)

In this darkly comic vision of "the power of Christian Europe" (18), Crane reiterated his view of men as "little souls who thirst for fight" ("War is Kind"). Pathetically confident that they can determine their own fate, these little creatures were "born to drill and die" in the warring universe that Crane projected in such other poems as "The Trees in the Garden Rained Flowers," where the "beautiful strong" prevail. In Crane's ironic view of the Concert of Powers, even the "hoary" admiral (and, implicitly, perhaps, even Captain Alfred Thayer Mahan, whose Darwinist theory of sea power was dramatically verifiable in such scenes) does not grasp the human reality of the power he commands, as Crane depicts it within the breast of a single "middy." He is "smaller than a sparrow," but he had "a man's eye," and when "this tot put a speaking tube to his mouth," it was "like hearing a canary bird swear."

> Of course, there is no more fiery-hearted scoundrel in the fleet of the Powers than this babe. Of course he would drop to his knees and pray his admiral a hundred prayers if by this he could be at his station on the Camperdown and have her move into action immediately. Against what? Against anything. This is of the traditions that perforce are in the breast of the child. They could not be cut out of it under these circumstances. If another child of the Camperdown should steal this child's knife he might go to a corner and, and perhaps, almost shed

tears, but no hoary admiral can dream of the wild slaughter and Hades on the bosom of the sea that agitate this babe's breast. He is a little villain. And yet may the god of all battle that sits above the smoke watch over this little villain and all bright little villains like him. (16)

Crane's description of this dark comedy ends as the *Guardiana* pulls out of Suda Bay: "In the twilight, the fleet was only a great black thing, and afterward it was nothing. The hand of Europe was hidden by the hills lying in peace" (19).

Scarcely a year after his arrival at Suda Bay, Crane, back in England, was rushing off to cover the Spanish-American War, "ready," as Conrad recalled, "to swim the ocean" (Stallman 347). When he arrived in New York, he attempted to enlist in the navy but, failing the physical examination, went to war again as a correspondent. There he wrote a number of other dispatches in which he described the great modern warships (particularly the new torpedo boats and the destroyers, with their engines of 6,500 horsepower and speeds of 31 knots) and the great enterprise of warship building in Yarrow, "the maker of knives for the nations": "If Russia fights England, Yarrow meets Yarrow; if Germany fights France, Yarrow meets Yarrow; if Chili fights Argentina, Yarrow meets Yarrow" (*War Dispatches*, 112–16). And, of course, he went to the front, needlessly risked his life, reported the Battle of San Juan, and distinguished himself as one of the outstanding war correspondents in history.

It is noteworthy that Crane and his fellow correspondents in the Spanish-American War—Paine, Davis, and Norris—all wrote sea stories. Even in that highly energetic period, as the world steamed into the twentieth century with the intensity reflected in these men's careers, their instincts drew them to the sea experience as well as to war. In these experiences they seemed to find the "life" that had eluded an earlier generation. These men were of the "new type" that, according to Henry Adams's "law of acceleration" in history, were in 1905 being demanded by "New York . . . and all the new forces": "a man with ten times the endurance, energy, and will and mind of the old type" (Adams 499). Like William Dean Howells and Henry James (who developed *The Ambassadors* from the "germ idea" he had found in Howells's remark to Jonathan Sturges, "Oh, you are young, you are young—be glad of it and live. Live all you can: it's a mistake not to. . . . It has gone past me—I've lost it. . . . Live!"), Henry Adams greeted the new century with the sense that he had "no motive—no attraction" (James, *Notebooks*, 226; Adams 505). He could only wonder whether he and others of his generation might find, if they could return on their centenary, in 1938, "for the first time since man began his education among the carnivores . . . a world that sensitive and timid natures could not regard without a shudder" (Adams 505). But in their tendency to rush into life and capture it most vividly in the sea or war experiences, these "new" men of Crane's generation exemplify more than a generational difference between themselves and Howells, James, or Adams. They also represent a tendency within a discernible group of American writers of all generations—among whom those in the tradition of American sea fiction are prominent—who have sought to grasp the essentials of life through direct experience, rather than through passive contemplation or a narrator's detached observation: Thoreau, for example, in his intent to "drive life into a corner," as opposed to Ralph Waldo Emerson; Dana or Melville, in Ishmael's pursuit of the "ungraspable phantom of life" and Ahab's hunt, as opposed to Hawthorne; Mark Twain as opposed to Henry James; Hemingway as opposed to T. S. Eliot. Although Crane did not recognize a tradition of "sea-brothers" who inspired him to write of the sea (there is no indication, for example, that he knew Melville), he definitely inspired many who followed him—for example, Jack London, Richard Matthews Hallet, and Hemingway. And in his last years, largely on the basis of what he had done in "The Open Boat" and what he had seen in *The Nigger of the "Narcissus,"* he established a brotherly relationship with Joseph Conrad that overcame the considerable differences in age and culture that might have separated them. In this unusually close relationship there was a passionate and mutual admiration like that which was only anonymously and one-sidedly expressed in Melville's "Hawthorne and His Mosses." In their letters to each other, both Crane and Conrad used extravagantly religious language to express their admiration for each other similar to that Melville had used in describing Hawthorne's Christlike genius. Urging his readers to accept this American Shakespeare, Melville wrote that, "by confessing [Hawthorne] you thereby confess others. You brace the whole brotherhood. For genius, all over the world, stands hand in hand, and one shock of recognition runs the whole world round" (*MD*, 547). Of his response to *The Nigger of the "Narcissus,"* Crane wrote to Conrad:

> The simple treatment of the death of Wait is too good, too terrible. I wanted to forget it at once. It caught me very hard. I felt ill over that thread lining from the corner of the man's mouth to his chin. It was frightful with the weight of a real death. By such means does the real writer suddenly flash out in the sky above those who are always doing rather well. (*Letters*, 150)

And in response to what he had seen in Crane, Conrad wrote:

> I am envious of you—horribly. Confound you—you fill the blamed landscape—you—by all the devils—fill the seascape. The boat thing is

immensely interesting. I don't use the word in its common sense. It is fundamentally interesting to me. Your temperament makes old things new and new things amazing. I want to swear at you, to bless you—perhaps to shoot you—but I prefer to be your friend.

You are an everlasting surprise to me. You shock—and the next moment you give the perfect artistic satisfaction. (*Letters*, 154)

In Conrad's description of his "intimacy" and his "brotherly" relationship with Crane (in his "Introduction" to Beer), it is clear that his high regard for the other's "humanity" ("it was a shining thing without a flaw") was deeply associated with the sea experience that drew these men to each other. Conrad recalled that in one of their visits, during which they sometimes actually worked together in the same room, Crane "looked harassed."

I, too, was feeling for the moment as if things were getting too much for me. He lay on the couch and I sat on a chair opposite. After a longish silence in which we both could have felt how uncertain was the issue of life envisioned as a deadly adventure in which we were both engaged like two men, trying to keep afloat in a small boat, I said suddenly across the width of the mantel-piece,

"None of them knew the colour of the sky,"

quoting the famous first line of "The Open Boat" (Beer 14). And, recalling a later experience between them, at a time when neither "saw the colour of the sky!" he wrote that "it stood already written that it was the younger man who would fail to make a landing through the surf" (Beer 31). And, on Crane's part, his affection and admiration for Conrad are memorably recorded in his passionate defense of *The Nigger of the "Narcissus"* at a literary luncheon one day when his friend Harold Frederick had demeaned it: shattering "a dessert plate" with the butt of his revolver, he "yelled," "you and I and Kipling couldn't have written the Nigger!" (Beer 165). And in the last letter he wrote, a note to Sanford Bennett, he asked "the last favor": "I have Conrad on my mind very much just now." Fearing that Conrad might never "be popular outside the ring of men who write," he asked that Bennett help "pull wires for a place on the Civil List for Conrad" (*Letters*, 283–84). Less than three weeks later, having crossed the Channel to the sanitarium in the Black Forest, where he died, Crane dreamed of changing places in "The Open Boat."

In writing the story of "the best experience of his life," Crane wanted desperately to get it "*right*," from Captain Murphy's point of view. Of course he wanted to please Murphy, whom he revered in the story and honored in his dedication to *The Open Boat and Other Stories*. But he seems mainly to have wanted Murphy's assurance, as an experienced seaman, that he had handled the sea materials correctly. He was obviously proud of having signed on as an able seaman and of "doing a seaman's work . . . well," as the cook reported (Stallman 248). The experience meant far too much to him to risk having his story discredited as a land-lubber's view of the sea. He needed no assurance that he was a brilliant reporter. With Murphy's assurance that "you've got it right, Steve. That is just how it happened," he could confidently claim—like any experienced seaman in the tradition of American sea fiction—that he had been there, that his story was authentic. Thus in his subtitle for "The Open Boat," "A Tale Intended to Be After the Fact: Being the Experience of Four Men from the Sunk Steamer *Commodore,*" there is something like the young Melville's claim in the first sentence of *Typee* that the story of his "six months at sea!" would not resemble the tales of "state-room sailors" about "the privations and hardships of the sea" on "a fourteen-days' passage across the Atlantic." As Crane wrote, "In a ten-foot dinghy one can get an idea of the resources of the sea in the line of waves that is not probable to the average experience, which is never at sea in a dinghy" (pt. 1). No seaman has ever faulted Crane's presentation of nautical reality in "The Open Boat." Only an occasional unenlightened critic has argued that Crane failed "to achieve circumstantial verisimilitude" in his story, that the men's "physical hardships" in the dinghy were "grossly exaggerated."[1]

But if Captain Murphy could assure Crane that he had got the facts of their experience right, it would take a much more sensitive reader—one like Captain Conrad—to appreciate Crane's success in launching his story immediately into the much higher realm of experience that is indicated in the first sentence by "sky." From this first moment, after which there will be considerable scanning of the heavens, "The Open Boat" proceeds as a traditional sea journey to knowledge, and the knowledge it attains is equally as mysterious or religious as that envisioned in other great American sea journeys—in Cooper's *Sea Lions,* for example, or Melville's *Mardi* and *Moby-Dick,* or Hemingway's *Old Man and the Sea.* The great difference between Crane's sea journey and these others is that, in its more purely autobiographical approach, it dramatizes an experience like those William James would describe two years after Crane's death in *The Varieties of Religious Experience.* The most intense moment of this experience in the story occurs in part 6 when the correspondent, having discovered "the pathos of his situation," has a vision, or what James Joyce might have called an "epiphany": a verse "mysteriously" entered his head, and he "plainly saw" a comrade, the soldier in Algiers whose death prefigures Billie's. This ex-plicitly visionary moment is exactly the kind of "religious experience" that James had in mind in defining such experiences as "*the feelings, acts, and experiences of individual men in their solitude, so far as they apprehend them-selves to stand in relation to whatever they may consider the divine*"; and he defined "divine" as that "primal reality" that "the individual feels impelled to respond to solemnly and gravely, and neither by a curse nor a jest" (31, 38). Such experiences, James was almost "appalled" to discover, involved much "sentimentality" and "emotionality," and he realized that "in all these matters of sentiment one must have 'been there' one's self in order to understand them" (486, 325).

The religious experience Crane dramatizes in "The Open Boat" is certainly not religious in the conventional sense. Long before he boarded the *Commodore*, this son of a Methodist minister had already journeyed into another universe and imagined that "God Lay Dead in Heaven." For this reason, God is conspicuously absent in "The Open Boat," and the correspondent does not think to pray. In the place of prayer, there is "a great deal of rage" that "might be formulated thus: 'If I am going to be drowned . . . why, in the name of the seven mad gods who rule the sea, was I allowed to come thus far and contemplate sand and trees? . . . It is preposterous. . . . The whole affair is absurd'" (pt. 4). Yet before the journey's end, this rage subsides and the correspondent responds, as William James would characterize such experiences, "solemnly and gravely, and neither by a curse nor a jest" (*Varieties*, 38). That is, in this journey, Crane came to recognize the kind of "religious values inherent in actual experience" that John Dewey would describe in *A Common Faith* (1934). "The Open Boat" capitalizes on the simple but enormously symbolic situation that Dewey imagined when he wrote—as though he had this story in mind—that "whether or not we are, save in some metaphoric sense, all brothers, we are at least all in the same boat traversing the same turbulent ocean. The potential religious significance of this fact is infinite" (85).

But if "The Open Boat" is a traditional sea journey that attains an unconventional sense of religious values or of "primal reality," as James might have preferred to put it, the values themselves are scarcely new. Indeed, centering as they do on a "brotherhood of men," they cohere in Crane's imagination in a way that reflects the traditional Christian realities that he knew as a boy. In his actual experience in the boat, he found a real captain who was also a kind of Father, a brother in Billie, who was also miraculously and "meekly" a kind of Son, and a "mysterious," ghostly sense that they were one. All this not despite but rather because of the bitter sense of his refrain "God is cold. . . . God is cold. . . . God is cold" (in his poem "A Man Adrift on a Slim Spar," which he wrote at the same time that he was writing "The Open Boat").

Perhaps it is because Crane has come to be identified with some of his more famous expressions ("God Lay Dead in Heaven" or "God is cold") that there is considerable disagreement about the values he envisions in "The Open Boat," or even about whether the story affirms *any* values. One critic, for example, writing from a conventional religious point of view, complained that "in Crane's view evidently no valid insight or awareness . . . can be derived from human experience" (Brennan 194, 196). And, focusing on the story's initial sense that "none of them *knew*" (my emphasis), another critic has argued that the story's "epistemological emphasis" points to "man's limited capacities for knowing reality" (Gerstenberger 557). Such interpretations obscure Crane's efforts to show how his correspondent did come to know reality (in the ultimate sense that James had in mind when he wrote *The Varieties of Religious Experience*) and his efforts to show that the *only* valid kind of knowledge is experience. The best critical approach to this problem is to recognize, as Conrad seems to have, that the story is a traditional sea journey to knowledge and to note that in its first sentences it links the concepts of "experience" and "knowledge." Crane's first sentences extend his subtitle's emphasis on factual experience and begin systematically to identify what can be "known" with what can be "experienced."

The statements "None of them knew the colour of the sky" and "all of them knew the colours of the sea" develop the initial emphasis on experience by playing on the primary sense of "to know" as "to perceive" or "to experience." Crane's desire to identify knowledge and experience in this way undoubtedly reflects his urgent sense that "this was the best experience of his life." But, also, the emphasis he gives this idea is necessary, in part, because he writes in English. In our language, the single word "know" has two main senses, which in French or German, for example, are reflected in the different words *connaître* and *savoir* or *kennen* and *wissen*. Quoting the *Encyclopaedia Britannica*, the *Oxford English Dictionary* (*OED*) notes that the word "know" is considered by some to have "two main meanings: 'to *know* may mean to perceive or apprehend, or it may mean to understand and comprehend. . . . Thus a blind man, who cannot *know* about light in the first sense, may *know* about light in the second, if he studies a treatise on optics.'" Accordingly, the *OED*'s first sense for "know" is "to perceive (a thing or person) as identical with one perceived before . . . ; to identify." Its second sense is "to be acquainted with; to be familiar with by experience or through information or report" (as in *connaître* or *kennen*); and its third sense is "to have cognizance of through observation, inquiry, or information" (as in *savoir* or *wissen*).

Throughout "The Open Boat," Crane uses "know" in a way that excludes the *OED*'s third sense of the word. From the first sentence to the last, he systematically denies his men the verifiable knowledge that "cognizance," "observation," or "inquiry" imply. Instead, he makes them confront what we normally think of as the unknown or the unknowable—as when they attain a "new ignorance of the grave-edge" (pt. 7)—and leaves them only with the kind of knowledge that we refer to in such expressions as "I have known sorrow," that is, "I have felt or experienced sorrow." The story's path to this knowledge is easily traced: it begins with the curious formulation about *knowing* colors and leads the correspondent to the moment when, having *felt* nature's cold indifference to his pleas, he can come to "know" "the pathos of his situation" (pt. 6). In bringing together "know" and "pathos" in this crucial moment, Crane underscores the meaning of "experience" in "The Open Boat": as "to know" carries the primary sense "to experience," so does "pathos," whose root extends to the Greek *paschein*, "to experience, suffer." Like Gloucester and King Lear, Crane's correspondent has come to "see feelingly." Thus, having heard "the great sea's voice" at the end of the story, he and the other survivors "*felt* that they could then be interpreters" (my emphasis).

Whether Crane consciously played on the etymological link between "pathos" and "experience" in "The Open Boat," it is impossible to tell. But clearly he was building toward the correspondent's moment of vision in part 6. And his next step in dramatizing the development of this religious experience was to depict in his characterization of Captain Murphy a nearly heroic figure who embodies religious values that derive directly from actual experience. Throughout the story, Crane emphasizes that the captain steadies the men with his constant calmness and serenity. Speaking of the "personal and heartfelt" quality in the captain's voice and of the men's obedience to him, Crane tells us that "after this devotion to the commander of the boat, there was this comradeship, that the correspondent, for instance, who had been taught to be cynical of men, knew even at the time was the best experience of his life" (pt. 3). The captain will become an object of devotion, and Crane's understanding of the captain's heroism is indicated in his initial portrait. Crane sets it off from the others' portraits by placing it last, by making it longer and more detailed than the others, and by rendering it in sounded, rhythmic language:

> The injured captain, lying in the bow, was at this time buried in that profound dejection and indifference which comes, temporarily at least, to even the bravest and most enduring when, willy-nilly, the firm fails, the army loses, the ship goes down. The mind of the master of a vessel is rooted deep in the timbers of her, though he command for a day or a decade; and this captain had on him the stern impression of a scene in the grays of dawn of seven turned faces, and later a stump of a topmast with a white ball on it, that slashed to and fro at the waves, went low and lower, and down. Thereafter there was something strange in his voice. Although steady, it was deep with mourning, and of a quality beyond oration or tears. (pt. 1)

This is memorably poetic prose, as many have noted, and it clearly conveys how strongly Crane felt about the captain. But it is important to note that the qualities that underlie the captain's heroic embodiment of religious values are that he is already injured, that his "mind is rooted deeply in the timbers" of his vessel, and that he is moved to deep mourning by having witnessed the suffering on the "seven turned faces" (of the men who actually went down with the *Commodore*). By virtue of his injury, he has suffered or "experienced." And his suffering for others, his resulting deep mourning that is "beyond oration or tears," is distinctly different from the correspondent's repeated useless ragings to an empty sky about "the seven mad gods who rule the sea." The correspondent will eventually experience a similar feeling, but only after his dark night alone. Crane's remark about the captain, "Thereafter there was something strange in his voice," parallels his later remark about the correspondent, "Thereafter he knew the pathos of his situation." But that the captain's mind is "rooted deep in the timbers" of his vessel, that he is deeply in touch with his actual situation, is his prime heroic characteristic. And it is through this trait that Crane dramatizes the difference between the captain and his men early in the story when they encounter some sea gulls.

The gulls, with their staring, "black bead-like eyes," seemed "uncanny and sinister in their unblinking scrutiny, and the men hooted angrily at them." But when one attempts to land atop the captain's head, Crane uses the crisis to characterize the captain's steadying grasp of reality:

> "Ugly brute," said the oiler to the bird. "You look as if you were made with a jackknife." The cook and the correspondent swore darkly at the creature. The captain naturally wished to knock it away with the end of the heavy painter, but he did not dare do it, because anything resembling an emphatic gesture would have capsized this freighted boat; and so, with his open hand, the captain gently and carefully waved the gull away. After it had been discouraged from the pursuit the captain breathed easier on account of his hair, and the others breathed easier because the bird struck their minds at this time as being somehow gruesome and ominous. (pt. 2)

The captain is worried about his hair; his mind, unlike the others', is not susceptible to fearful fantasies that might have caused the boat to capsize. Crane's point is that, at this early stage in his experience, the correspondent has a long way to go before he will be able to direct his own mind away from the empty sky at which he rages and thereby come to know the pathos of his actual situation. Nor does the captain lose his grip even when faced with the possibility of his own death; he calmly accepts the likelihood that they will capsize in the surf, saying to the others, "If we don't all get ashore . . . I suppose you fellows know where to send news of my finish?" They exchange the necessary information, and Crane again distinguishes the captain from the men by remarking that "there was a great deal of rage" in their reflections, which he expresses in the refrain (used here for the first of three times), "If I am going to be drowned," and so on.

This raging ends here in its first instance in a flat denial of reality: "She cannot drown me" (pt. 4).

Despite his injury, or because of it, the experienced captain retains his heroic grasp of reality. He knows where he is and helps the men find their own bearings: "'See it?' said the captain," once, pointing toward the lighthouse. "'Look again. . . . It's exactly in that direction.'" Crane comments, "It took an anxious eye to find a lighthouse so tiny" (pt. 2). And even in the whirling surf, with "his face turned away from the shore" toward his men, the captain repeatedly calls, "Come to the boat!" This selfless, experienced "iron man" to whom the men are so devoted exerts a growing influence over them that is most apparent in the "curiously ironbound friendship, the subtle brotherhood of men" that develops among them. In a very definite sense, Captain Murphy fathers this "subtle brotherhood."

"After" the crew's "devotion" to Captain Murphy ("it was more than a mere recognition of what was best for the common safety"), "there was this comradeship" that the correspondent sees pictured in the other men, asleep underfoot as he rows: "The cook's arm was around the oiler's shoulders, and, with their fragmentary clothing and haggard faces, they were the babes of the sea" (pts. 3, 5). Largely because of the captain's influence, then, the correspondent ceases his raging and fully enters this childlike and innocent brotherhood of seamen. Gradually Crane introduces a refrain about the men's prolonged rowing that will eventually displace the refrain of rage: "If I am going to be drowned . . . why?" He uses the new refrain three times in parts 3 and 4, first in an extended way: "The oiler and the correspondent rowed. And also they rowed. They sat together in the same seat, and each rowed an oar. Then the oiler took both oars; then the correspondent took both oars; then the oiler; then the correspondent. They rowed and they rowed." This refrain gives way to the simpler refrain that appears three times in parts 5 and 6, first when the oiler, overpowered and blinded with sleep, "rowed yet afterward": "Then he touched a man in the bottom of the boat, and called his name. 'Will you spell me for a little while?' he said meekly." The correspondent replies, "Sure, Billie." And then, after his dark night alone (he "thought he was the one man afloat on all the oceans"), he speaks into the bottom of the boat, "Billie! . . . Billie, will you spell me?" The oiler replies, "Sure." And before their last day dawns, they change places again in the open boat:

> "Billie! . . . Billie, will you spell me?"
> "Sure," said the oiler. (pt. 6)

The essential values of Crane's brotherhood are sealed in these exchanges between Billie and the correspondent. And yet, as Crane emphasizes in the narrative development of his story, it is only in the intensity of his religious experience in part 6 that the correspondent can "plainly" see and articulate the significance of what he had come to feel. His vision of a dying "comrade" and of himself taking "that comrade's hand" is "an actuality—stern, mournful, and fine." And Crane explicitly articulates the change that this vision brought about in the correspondent: he "was moved by a profound and perfectly impersonal comprehension. He was sorry for the soldier of the Legion who lay dying in Algiers."

Crane's short sea journey took him exactly this far: from the condition of one "who had been taught to be cynical of men" to that of a man who had been "moved" to feel sorrow for another. But scholarly commentary on "The Open Boat" often fails to weigh the profound effect that this actual brief voyage had on Crane, as dramatized in his story and in his deathbed dreams of changing places in an open boat. In a cold analysis of the correspondent's epiphany in part 6, J. C. Levenson, for example, cannot imagine that Crane sought here to re-create the deeply emotional and mysterious experience that the story clearly presents as "actual." Rather, Levenson argues that Crane pauses here—in the most intense moment of the most sincerely personal story he ever wrote—to "establish" with "irony and intelligence" a "relation between the subjective colouring and the objective facts." That is, Crane calls up the "tears and flapdoodle" of "Caroline Norton's sappy and very popular ballad" to make a "direct hit at popular culture" and scorn "the sentimentally bemused" (Levenson lxiv).

Stephen Crane was certainly a master of irony, and there are many ironic touches in "The Open Boat." The ironic approach is conventional in short stories that emphasize a character's initial blindness before his or her epiphany. James Joyce, the master of this kind of story, also used a popular song by Caroline Norton to portray the prolonged blindness of the boy in "Araby." Joyce does not quote "The Arab's Farewell to His Horse," but his ironic reference to it serves to indicate, as Crane does in "The Open Boat," how his character proceeds from his blind state toward an epiphany. In Crane's story, the correspondent's epiphany includes his recollection of the poem, but with a new sense of the relevance of its sentimental message to his present situation. When the epiphany does come in Joyce's stories and "The Open Boat," the emotional gravity and religious possibilities of such moments (as suggested in "epiphany") are clear, and the irony of the individual's initial blindness to his actual condition has no further basis. The central irony in "The Open Boat" exists—emphatically—in the correspondent's comic raging at the heavens. And this raging ends when he "feels" nature's "word . . . to him" in the "high cold star on a winter's night." Crane's use of "thereafter" at this moment ("thereafter he knows the pathos of his situation") underscores the change that comes about in the correspondent and within the narrative's tone—just as, earlier in the story, after the captain had watched his ship go down with seven men, Crane wrote that "thereafter there was something strange in his voice"; it had become "deep with mourning, and of a quality beyond oration" (pt. 1). Now, from this point (pt. 6) on in the story, the narrative, centered in the correspondent's consciousness, moves beyond the correspondent's ironic ragings to his new "profound and perfectly impersonal comprehension." His experience has made it impossible for him any longer to respond to life with either "a curse [or] a jest," to use James's terms for such experiences; rather, the narrative proceeds with an appropriate degree of solemnity and gravity toward the moment when Billie's "still and dripping shape was carried slowly up the beach" (pt. 7).

It is a gross misreading of "The Open Boat" to deny the emotion, mystery, and sentiment in the correspondent's vision in part 6; these are natural and essential accompaniments in the epiphany or "religious experience" that William James would have recognized partly *because* of its "sentimentality" and "emotionality" (*Varieties*, 486). Readings of the story that do not recognize the correspondent's epiphany for what it is—a newly apprehended sense of the "divine" or of "primal reality," as James would say—can grasp neither the enormous personal significance of Crane's experience nor the story's development as a traditional voyage from its initial moment when "none of them knew the colour of the sky." Such readings would suggest that Crane's brief sea journey led him not to a knowledge of "the pathos of his situation," as he said, but to the bathos.

Perhaps it is true, as James said, that "in all these matters of sentiment one must have 'been there' one's self in order to understand them" (*Varieties*, 325). In writing "The Open Boat" Crane was certainly aware that he might be unable to reach the reader who had not "been there," whose "mind unused to the sea" could not grasp even the simple realities of the sea that he presented. As he wrote in "War Memories," "we can never *tell* life, one to another" (*Wounds in the Rain*, 229, my emphasis). But compelled, after the *Commodore* sank, to re-create the best experience of his life, he told of the intimate proximity of four men in a boat. Depicting their devotion to the captain, their shared labor, and their huddling together and touching each other for warmth, he dramatized the physical reality of the spiritual fact: "The subtle brotherhood of men . . . dwelt in the boat, and each man felt it warm him." The shocking success of his effort, as Conrad suggested, earned him a place in the brotherhood of American writers who have "been there," at sea, and honored the brotherhood of seamen they knew. This is a constant impulse in the tradition of American sea fiction, from Melville's chapter "A Squeeze of the Hand" in *Moby-Dick*, through successive scenes in Crane, Thornton Jenkins Hains, Bill Adams, Lincoln Colcord, Richard Matthews Hallet, and Hemingway. And as each of these men would know, the brotherhood's vital source is itself constant in the sea experience of any time, as one can feel it, for example, in the fisherman's story from *The Alaska Fisherman's Journal* of November 1978. Reporting how the fishing vessel *Marion A* sank in Geese Channel off Kodiak Island, the *Journal* quoted the lone survivor. His friend Jerry helped him disentangle and climb into the single survival suit that floated to the surface after the *Marion A* went down. The captain had already disappeared. Then:

> "I told Jerry to hold around my waist. He kicked while I kicked and swam. I told him to keep kicking.
>
> "We were closer to the island side and I wanted to go that way but the wind was blowing us (in the opposite direction). Every time I tried to turn into it, Jerry would say, 'Just go with the tide, go with the wind.'
>
> "Well, he only said it a couple times. . . . Jerry slowed down. Started talking real slow. He knew it and I knew it: It was going to take too long to hit land.
>
> "He said, 'I love you, Joe.' I said, 'I love you, too.' He kissed me on the cheek and I kissed him on the cheek. I said, 'We're going to make this. Just keep kicking. Open your eyes.' I held him until he collapsed in my arms and then I held him longer. I was sure he was dead. I finally let go."

6

Jack London in the Tradition of American Sea Fiction

> And at last my dream would be realized: I would
> sleep upon the water. And next morning I would
> wake upon the water; and thereafter all my days
> and nights would be on the water.
> —Jack London, *John Barleycorn*

During the last two decades, Jack London has emerged as a much more significant American writer than critics were prepared to admit during the half-century following his death.[1] But it is a strange and unfortunate oversight that the author of *The Sea-Wolf* has never been fully recognized as a major writer in the tradition of American sea fiction. The most obvious reason for this oversight is the mistaken assumption that the tradition virtually ended with the publication of *Moby-Dick*. Also, like Cooper, who came to be identified with but one part of his work (the Leatherstocking series), London has become known mainly for his Alaskan stories, particularly *The Call of the Wild*. Furthermore, the sheer volume and range of London's work has confused many of his critics, leaving his own figure as an important sea writer enshrouded, like the sealing schooner *Ghost* in one of the great fogbanks of the Bering Sea. In his meteoric sixteen-year career, this most energetic writer of the "Strenuous Age" produced over fifty books, Earle Labor reminds us, "with an astonishing range of subjects: agronomy, architecture, astral projection, boating, ecology, gold-hunting, hoboing, loving, penal reform, prize-fighting, Socialism, warfare" (viii). Labor presents this impressive list in alphabetical order, but it should be rearranged and the subject "boating" replaced at the head of the list with The Sea. For like Dana, Melville, and others who are now unknown, London entered the literary world by way of the sea, and he remained until his death a more potent force in perpetuating the tradition of American sea fiction than we have yet recognized. From his seventeenth year, when he published his first story, "Typhoon Off the Coast of Japan," until he wrote his last story, "The Water Baby," he turned repeatedly to the sea in his efforts to grasp the essential reality of our existence.

Like the other great figures in our tradition of sea literature—Philip Freneau, Cooper, Dana, Melville, Crane, Joshua Slocum, O'Neill, Hemingway, and Peter Matthiessen—London wrote from direct experience of the sea and was inspired by other writers in the tradition who had sailed before him. But excepting only Freneau and Slocum, none of these writers can claim to have drawn on so broad and varied a basis of firsthand sea experience. As a boy London was an estimable small boat sailor in San Francisco Bay, where he won local fame as "prince of the oyster pirates" and served on the California Fish Patrol. At seventeen he sailed before the mast as an able seaman on the sealing schooner *Sophia Sutherland,* and at twenty-one he steamed and, on the last leg, reportedly sailed in an Indian dugout canoe from San Francisco to Dyea, Alaska.[2] Following a two-thousand-mile journey in a hand-hewn boat down the Yukon River from Dawson to St. Michael, he worked his way back to British Columbia passing coal on an ocean steamer. Later he would sail as a passenger on innumerable coastal and transoceanic voyages by steamer and would continue until the end of his life to sail his own small boats in the waters of San Francisco Bay. Finally, in addition to the famous eighteen-month cruise that he logged in *The Cruise of the Snark,* he fulfilled a lifelong dream in 1912 by sailing from Baltimore to Seattle on a five-month voyage around Cape Horn. He was our last major writer to make the passage and tell the story before steam power and the Panama Canal left buried at sea one of our literature's earliest and most compelling tales of mythic proportions.

In addition to this impressive firsthand sea experience, London drew heavily on his experience with sea literature. In the first place he read Melville. In fact, as Charles N. Watson, Jr., has emphasized, London should be credited with having read *Moby-Dick* "more creatively than any novelist" before him and "at a time when few readers remembered Melville at all" (61, ix). But he also read widely and deeply in Cooper, Dana, Frederick Marryat, Algernon Swinburne, John Masefield, Robert Louis Stevenson, Rudyard Kipling, and his contemporaries, Crane, Norris, Slocum, Morgan Robertson, and Conrad. Of these, he was most inspired and influenced by Melville, Dana, Slocum, and Conrad. But London's sea fiction bears the unique stamp of his own genius, and his notable work in the field includes not only his masterpiece, *The Sea-Wolf,* but the neglected novel, *The Mutiny of the Elsinore* (1912), and such memorable stories as "The Seed of McCoy," "Make Westing," "The Heathen," "The 'Francis Spaight,'" "The Sea-Farmer," "Samuel," and "The Water Baby." In addition to a number of other good but less notable sea stories, including "Under the Deck Awnings" and "The Pearls of Parlay," he produced a fine boys' book in *The Cruise of the Dazzler* and the collections of boys' stories of his own boyhood contained in *Tales of the Fish Patrol* and *Dutch Courage and Other Stories*. Finally, he produced several stories and books that are shaped significantly by the sea, even though they cannot be described as pure sea fiction; the most important of these are *The Cruise of the Snark* and *Martin Eden*, but there are as well *John Barleycorn*, "An Odyssey of the North," *Jerry of the Islands*, and *Michael, Brother of Jerry*.[3]

Clearly, Jack London had more to say about the sea than can be fully represented in a single chapter, but perhaps a brief examination of four of his sea pieces—*The Sea-Wolf*, *The Mutiny of the Elsinore*, *Michael, Brother of Jerry*, and "The Water Baby"—will reveal what he saw in the sea that drew him so constantly to it and what he contributed to the tradition of American sea fiction.

Like so many memorable American novels, *The Sea-Wolf* is great but flawed. Its estimable energies, like those of *Huckleberry Finn*, for example, are sadly dissipated in the closing chapters. One of London's disciples, Jan de Hartog, put it distinctively. Remarking that "the best reading matter at sea is Jack London," he explained the circumstances under which he first read *The Sea-Wolf*. "In sharp competition with the cook's digestion; owing to the fact that he tore out about fifty pages per book, I rarely managed to catch up with their endings. I was thus spared Jack London's women, who come in at the end of his books and spoil them" (351–52). But most readers can agree with Ambrose Bierce's remark that the novel's "great thing—and it is among the greatest of things—is that tremendous creation, Wolf Larsen. . . . The hewing out and setting up of such a figure is enough for a man to do in a life-time" (quoted in Foner 61–62).

Wolf Larsen is certainly London's greatest creation of the sea, and the purpose of my limited remarks about him here is to emphasize his uniqueness among sea captains as a creature of the water. Despite his many resemblances to Captain Ahab and the influence of *Moby-Dick* on *The Sea-Wolf*, Larsen is certainly more than a mere copy of Ahab or even "the Captain Ahab of literary Naturalism."[4] With Ahab and a more recent American sea captain, Captain Raib in *Far Tortuga*, Wolf Larsen stands on his own legs (as he would have put it) as one of America's great characters in literature. He is, admittedly, a descendant of Ahab, but Jack London is his father, and he was shaped by London's own times and preoccupations as surely as Ahab was shaped by Melville's. Larsen's unique watery nature is a reflection of London's effort to represent concretely in his character the essential biological reality of all life as it had come to be understood forty-three years after the appearance of the *Origin of Species*. Darwin had first appeared in the tradition of American sea fiction in the 'Extracts" of *Moby-Dick,* where (eight years before the *Origin of Species*) Melville quotes briefly from "Darwin's Voyage of a Naturalist"; but Darwin's profound influence on the tradition begins in *The Sea-Wolf.* Henceforward in the tradition, the sea as the source of all life on earth would often influence the portraits of seamen by revealing—as in Wolf Larsen—the primordial sea-animalness of man. Such would be the case in Hemingway's portrait in *To Have and Have Not* of Harry Morgan, whose prodigious lovemaking is compared to that of a loggerhead turtle; or, more subtly, in Peter Matthiessen's portrayal of his fishermen in *Far Tortuga.* In *Moby-Dick,* Melville had emphasized the bloody sharkishness of life, but he could not see, as London could in 1904, how the salt sea reflects the harsh reality of biological time rather than an ambiguous promise of eternity.[5] Melville's wonderful sensitivity to the water finds expression not through Ahab, who is maddened by the ambiguity of life, but rather through Ishmael in his sense of the "sweet mystery about this sea, whose gently awful stirrings seem to speak of some hidden soul beneath" ("The Pacific"). And whereas Ishmael is *drawn* to the water, where he sees reflected the "image of the ungraspable phantom of life" ("Loomings"), Wolf Larsen is *of* the sea.

Larsen's entry into our literature is significant. We see him first as he glances "out over the water" (9). There is "life and death" in his "gaze," and "deep thought"; and when his "gaze [strikes] the water," he finds there the shipwrecked Humphrey Van Weyden, afloat "in the midst of a gray primordial vastness." Thus Wolf literally saves Humphrey from drowning in San Francisco Bay, but London's figurative meaning is that Wolf will save Humphrey by causing him to go through the process of evolution aboard the "miniature floating world" of the sealing schooner *Ghost,* the actual process of life that Van Weyden, a "romantic," sophisticated "landsman," has somehow escaped (25). As Humphrey Van Weyden begins to regain consciousness aboard the *Ghost,* he will awaken to what is for him a new reality. In his first dreamy sense of "swinging in a mighty rhythm through orbit vastness," of being "lapped in the rippling of placid centuries," we can see London's first attempts to breathe new life into him (10). Moments before the collision, Humphrey had imagined that he rode "through the gray shadow of infinite mystery" (i.e., the fog) on a "steed of wood and steel" like a man, a "mere mote of light and sparkle" (5). Now he will awaken to the twentieth century, when men would be depicted as Stephen Crane had depicted them in "The Blue Hotel," for example, as so many "lice" clinging to a "whirling, fire-smote, ice-locked, disease-stricken, space-lost bulb" (*Tales,* 165). (Crane's sense of the species' origin was not as acutely biological as London's, nor is it reflected at all in "The Open Boat"; but he saw that the "black riders came from the sea.") And because London's sense of the new reality—the flux, the biological strife and instability—was always most intensely clear to him at sea, Humphrey Van Weyden opens his eyes to see that "his mighty rhythm was the lift and forward plunge of a ship on the sea" (10).

Humphrey has embarked on a traditional sea journey to knowledge, and his course is charted in the "life and death" he first sees in Wolf's gaze. But before London allows Humphrey to look more deeply into Wolf's eyes, he forces him to witness a reenactment in flesh and blood of the eternal drama, *life* in Wolf's flesh confronting *death* in the "diabolical grin" of the dead mate. Humphrey's first impression of Wolf's "strength" is that it is "the essence of life . . . the potency of motion, the elemental stuff . . . of life," that "which lingers in a shapeless lump of turtle meat and recoils and quivers from the prod of a finger" (14). But despite Wolf's Mesozoic vitality and even the "thunderclap" and "electric sparks" in his oaths, the dead mate's grin of "cynical mockery and defiance" makes *him* "master of the situation" (15–16). The great sea captain is a mere survivor, left to create order in his "miniature floating world" and to instruct his new cabin boy. And Humphrey certainly has much to learn from Wolf, something that he first senses is beyond "sounding," something asleep "in the deeps of [Wolf's] being" and that is reflected in his eyes: "a baffling protean gray which is never twice the same . . . gray, dark and light, and greenish-gray, and sometimes of the clear azure of the deep sea" (18–19). When Humphrey does first look "steadily" into Wolf's "cruel gray eyes," he sees no sign of the "light and warmth of a human soul," only the "cold" and "gray" of "the sea itself" (24). Thus it is that London ends his introduction to this allegorical voyage, before the *Ghost* enters the "lonely Pacific expanse," by arranging for Wolf to express the sum of his wisdom and sea experience— all that was contained in his first gaze of "life and death" and all that he can ever teach Humphrey about reality. Presiding over the sacred ceremony, while "the wind shriek[s] a wild song through the rigging" and the men sway "in unison to the heave and lunge of the deck," Wolf says it all: "And the body shall be cast into the sea" (25–26).[6]

By the end of chapter 12, a "carnival of brutality," Humphrey has begun to learn about the "realities of life"; he sees himself now as "Hump, cabin boy on the schooner *Ghost*," and affirms, "Wolf Larsen [is] my Captain" (79, 86). Then, by the beginning of chapter 16, having evolved far enough for Wolf to congratulate him for having discovered his own legs, Hump is the *Ghost's* mate. The crucial steps in his development were his descent into "the inferno of passion" and violence in the forecastle and his being "deluged" by Wolf's arguments that "might is right." Also, he had heard Wolf speak of his own death, which, inevitably, would be "at sea": then he would "cease crawling" and "be acrawl with the corruption of the sea," the "strength and movement of [his] muscles" then only "strength and movement in fin and scale and the guts of fishes" (94, 77, 54). And Humphrey had viewed and touched the "terrible beauty" of Wolf's naked body, the supreme "mechanism of the primitive fighting beast" (102). His physical evolution now complete, Hump is aware that he will never be the "same man," and he is grateful to Wolf for opening up for him the "world of the real" (109). Soon, of course, Maud enters the novel, but before London subjects Hump (and his readers) to her disappointing spiritual influence (she is the permanent "etherealized essence of life . . . in the changing order of the universe" [190]), he celebrates Hump's new manhood in a ceremonial storm scene that illuminates Wolf Larsen's watery powers.

Wolf's stormy nature is repeatedly emphasized in the prophecies of the character Louis: "Look out for squalls," he warns Hump (74). So it is appropriate that in the great storm scene of chapter 17 we see Wolf as he is most fully himself; here also we see London most fully himself as a sea-writer. At once "joyous" and "ferocious," Wolf is "thrilled and upborne with knowledge that one of the great moments of living, when the tide of life surges up in flood, was upon him" (111). In the "purplish light" of the coming storm, "Wolf Larsen's face glowed and glowed" as if "encircled by a halo" (112). The ensuing storm scene is one of the most memorable in literature, but my point is that it is more than an exciting true picture of a storm, drawn from the author's own sea experience: it is a celebration of the ultimate experience that London could imagine in life. Knowing that the sardonic grin of death is the final master of man, London celebrates not resurrection but survival—the Ghost's repeated "miracle" of being "buried beneath the sea" and then righting herself and breaking, "like a whale's back, through the ocean surface" (114, 117).[7] From his lofty perch in the crosstrees, Hump sees the Ghost "against the foaming sea as she [tears] along instinct with life" (113). When a huge wave overtops the schooner, he gazes "sheer up into it . . . a rushing green backed by a milky smother of foam" (115). Then "under water," he fears the "terrible thing . . . being swept in the trough of the sea"; but he is "pounded," "dashed," "turned over and over," and he breathes "the stinging salt water into [his] lungs" before finally envisioning Wolf "standing at the wheel in the midst of the wild welter" (115). By taking the salt water into his lungs, by clinging to the image of Wolf, and by struggling to fulfill his order—"get the jib backed over to windward"—Hump survives this deluge (115). And when the Ghost is repeatedly submerged, he

> felt strangely alone with God, alone with him and watching the chaos of his wrath. And then the wheel would reappear, and Wolf Larsen's broad shoulders, his hands gripping the spokes and holding the schooner to the course of his will, himself an earth god, dominating the storm, flinging its descending waters from him and riding it to his own ends.

And oh, the marvel of it! That tiny men should live and breathe and work, and drive so frail a contrivance of wood and cloth through so tremendous an elemental strife! (117–18)

It is a mistake to see such storm scenes and feats of seamanship in London's fiction as mere romantic adventure, the boy's way to manhood, even though we know how thrilled the seventeen-year-old Jack had been in proving himself an "able-bodied seaman" by steering the *Sophie Sutherland* through a night of storm. In fact, such scenes and the logic underlying them provide a clear view of London's deepest understanding of the sea and a clear measure of the distance between himself and Melville as sea writers of different times. Great storm scenes make up a very small part of *Moby-Dick*, and serve (as in "The Candles") to highlight the spiritual struggle between Ahab's doubt and Ishmael's faith, a struggle that is subsumed in Ishmael's meditative wonder, his sense of the sea's "sweet mystery" (The Pacific"). Ahab's death and Ishmael's survival constitute a spiritual affirmation that London could not accept. Despite his acknowledged love for Melville and the apparent influence of *Moby-Dick* on *The Sea-Wolf*, London's only explicit reference to *Moby-Dick* registers his objection to its "imaginative orgies."[8]

London always strove to dispel the sea mysteries that he felt were embodied in the traditional romantic sea stories. In his autobiographical story "That Dead Men Rise Up Never," for example, he confesses that he had felt the "fibre-instinct of ten thousand generations of superstitious forebears" and imagined that he saw the ghost of a shipmate (the bricklayer) whom he had helped bury at sea and whose bunk he had taken over despite the superstitious warnings of the other sailors (*Human Drift*, 46). The "ghost" proved to be only the play of moonlight in the *Sophia's* rigging. Similarly, *The Cruise of the Snark* dispels Melville's dream of the paradise of Typee and the fabled "horrors" of the leper colony at Molokai; and the name he chose for his famous boat, *Snark*, constitutes a grand, good-natured sneer at all who would romanticize the sea. The constant process of evolution was for him the essential reality in which he could express a kind of "faith." Its machinelike laws caused him to compare "the mechanism of the primitive fighting beast" he saw in Wolf's body to "the engines of a great battleship or Atlantic liner" (102). And the same biological laws drove the engines of evolution that would perpetuate the race through the love of Maud and Humphrey, sentimental and comic as it is. As he later wrote in *Martin Eden*, it had at first "struck him as ridiculous and impossible" that "in the fabric of knowledge there should be any connection whatever between a woman with hysterics and a schooner carrying a weather-helm or heaving to in a gale." But "Herbert Spencer had shown him, not only that it was not ridiculous, but that it was impossible for there to be no connection. All things were related to all other things, from the farthermost star in the wastes of space to the myriad atoms in the grain of sand under one's foot" (121).

The Mutiny of the Elsinore (1914, written ten years after he had fin-ished The Sea-Wolf and four years after he had abandoned the cruise of the Snark) is a far better sea novel than is generally recognized. Only Grant C. Knight, in a very brief footnote, has found it to be "one of the best sea stories in our literature" (132). It is seldom read today, and when it is, it is usually dismissed as an example of London's racism and his willingness late in his career to write anything that would sell. The novel does reflect the glare of Darwinian race theory that troubled the time, but the glare would soon lose its scientific luster and appear to be a "ghastly mistake," as Richard Hofstadter has explained (202). There is no need to apologize for London's having fallen for the idea of the "Yellow Peril." Although for a time it was widely accepted as part of the new theories of evolution, it seems likely that London would have come to deny it altogether. It is cer-tain, at least, that in The Mutiny of the Elsinore he came to express a very jaded view of the biological destiny that such theories projected for his race. Whereas in 1904 he had smiled at the love of Maud and Humphrey, in 1913 he would deride it in a mood of black comedy, even if he could not deny it. By this time, his faith in love as the mechanism of evolution, as well as his faith in the working class, had darkened. He had produced no son to carry on his line, and he could imagine a victory for the working class only in the distant future, after it had been ground under the totali-tarian iron heel and roused to resistance.

London always knew that mutiny is a natural state, as it is, for ex-ample, among the sled dogs in The Call of the Wild (GSW, 42). And he was well aware of the history of mutiny among men at sea. His point in The Mutiny of the Elsinore is that the real mutiny in nature is not at all like that depicted in traditional sea fiction. Thus his view of this modern mu-tiny of 1913 emphasizes both the degenerated state of the once great sailing ships and their sailors, and the brutal but regenerative forces of evolution.[9] The Elsinore is among the last of the old ships, and its officers, Captain West (accompanied by his daughter Margaret), and the mates, Mr. Pike and Mr. Mellaire, represent the old order. But the ramshackle crew is made up of "gangsters," "broken men and lunatics" (51). London's nar-rator, Pathurst, another gentlemanly writer like Humphrey Van Weyden, has gone to sea as a passenger because he has lost his "taste for [his] fellow man," for his career as an artist, and for women, whose "almost ferocious devotion to the destiny of sex" had become disenchanting (9). He is out-raged that Captain West's daughter is aboard, and he wonders, with the reader, "was there ever such a freight of human souls on the sea?" (98).

Captain West is an old aristocrat, cool and detached, who reminds

Pathurst of a "plantation" owner, a "samurai," or a "king"; he believes in God and is willfully blind to his mates' brutal exercise of authority (118, 77, 178). But this is his last voyage, for he dies before the *Elsinore* rounds the Cape, his death brought on by his awareness that he had committed a blunder in navigation. Both of the mates are old and both had served under a Captain Somers. London emphasizes the name, for he was aware of the alleged mutiny in the famous Somers affair of 1842, even though he could not have known that Melville, too, had worked with the idea in *Billy Budd.*[10] According to London's plot, Pike had been a favorite of Captain Somers, who had given him license to exercise severe discipline. But the mutinies Somers had suppressed inevitably overtook him; he was murdered, and Mr. Pike had vowed to spend the rest of his days at sea searching for the murderer. As it turns out, the *Elsinore's* second mate, with the suggestive name of Mellaire, was the murderer, and before he is found out, he warns Pike that the men "won't stand for this driving. . . . Times have changed . . . and laws have changed, and men have changed" (272). Of course, the mutiny must come, and when it does, Pathurst repeatedly remarks that this modern mutiny is "ridiculous and grotesque" (335). Eventually Pike and Mellaire disappear, apparently having killed each other in a death struggle that took them overboard. With all the members of the old order now buried at sea, the grotesque mutiny becomes even more ridiculous. For Pathurst ascends to the "high place," and with the help of Margaret—the "blind-instinctive race-mother"—he masters the mongrel crew in one darkly comic scene after another (100). At one point, Pathurst can "scarcely keep from laughing" at his own "ludicrous" exercise of brute authority, even as he relishes it under the "cool, measuring eye" of Margaret; and another scene is an obvious parody of the "crucifixion" and "resurrection" (325–26, 359–60). Finally, it is clear that Margaret and Pathurst will see the *Elsinore* safely in to Valparíso, where "the law and order that men institute" is sure to provide a happy ending; and as the book closes, we see Margaret and Pathurst "hidden in the darkness, clasped in each other's arms [talking] love and love plans" (369, 379). They will be married in Seattle, to which port the grotesque machinery of biology— "the destiny of sex"—will surely drive them. Pathurst, like many a good early twentieth-century hero, is happily caught by Margaret, one of the "instinctive huntresses of men" who hunt "with quite the same blind tropism that marks the pursuit of the sun by the sunflower" (52). Pathurst's last remarks, uttered between loving kisses, reveal London's ironic view of it all: "But I was stupid," he remarks; "'Oh, the weary, weary months' [he] complained"; "I am a fool . . . I am aware of only one thing: I want you. I want you"; "I stammered"; "she confirmed"; "I rattled on" (378).

The one minor character aboard the *Elsinore* whose point of view is reliable and with whom London is clearly sympathetic is Mulligan Jacobs, a pathetic creature of the abyss who "might have been an artist, a philo-sophic poet, had he not been born crooked with a crooked back" (372). Jacobs is well-read and he is particularly fond of Shakespeare (to whose Edmund the Bastard he seems related), Emile Zola, and Maxim Gorky. And he has the authority even to judge that "Joseph Conrad was living too fat to turn out the stuff he first turned out" (96). In short, he is London's ideal representative of the proletariat who *would* resist and eventually overturn the reigning order. "He was a direct actionist. The mass strike was the thing. Sabotage, not merely as a withdrawal of efficiency, but as a keen destruction-of-profits policy, was the weapon" (96). Drawing on such powers of bitter defiance, Jacobs successfully resists even Mr. Pike, and he stands in stark contrast to another of the *Elsinore's* crew, the type of mod-ern sailor with whom London had no sympathy, the "sea lawyer." Pathurst can see Jacobs only as a "filthy, malignant rat" and wonder at his powers of defiance: "How dare he—with no hope of any profit, not a hero, not a leader of a forlorn hope nor a martyr to God . . . how dare he . . . be so defiant?" (98). London's personal commitment to Jacobs is evident in Path-urst's description of his face, its "concentrated rage . . . on the verge of bursting into incandescence" (98). In all of London's sea fiction, only Wolf Larsen's face glows with such promise, and in the flesh of these two be-ings—one, the supreme product of physical evolution; the other, the com-bustive source of an inevitable social revolution—we see reflected all that remains for London of the mystic powers that Melville had seen in St. Elmo's fire—St. Elmo, the patron saint of sailors.

Thus it is that Mulligan Jacobs survives the *Elsinore's* modern mutiny and puts the new Captain Pathurst in his place: "An' who in hell are you an' your fathers? Robbers of the toil of men. I like them little. I like you and your fathers not at all. . . . To hell with you" (371). There is no ques-tion that London shares the "actionist" Jacobs's view of Pathurst, whose rise to brutal dominance parallels London's 1908 fable of the "cosmic pro-cess and purpose" of social evolution in *The Iron Heel* (Watson 121). Like Wickson in that novel, Pathurst gloats in his superiority over the "weak-lings and the rejected" aboard the *Elsinore*: "My heels were iron as I gazed on them in their peril and weakness" (197–98). Thrilled to have found that "culture has not emasculated [him]," Pathurst envisions himself and his "royal woman" holding "the high place of government and command until our kind perishes from the earth." But Jacobs's vision of him is pro-phetic: "You'll end in the darkness," he tells Pathurst, "And your dark-ness'll be as dark as mine" (336–37). It is a fitting end to the *Elsinore* affair that both Pathurst and Margaret remain "hidden by the darkness" as they rattle on to Seattle.

Despite the grotesque and comic allegory that thickens almost un-bearably toward the end of *The Mutiny of the Elsinore,* it is a very readable book with many of London's characteristically fine and authentic scenes of sailing in stormy seas and rounding the Horn. And, as an individual work in the tradition of American sea fiction, it is a landmark, rich with London's meaningful references to those who had sailed before him. Even Pathurst, the new American captain whose course toward the obscure ends of biological regeneration and race destiny was only recently charted, has a possible forebear within the tradition in Melville's Captain Amasa Delano, whose dubious heroics in preserving white supremacy were also performed with his eyes closed. Following Pathurst, later sea captains in American literature would reveal their authors' changing views of the Darwinian reality as it centers in sexual regeneration. The veil of Victorian tastes and editorial judgments that influenced London's presentation of the sex drama would be lifted, as theories of the aggressive race mother gave way to theories of the dominant, virile male; and the sea captain's authority would be associated, as it is in *To Have and Have Not* and *Far Tortuga,* not only with his seamanship but with his ability to survive in the elemental sexual competition of life.[11]

If *Michael, Brother of Jerry* (completed a year before, and published a year after London's death) is remembered at all, it is dismissed as a "mere dog story" or as London's exposé of the cruelty of trained animal shows.[12] But it is also the last novel in which London drew on the tradition of sea fiction to define man and his true place in nature. Following in the wake of *The Sea-Wolf* and the *Elsinore* mutiny, the first half of *Michael* projects London's ever-darkening allegory based on the "ship of fools" idea. As in *The Mutiny of the Elsinore,* he intensifies the allegory by centering it on critical references to the masterworks of nineteenth-century British and American sea literature, his constant purpose being, as it had been since *The Sea-Wolf,* to burn off the fog of romanticism that he felt had blinded the earlier writers. Here, in the dark months following the *Lusitania* incident, London wrote his versions of *Moby-Dick* and "The Rime of the Ancient Mariner."

He first signals his allegorical intent in chapter 9, where he introduces both the "Albatross" and "The Ancient Mariner." But the "Albatross" appears only briefly, as a warship—a "British cruiser of the second class"; what had been the romantic symbol of nature's inviolable mystic order is now for London a symbol of its actual order (59).[13] And London's twentieth-century "Ancient Mariner" is no wretched sinner but an ingenious survivor. He presents himself under the false name of Charles Stough Greenleaf, a name he compounded from "the pages of the history of the United States" (103). As we learn later, the Ancient Mariner had actually been born into a wealthy family and had "trod the quarterdeck" as a junior officer before he left the sea, squandered his wealth, and was eventually disowned by his wealthy family. He then spent six months in the poorhouse, where he learned his formative lesson—what it means to be "shut out from life" (103–6). Renewed by this descent into the abyss, he reentered society as a common laborer until he devised the confidence game of leading wealthy investors on long, futile sea searches for buried treasure he claims to have left on an uncharted island in the Pacific after being shipwrecked on the vessel *Wide Awake* in 1852. He tells his tale convincingly, making it as "literary" as possible. In this way, he makes a good living and does his money-hungry victims a favor: the long sea voyages are good for their health. This incredible Ancient Mariner, a benevolent confidence man who embodies the full range of American economic experience, is clearly "the finest man on board" London's "ship of fools" (90).

The ship's name, *Wide Awake,* is another of London's devices—as in the "white logic" or the character called "Burning Daylight"—to illuminate his fiction with the harsh reality of early twentieth-century thought and thereby to dispel the "imaginative orgies" he saw, for example, in *Moby-Dick.* Thus it is that in 1915 this "ship of fools" has its own encounter with a whale, and London's rendering of its disastrous end is both realistic and darkly comic. The catastrophe is brought on by one of the wealthy treasure hunters, who becomes frustrated in his efforts to paint the sea. When he fails to reproduce the "colour-delicacies" of "seminary maidens," he bursts into a "violent rage." Repeatedly on such occasions, he would tear up the attempted painting, "stamp it into the deck, then get out his large-calibred automatic rifle, perch himself on the forecastle head, and try to shoot any stray porpoise, albacore, or dolphin. It seemed to give him great relief to send a bullet home into the body of some surging, gorgeous-hued fish, and turn it on its side slowly to sink down into the death and depth of the sea" (94). Sometimes he would shoot at whales, despite the Ancient Mariner's grave warnings that whales have been known to sink such "full-rigged ship[s]" as the "whaler *Essex*" (95; again and again, as in this repeated reference to the *Essex* incident, London emphasizes his awareness of the tradition and his intention to extend it). But the frustrated painter will not believe such tales; he persists, eventually killing a helpless calf whose "grief-stricken" mother turns on the ship.

London's description of the calf's death, the cow's ramming and final sinking of the ship, and the crew's escape in the lifeboats is in stark contrast with Melville's melodramatic sinking of the *Pequod,* for the authors' purposes are different. Whereas Melville's whale, with all its power of divine retribution, sinks the *Pequod* in an instant, London's eighty-foot cow whale is only an eighty-foot cow whale: she finally succeeds in sinking the ship, but she is badly wounded herself, as in the actual *Essex* incident. And she takes no notice of the lifeboats: "It was from the huge thing, the schooner, that death had been wreaked upon her calf; and it was upon the schooner that she vented the wrath of her grief" (138). In contrast to

Moby-Dick, there is no cosmic justice here: the whale's tormentor escapes with the rest of the crew. London's description of the scene is flatly realistic, but though his sympathy for the whale is clear, he portrays the crew's escape in black comic tones. In their panic, they argue over the limited space and overload the boats with a "clutter . . . of men, provisions, and property" (133). When the first sailor ignores the captain's orders and, "sea-bag in hand," prepares to escape, another calls him "a rat leaving the ship." But the Ancient Mariner voices London's judgment of the incident: "We're all rats. . . . I learned just that when I was a rat among the mangy rats of the poor farm" (123–24). When the ship sinks, "only the whale" remains, "floating and floundering, on the surface of the sea" (138). The survivors are picked up two days later by the passing steamer *Mariposa,* none the worse for their adventure. And when they arrive in San Francisco, no one believes their tale: "Sunk by a whale? . . . Nonsense," exclaim the cub reporters and moviegoers, for whom "the real world and all its spaciousness does not exist" (143).

The constant lure of "the real world and all its spaciousness" that first drew the young Jack London to experience the sea for himself and to publish his story "Typhoon Off the Coast of Japan" took him to sea once again in the last story he wrote. "The Water Baby," which he finished the month before he died, has been cited as evidence of London's "rebirth" in 1916, his envisioning of a "saving illumination" in the "powerful energies" of the "Jungian subconscious" that could "triumph over the death-dealing wasteland" (McClintock 172–73). There is no question that London had become interested in Jung, that he was among the first American writers to be influenced by both Freud and Jung; but what he saw in Jung, as reflected in "The Water Baby," seems mainly to have corroborated the sense of reality he had already projected in *The Sea-Wolf.* The story brings together an old Hawaiian fisherman and a white narrator named Lakana (Hawaiian for London), who converse in the old man's canoe as he tends to his fishing lines. The story presents the vital old fisherman's songs of the Creation as being more believable than the account given in Genesis, and London admits that they are as reasonable as his own version based on early twentieth-century science. It is "funny," he remarks, that the Hawaiian myth is true to what he knows of "evolution," "astronomy," and "seismology," which teach "that man did run on all fours ere he came to walk upright, that . . . the speed of the revolution of the earth on its axis has diminished steadily, thus increasing the length of day, and that . . . all the islands of Hawaii were elevated from the ocean floor by volcanic action" (*Makaloa Mat,* 144–45).

But the energy of this story does not derive simply from London's sense that ancient myth and modern science point in the same direction. It is true that London senses a profound general wisdom in the old fisher-

And with his several ancient fangs [he] bit into the heart and the life of the matter.
    —Jack London, "The Water Baby"

man's humble sense that he is "of little worth, and . . . not wise," and in his Jungian mythic sense that the sea is his mother, "the milk giver, the life source" (144). But the old fisherman's long tale of the Water Baby is baffling and comically unverifiable, despite his claim to "know for a fact." The story's undeniable "facts" and its most intensely memorable imagery derive from direct observation, after Lakana bares his "eyes to the stab of the sun['s]" "glare on the water." Then he watches the vital old fisherman dive for a large squid:

> I saw him steady himself with his right hand on the coral lump, and thrust his left arm into the hole to the shoulder. Half a minute elapsed, during which time he seemed to be groping and rooting around with his left hand. Then tentacle after tentacle, myriad-suckered and wildly waving, emerged. Laying hold of his arm, they writhed and coiled about his flesh like so many snakes. With a heave and a jerk appeared the entire squid, a proper devilfish or octopus.
>
> But the old man was in no hurry for his natural element, the air above the water. There, forty feet beneath, wrapped about by an oc-topus that measured nine feet across from tentacle tip to tentacle tip and that could well drown the stoutest swimmer, he coolly and casually did the one thing that gave him his empery over the monster. He shoved his lean, hawklike face into the very center of the slimy, squirm-ing mass, and with his several ancient fangs bit into the heart and the life of the matter. (147–48)

This compelling scene (he had created a similar one in the story "Yah! Yah! Yah!") is one of the "great moments of living" in Jack London's sea fiction and, indeed, in the tradition of American sea fiction. It depicts the essential biological struggle that London had always recognized, and not at all a "struggle between the most fundamentally human desire for salvation and the most fundamentally human fear of damnation" (McClintock 174). The myths of "rebirth," "salvation," and "damnation" can never survive the harsh light of London's "white logic." For London, there is only the "elemental stuff itself," the vital life strength like that embodied in Wolf Larsen's flesh. And even if it "lingers" as in a "shapeless lump of turtle meat and recoils and quivers from the prod of a finger," it will very quickly be "acrawl" and give up even its final shapeless identity to "the corruption of the sea."

Through Jack London, the tradition of American sea fiction survived the passing of the great sailing ships. Sensing and responding to the sea's timeless influence on our lives, he was certainly ahead of his own time in retrieving for the tradition and our culture in general a sense of Melville's permanent value. And like his fellow writers before and after him in the tradition, he was of his own time in celebrating the ecstasy of survival, "the great moments of living" that he had known personally at sea and that revealed to him the essential reality: for the species, the constant lift and forward plunge of evolution; for the individual, only that "the body shall be cast into the sea." To Maud Brewster's question, "And immortality?" he would answer, with Wolf Larsen, "Bosh!" But it is revealing of London's feeling for the sea and for his great sea captain that Wolf Larsen's last word is not actually "bosh," as Humphrey reports it to be. A full week later, in response to the question, "Are you all there?" Wolf uttered his actual last word: "Yes" (*Sea-Wolf*, 248–50). Always, even at the moment of his own entry into "the vastness and profundity of the quiet and dark" that finally overtakes Wolf, Jack London affirmed his readiness to go to sea, to search for and perhaps grasp yet another of the "great moments of living" that he found at sea and in his fellow writers' tales of the sea: "The last work in which he read that night" he died, as Charmian London reported, "was 'Around Cape Horn, Maine to California in 1852, Ship *James W. Paige*'" (*Book of Jack London*, 2:385).

7

From Sail to Steam: Sailor-Writers of the 1860s and 1870s

By 1851, when Melville published *Moby-Dick* and Donald McKay's *Flying Cloud* sailed for Cape Horn and San Francisco, the age of sail and the golden age of American sea fiction had begun to pass. There can never be another *Moby-Dick* or *Flying Cloud.* But Melville lived for forty more years, finally returning to the sea and to writing about it. And after the Civil War there was a resurgence of sailing ship activity in America. McKay built his last ship, *Glory of the Seas,* in 1869 (in 1874 she sailed from New York to San Francisco in ninety-four days), and not until some time after she was burned for her copper in 1922 did commercial sailing ships disappear from American waters. In the intensifying competition between sail and steam, sailing ships survived by scrambling for the last viable markets, carrying grain and wool, sugar, oil, guano, and ore. And even after the opening of the Panama Canal in 1914, some—like the *Star of India* and the *Glory of the Seas*—could still survive by hauling lumber or canned salmon.

During this period there was also a resurgence of interest in writing about the sea. In 1900 Joshua Slocum capitalized on this resurgence, and contributed a great deal to it, by publishing his *Sailing Alone Around the World.* And before Melville died several young men had already begun careers at sea that would eventuate in a new wave of American sea fiction that began to appear in the late 1890s. These men, born between the 1860s and 1890s, went to sea for the same reasons that Dana and Melville did, and for new reasons as well: they had the examples of Dana and Melville, and they found in the sailor's life an escape from the complexities of an increasingly industrial culture. Moreover, realizing that sailing ships were disappearing before their eyes, they rushed to experience that way of life, romanticized as it certainly was, before it passed utterly away. And some went on to make short careers in steam. Then, after their work at sea, they found a readership between the 1890s and 1930s that thirsted for their adventurous tales of a simpler existence, a readership much like that to which the local colorists had already appealed. Even though, when returned from the sea, many of these writers were still young men, they could write as *experienced* men, even as old salts from the already ghostly past of sail. The chief impulse in many of their stories was to elegize this past. At the same time, in following Dana and Melville by writing of their experiences as young men at sea, these writers told a new story that made a great deal of sense to their new audience. The manhood and independence a young man might acquire by going to sea in the 1890s was quite different from what it had been for Dana and Melville in the 1830s and 1840s. After the *Origin of Species* and the *The Descent of Man,* the brutalities of sea life that had struck Dana and Melville as being monstrously inhuman now seemed merely an undeniable attribute of manhood as it could be understood to exist in the evolutionary stream. Indeed, Jack London's young sailor Martin Eden speaks for all the sailor-writers from the 1890s to the 1930s when, addressing the Berkeley professor, he charges, "you lack biology." He had learned from Herbert Spencer "that evolution was no mere theory. . . . There was no caprice, no chance. All was law. It was in obedience to the same law that the bird flew, and it was in obedience to the same law that the fermenting slime had writhed and squirmed, and put out legs and wings, and become a bird." Charging that the professor "lacked biology," Eden was not simply bullying him but urging him to consider "biology in its larger aspects," that is, "the real interpretive biology, from the ground up . . . up to the widest aesthetic and sociological generalizations" (*Martin Eden,* 243, 120, 244). In the sea fiction of this period the biological theme runs deep, from the brutalities of bucko mates to the larger economic and "sociological generalizations" from which emerged the seaman as "hairy ape."

These writers' immersion in the rugged sea life of their times seemed resoundingly to corroborate the widely accepted Darwinist interpretations of life. The sailing ships themselves were engaged in a fiercely competitive economic struggle to survive. And conditions aboard the modern sailing ships clearly dramatized the physical, biological reality that underlay the larger, more abstract theories of economic competition. Yankee skippers had always had reputations as "drivers," but in the last days of sail they drove harder or gave way to steam. These "were the days of *large* ships and *small* crews," as Felix Riesenberg explained in *Under Sail* (1918), based on his own experience, largely on his having sailed before the mast around Cape Horn in 1897 on the *A. J. Fuller:*

> In clipper days, a flyer like the *Sovereign of the Seas* carried a crew of *eighty* seamen, and most of them were as rated—A.B. The ship *A. J. Fuller,* in the year 1897, left the port of New York, for the voyage around

Cape Horn to Honolulu with *eighteen* seamen, counting the boy and the carpenter, the *Fuller* being a three skysail yard ship of 1,848 tons register. (6–7)

Riesenberg then compares the size and crew of the *Sovereign of the Seas* with those of the *A. J. Fuller:*

Ship	Sovereign of the Seas	A. J. Fuller
Length	258 ft.	229 ft.
Beam	44 ft.	41.5 ft.
Draft	23.5 ft.	18 ft.
Register Tonnage	2,421 tons	1,848 tons
Crews—		
Master	1	1
Mates	4	2
Boatswains	2	–
Carpenters	2	1
Sailmakers	2	–
Able Seamen ...	80	16
Boys	10	1
	101	21

This condition, of small crews and large ships, brought to the seven seas a reputation for relentless driving and manhandling that has clung to the minds of men as nothing else. The huge American ships were the hardest afloat, and that remarkable booklet, "The Red Record," compiled by the National Seamen's Union of America, in the middle nineties, carries a tale of cruelty and abuse on the high seas that must forever remain a blot upon the white escutcheon of sail.

These ships bred a sea officer peculiar to the time—the bucko mate of fact as well as fiction. These were hard fisted men, good sailors and excellent disciplinarians, though they lacked the polish acquired by sea officers of an earlier day when the sailer was often a passenger carrier, and intercourse with people of culture had its effect upon the men of the after-guard. (8)

And if the writers of these years felt that their elemental existence aboard such ships was clearly a struggle for survival, the world's seas were alive with the great naval ships that were engaged in the larger international struggle for dominance upon which Alfred Thayer Mahan had based his extensive Darwinist analyses of sea power in history. In their experiences as war correspondents in the Caribbean and the Pacific, Stephen Crane and Jack London were firsthand witnesses to incidents that were related to the struggle for sea power. And in the fiction of the less well-known writers I discuss in these chapters, the international struggle for sea power is clearly reflected in references to Admiral George Dewey, the *Merrimac,* the *Maine,* Santiago, Havana, and Manila.

Finally, another aspect of the Darwinian interpretation of life—that pertaining to "sexual selection"—figures far more prominently in the plots of these sea stories than do the ideas of sea power. Like the plots of London's *Sea-Wolf* and *Mutiny of the Elsinore,* or Frank Norris's *Moran of the Lady Letty,* many others in the sea fiction of this period appeal not only to the reading public's desire for tales of romance but also to the more serious reader's awareness that the struggle for life involved not only "natural selection" (or Spencer's popularized phrase "survival of the fittest"), but "sexual selection," as Darwin had developed that idea in *The Descent of Man, and Selection in Relation to Sex* (1871).

In many sea stories during this period, a young seaman's struggle to survive and become a man is inseparably linked with his struggle to win a mate. This struggle, necessitated by the "law of battle" that Darwin discusses in *The Descent of Man* (573–75), is not only brutal but sometimes darkly comic, as when Jack London and Richard Matthews Hallet see in it a means of parodying the violent rituals of courtly love. Often, the individual's struggle is presented in the larger context of racial evolution; and frequently, as such plots unfold, the merely brutish competitor or, in evolutionary terms, the "degenerate" (as in the "hairy ape"), loses the struggle. That this should pertain—as, for example, in Humphrey Van Weyden's defeat of Wolf Larsen in the struggle for Maud, or in the cases of Richard Matthews Hallet's young seamen or, inversely, in Eugene O'Neill's Yank— is determined not only by the author's hopes to please his readers but by Darwin's surmise in *The Descent of Man* that the loss of body hair in the evolution of man resulted (as in the development of breeding plumage among birds) from a long series of mates who selected each other because of their relative hairlessness (613–18).

But though it is true that the frequency of female participants in the fictional sea voyages of this period resulted largely from efforts to please the reading public and to reflect an evolutionary reality, it is also true that many women were to be found at sea during these years. Not only were women passengers on the packets and liners, but also they often sailed with their husbands and families in the merchant trade. In such circumstances, both Joanna and Lincoln Colcord were born at sea in the early 1880s, their mother, Jennie, having accompanied their father, who captained the bark *Charlotte A. Littlefield* in the China trade. And in a famous incident in 1866, when Captain Patten of the clipper *Neptune's Car* collapsed, his wife, Mary, took command of the *Car* and navigated it safely around Cape Horn and in to San Francisco.

The sea fiction I discuss in the following pages is so strongly given to the broad theme of the struggle for survival during the last years of sail that it will often seem dated and distorted to readers from our late twentieth-century point of view, especially to those who prefer stories from the golden age of sail. But the last years of sail were a time of "nautical darkness," as one writer put it (Hallet, *The Lady Aft*, 116). All the sailor-writers of these years were painfully aware of this "darkness" and treasured that literature of an earlier age when Dana, for example, could depict "the sea life of his time" with what Jack London termed "untroubled vision" (*The Human Drift*, 102). If we acknowledge the underlying reasons for the dark and troubled vision that is projected in the sea fiction from this period, we can more fully value the picture it gives us of the actual sea life of those times. And some of the best writers in this group—Thornton Jenkins Hains, Arthur Mason, Lincoln Colcord, or Archie Binns—occasionally achieved a simplicity of style and vision that illuminated both their work and their dark times. One should not turn to these sea stories in hopes of finding another Melville or *Moby-Dick*. But for readers who are interested in the tradition of American sea fiction, the literature of these years is crucial. For students of American literature in general, the sea fiction from this period will be of interest at least because, like the mass of regional or local color fiction that was produced in America between the Civil War and World War I, it fills in our picture of the nation's experience, its mind and mood, during those years. And for any lover of sea stories or any reader who is simply curious about American sea experience during the last years of sail, there are treasures here.[1]

Morgan Robertson (1861–1915)

With his ten years before the mast, Morgan Robertson was more completely a working sailor than most others in the tradition of American sea fiction, and his fourteen books firmly establish his claim as one of the tradition's memorable minor writers. He is a true representative of his time, the "Strenuous Age." The wide range of his working experiences, the variety of ideas he incorporated in his fiction, and the structure of his tales—devoted as they are to headlong, episodic action: all these exemplify the "rush of experience" that was characteristic of his time (Martin, *Harvests*, 21). Robertson was a sailor on both sailing ships and steam, and at other times he was a cowboy, a swimming instructor, a watchmaker, an inventor, and an author. His fiction was shaped by the Darwinian biological reality he saw at work not only in the individual's struggle to survive but in the larger spheres of social and international struggles for power. But he was also interested in psychology, from the older concepts of phrenology to the newer ideas involving the psychology of the subconscious, and he wrote extensively of the more legitimate sciences of chemistry, hydrology, and the physics of light and sound.

Whether or not Robertson will ever find a permanent, minor place in our literary histories as a representative spirit of his time, it is certain that he earned a measure of recognition and respect from a number of his more famous contemporaries, like Jack London (who owned two of his books) and Booth Tarkington, Richard Harding Davis, Joseph Conrad, and William Dean Howells, the last four of whom are said to have assisted in the publication of an edition of Robertson's works after his death.[2] Robertson published more than two hundred stories in such journals as the *Atlantic Monthly, Harper's Monthly Magazine, Colliers's Weekly,* and the *Saturday Evening Post* and three novels. But his chief contributions to the tradition of American sea fiction can be grouped within two general areas. The first of these is a series of speculative fictions—during a profoundly revolutionary period in maritime history—on future sea experience. The second is "sea comedy," as George M. Hunter, the editor of *Seaman's Magazine,* described it (Hunter 317).

The most notable of his fictional speculations is *Futility: Or, The Wreck of the Titan* (1898), and had he written only this book, Robertson would still be of interest today, for in *Futility* he foretold the *Titanic* disaster by fourteen years. His great ship, the *Titan,* was embarking on its fourth Atlantic crossing. "She would land her passengers three thousand miles away with the promptitude and regularity of a railway train," for her officers were determined to break the record she had established on her maiden voyage (3). The novel begins:

> She was the largest craft afloat and the greatest of the works of men. In her construction and maintenance were involved every science, profession, and trade known to civilization. On her bridge were officers, who, besides being among the pick of the Royal Navy, had passed rigid examinations in all studies that pertain to the winds, tides, currents, and geography of the sea; they were not only seamen, but scientists. The same professional standard applied to the personnel of the engine-room, and the steward's department was equal to that of a first-class hotel. (1)

Acknowledged to be "unsinkable—indestructible, [the *Titan*] carried as few boats as would satisfy the laws" (2). Thus, when she hits an iceberg at top speed in the North Atlantic, there are few survivors. As Paul R. Ryan noted in an issue of *Oceanus* devoted to the *Titanic's* discovery in 1985:

The similarities between [Robertson's] *Titan* and the real *Titanic* are uncanny:

	Titan	*Titanic*
Ship length	800 ft.	882.5 ft.
Tonnage displacement	75,000	66,000
Propellers	3	3
Speed of impact	25 knots	22 knots
Number of passengers	3,000	2,340
Number of lifeboats	24	20
Month of sinking	April	April (6)

Aside from *Futility*'s "uncanny" foretelling of the *Titanic* disaster, it is for other reasons a notable book within the tradition of American sea fiction. It was the first American sea novel to present the struggle between sail and steam within the full context of Darwinian theory, from the hero's (Lieutenant Rowland) defeat in the sexual competition for a mate, to the *Titan*'s principles of navigation, to the final legal and financial struggles between the *Titan*'s owners and the insurance broker. Robertson also depicted the *Titan*'s internal workings with imagery that would prevail in the tradition for the next four decades:

> Fifty feet below her deck, in an inferno of noise, and heat, and light, and shadow, coal-passers wheeled the picked fuel from the bunkers to the fire-hold, where half-naked stokers, with faces like those of tortured fiends, tossed it into the eighty white-hot mouths of the furnaces. In the engine-room, oilers passed to and fro, in and out of the plunging, twisting, glistening steel, with oil-cans and waste, overseen by the watchful staff on duty, who listened with strained hearing for a false note in the confused jumble of sound—a clicking of steel out of tune, which would indicate a loosened key or nut. (4)

In view of Robertson's career in both sail and steam, it is fitting that this monstrous ship should run down and sink a sailing ship before its own fatal collision. Rowland, formerly a man-of-war's man, was in the crow's nest when the *Titan* struck and cut the sailing ship in half. He reported the ship as soon as he had sighted it, but it was too late. He heard the "shouts and shrieks" of the sailors aboard it and saw its two halves "swallowed in the blackness astern" (10–11). Later, having refused to cooperate with the captain's effort to cover up the incident and his failure to attempt a rescue, Rowland becomes doubly dispossessed. Already he had seen among the passengers the former lover who had rejected him for the wealthy husband who now accompanies her, and now the captain will drug him and portray him as a drunkard to discredit his testimony. When, in a half-drugged hallucinatory state (the captain's plan to drug him had been accidentally interrupted), Rowland tries to decipher the meaning of his existence, Robertson's full design comes into focus. Rowland sees his rejection as "part of a great evolutionary principle, which develops the race life at the expense of the individual" (22). Seeing himself as one "unfitted to survive" and denying the existence of "a merciful God—a kind, loving, just and merciful God," he bursts "into a fit of incongruous laughter" (22). "'The survival of the fittest,' he rambled, as he stared into the fog; 'cause and effect. It explains the Universe—and me'" (23–24).

But Rowland does survive the *Titan's* collision with the iceberg. He even manages to save his former lover's child and reach the iceberg, where, incredibly, he kills a polar bear but loses an arm in the struggle. Then, immediately after he had prayed to "the God that he denied," though only for the sake of the child and her mother, the "moon-lit fabric" of a bark came into view, and they were rescued (38). In the succeeding legal and financial struggles between the villainous insurance broker, the *Titan's* owners, and the captain of the ship the *Titan* had run down (miraculously, he too had survived), a melodramatic justice is achieved. As in most of his other tales, especially the comic ones, Robertson projects a view of life in which the Darwinian order and "cause and effect" prevail—but in ways that favor the simple working seaman (as opposed to captains and, especially, ship owners) and preserve the possibility of both an inscrutable Providence and a marketable plot for his turn-of-the-century audience.

After *Futility*, Robertson's speculations on future developments at sea were shaped largely by the widespread interest in Captain Alfred Mahan's histories of sea power and by his own special interest in the submarine. The submarine as a military weapon had been known in America since David Bushnell built the *Turtle* in 1775. But in the era of sea power it had become a frightful, practical reality that would lead not only to the sinking of the *Lusitania* but to history's greatest disaster at sea, the sinking of the *Wilhelm Gustloff* in 1945, when seventy-seven hundred refugees were lost. Robertson became fascinated with the technology of submarines and, for a time, with the possibility that they would put an end to the great battleships. In 1904 he published an article in the *World's Work* titled "Will Battleships Be Obsolete?" and, working for a short time for the U.S. Navy, he invented and built the first periscope. With his typical bad luck, however, he was denied the patent rights that might have made his fortune. Also, his interest in the physics of light and sound led to his fictional speculations on technologies that resemble modern radar and sonar.

The settings for these stories of future naval wars project Captain Mahan's Darwinist view of international struggle. "Beyond the Spectrum," for example, is set in a time when

the long-expected crisis was at hand, and the country was on the verge
of war. Jingoism was rampant. Japanese laborers were mobbed on the
western slope, Japanese students were hazed out of colleges, and Japanese children stoned away from playgrounds. Editorial pages sizzled with
burning words of patriotism; pulpits thundered with invocations to the
God of battles and prayers for the perishing of the way of the ungodly.
(*Over the Border,* 207)

Elsewhere—in a story set in the more distant future than that presented in
"Beyond the Spectrum" or "The Last Battleship" (in *Over the Border*),
when the battleship *had* become obsolete, Robertson depicted the resump-
tion of war that follows inevitably when technology had produced the kind
of vessel he features in "The Submarine Destroyer" (in *Land Ho!*). This
tale opens in a time of "peace," when the "bone-yards [of] old leviathans"
testified to "a barbarous past when men fought with twelve-inch guns":
"The United States had absorbed her trusts and was deporting the negro—
a ten years' job, nearly done." Russia and the rest of the world were threatened by "China's open door policy": "The overflowing millions of the
prosperous land poured forth to people the earth" (220–22). But the
United States meets "unexpected and strenuous objection[s] from the remnant of her black population" and from Japan, which is threatened by the
American effort to deport "every Celestial below the rank of diplomat" to
China (222). In "The Submarine Destroyer," America's plan to be "happily rid of the Dark Destroyer and the Yellow Peril at one move" is complicated when the American submarine escorting the transported refugees
encounters a strange new craft that "can catch and destroy any submersi-
ble afloat or submerged" (227). When the American commander of the
submarine realizes with a "shudder" the inevitable consequences of this
development, he calls to the inventor of the new craft, "You are not a
benefactor of humanity. . . . You bring back the battleship—and war
upon the sea" (227).

In such tales, Robertson presents a grim comedy of man's pretense
that he can achieve civilization and peace outside the Darwinian order.
But in many other stories, his tone is more overtly and lightheartedly
comic. Typically, in these stories, his comic subjects involve a simple
sailor's genius for survival in a variety of crises at sea. He survives because
he *is* an "able-bodied sailor," and in his survival he often demonstrates his
superiority to the mates, captains, or ship owners who abuse him. Finnegan, in "The Subconscious Finnegan" and "A Chemical Comedy" (in
Down to the Sea), and Scotty, in "The Dollar," "The Shipowner," and
"The Wave" (in *Land Ho!*), are such comic survivors. In other comic tales
he portrays the yachtsman's ineptitude at sea, as in "Polarity: A Tale of

Two Brunettes," in *Shipmates;* the comic war between the sexes, as in "Primordial," in *Where Angels Fear to Tread,* or "The Honeymoon Ship" and "Three Laws and the Golden Rule," in *Three Laws and the Golden Rule;* or the Darwinian order itself, as in "The Mutiny" in *Down to the Sea.*

"The Mutiny" is one of his most bizarre and, from the point of view of traditional sea fiction, amusing tales. Robertson is the first writer in American sea fiction to exploit the comic possibilities of Darwinian theory (although Jack London would soon do so to a limited extent in *The Sea-Wolf* and, in a thoroughly jaded way, in *The Mutiny of the Elsinore*). In Robertson's mutiny, Fleming, a shipwrecked sailor on the African coast, ships as first mate on the brig run by Captain Bruggles. Bruggles is a giant, "almost seven feet tall," massively but perfectly developed, and with "the grim dignity of a lion" (276–77). When Fleming goes aboard he is astounded to see not only that the captain's beautiful daughter is aboard but also that she is the lover from whom he had been separated some time before. She is now her father's terrified captive on a ship crewed by giant apes. When Bruggles musters the crew, he warns Fleming that to get their attention and respect, he must thump each one on the head, "about as hard as you'd hit a nail with a hammer; it won't hurt 'em" (285). Bruggles introduces Fleming to "Haeckel," who grins and blinks when the captain strikes him on the head with a handspike. Fleming meets "Darwin, Huxley, Tyndall, Spencer, and Marsh": "'I've named them after the leading evolutionists,' said the captain, as we returned to the poop; 'but I doubt that they'd feel complimented.' I was too weak in my knees and dizzy in my head to ask whether he meant the scientists or his pets" (287).

The captain assures Fleming that animals cannot be controlled by either "kindness" or "severity" alone: "But, combine the two, and you have the working rule which made the Christian religion the greatest force for civilization the world has known—hope of reward and fear of punishment. It will civilize a devil out o' hell" (287). The system works tolerably, except for the ape "Spencer, survival of the fittest," who dominates the others, leads the eventual mutiny, kills the captain, and remains in control of the ship when Fleming and the girl finally escape by boat. Looking back at the brig, Fleming says, "There's Spencer out on the jib-boom, and the female on the spanker-boom. It's a horrible courtship" (312). Soon Fleming and his own lover are rescued by a "French schooner-of-war—one of the slave-trade police of the African coast" (312).

The full range of Robertson's work cannot be contained within these two areas of speculative and comic fiction. In some of his tales, for example, he manages somewhat to subdue the "rush of experience" and ideas that often clutter his work. Then, as in "Through the Deadlight" (in *Three Laws*) or "The Enemies" (in *Down to the Sea*), he achieves a simplicity of action and tone that can be affecting. Of his work in general, the earliest pieces, especially *Futility*, show promise and convey the passion, intensity, and exuberance that we recognize in the early work of other careers, as in *Maggie*, for example, or *Mardi*. But Robertson was no Crane or Melville. In his later work, as in his expansion of the early and rather successful story "Where Angels Fear to Tread" into the novel *Sinful Peck*, we sense an older, more market-wise approach. The rush of experience in the plots he devised and the ideas he employed seem mechanical and jaded: he was caught up in the competitive race into print that destroyed many writers' careers during his time. Unlike the more talented and powerful Jack London, who made a fortune in the same race and found the emptiness of it, Morgan Robertson barely survived before he exhausted his energies and ended in poverty. The circumstances of his death moved the *New York Times* to comment on the lamentable conditions of Robertson's and other American writers' lives ("Literature and Its Rewardings"). On its front page of the previous day, 25 March 1915, the *Times* had reported Robertson's death in a story headlined "Morgan Robertson Dies Standing Up." The story described how he was discovered leaning up against a bureau in his shabby Atlantic City room, gazing out to sea.

Thornton Jenkins Hains (1866–?)

Thornton Jenkins Hains is virtually unknown today; the sketchy biographical information available on him includes neither a full account of his sea experience nor any record of his last years. He began his career as a writer in the late 1880s, and by 1912 he had produced several sea books, among which two deserve permanent places in the tradition of American sea fiction: *The Strife of the Sea*, stories (1903) and *The Voyage of the Arrow*, a novel (1906). Of his other works, one, at least, a collection of stories, is especially noteworthy: *The White Ghost of Disaster: The Chief Mate's Yarn* (1912). Hains's stories clearly reveal that he had considerable sea experience, but we know only that he was "a licensed navigator of oceans for vessels of more than 700 tons gross," that he held "both English Board of Trade and American navigator's licenses," and that he was "owner and master of many small vessels" (*Who Was Who in America*, 4).

The Strife of the Sea is a unified collection of eleven stories of various sea creatures, from seabirds and fish to fishermen and whales. Together, the stories constitute something like a *Call of the Wild* of the sea, though they owe nothing to London's story, which appeared in the same year. Struggling, surviving, succumbing, evolving, each of the human and ani-

*[He] shot straight downwards upon the doomed
fish. It was literally a bolt from heaven out of
a clear sky.*
—Thornton Jenkins Hains, *The Strife of the Sea*

mal characters acts out his own story in the larger biological plot of life. An old pelican in the first story, for example ("The Old Man of Sand Key"), surveys the gulf waters:

> Here and there a large barracouta or albicore would dart like a streak of shimmering silver through the liquid, and the old man would cast his glance in the direction of the vanishing point with a ready pinion to sweep headlong at the mullet or sailor's choice that was being pursued. (12)

Again, when a "slight ripple showed upon the surface of the quiet sea,"

> the pelican sighted it and stood away toward it, for it looked like a mackerel that had come to the surface to take in the sunshine and general beauty of the day. In a moment the old man had swung over the spot at a height of about a hundred feet; then suddenly folding his wings, he straightened out his body, opened his beak, and shot straight downwards upon the doomed fish. It was literally a bolt from heaven from out of a clear sky. (13)

As Hains renders it, the pristine violence of this order proceeds with the calm majesty of the pelican's flight. And when the pelican himself is torn in a fierce battle with two eagles who pirate his catch, Hains accepts the inevitable but reserves for his old man a peaceful and dignified end; on the beach, the dying pelican "drew his head back and held himself dignified and stately as he walked to the edge of the surf. There he stopped, and as the flaming orb sank beneath the western sea, the old man stood watching it as it disappeared" (32). Similarly, after a giant ray is destroyed in a wild battle with a fear-crazed fisherman, the sea has its way: "He sank slowly down upon the clean sand below, and the ground-sharks of the reef came silently into their feast" (74).

In two of these stories, "The Loggerhead" and "A Tragedy of the South Atlantic," a loggerhead turtle and an old finback whale endure the strife of the sea, even—Hains emphasizes—their encounters with man. Hains very tentatively speculates here on the possibility that life might evolve into a more peaceful order. With their great size and longevity, the loggerhead and whale exist in a serene state in which they seem to feed not so much on life as on their dreamy contemplations of earth's beauty. In his own projected dream of their conscious states, Hains envisions a life in which the loggerhead, for example,

> had no trouble getting enough to eat without fighting for it. It seemed a great waste of energy to be eternally chasing other and weaker creatures, and now he had drifted instinctively back to the habits of his

Both eagles came at him at once, uttering hoarse cries . . . .
—Thornton Jenkins Hains, *The Strife of the Sea*

forefathers. He took things very coolly. When a savage shark or albicore made a strike at him he did not retaliate by snapping at them with his huge beak. . . . He simply hauled in his paddles and stump of a tail to the sheltering safety of his armor . . . [drawing in his head] until his ugly beak and steady eyes looked out of a sort of cavern. . . .

After they had gone away he would slowly and lazily shove out his paddles again and proceed to scull himself leisurely on his way, his small, dull mind undisturbed at the affront. Such creatures were a nuisance to him, but they were in existence and it was not for him to worry because they were. He would go along in the sunshine and soft air in his easy way, and when these no longer attracted him he would draw in his head, upset himself, then, thrusting it forward again, go sculling for the cool depths where he would spend many hours among the beautiful marine growths fathoms below the surface upon the coral reef, and where the faint light of the sun filtering down made objects dim and uncertain. All was quiet here, and it was the ideal place for repose. (144–45)

Earlier in the story the loggerhead had easily survived confrontations with man. A conch fisherman had given up in his efforts to turn the six-hundred-pound turtle onto his back, going on to capture others of more manageable size; and another conch had ignored the turtle and merely probed the sand in search of eggs. But in the concluding episode, the turtle becomes involved in a more formidable struggle with men when he is caught in a seine. In surviving this battle, too—because the fishermen finally discover that he is a useless loggerhead and not a prized green turtle—he inadvertently frees the other creatures from the seine. The scene is unique in Hains's detailed portrayal of netted fish from the fishes' point of view and in its envisioning a comic disruption of man's deadly, efficient participation in life's hunt. Some of the entrapped fish "swerved at the line and flowed past in a solid phalanx of shimmering silver to swim back and make a new trial" (155). Now,

the mullet and whiting were . . . leaping by scores over the corked line. Their active life had made them fleet and strong. They had fought for existence from the beginning, and the trap about them was but another of the many obstacles they must surmount if they would endure. They were terrified, but they acted quickly and sensibly, their fright not causing them to overlook any possible means of escape. They were getting clear in spite of the shouting men who were now hauling line as fast as they could. Several large skates and a couple of flounders who had lived up the slue were vainly trying to burrow under the heavy leadline that swept the bottom. The loggerhead noticed them as he passed, but they paid no heed to him. A troop of crabs were being hustled along the bottom by the weighted line. They were snapping at everything that came in their reach.

> The loggerhead began to get anxious to go away. He made a savage lunge at the meshes closing about him and he drove his head through a great rent he made with his beak. His paddles, or flippers, however, caught in the snare and he struggled wildly and with gigantic power to get through. His tremendous struggles soon drew the corked line below the surface and brought the fishermen hurrying in their boats to find out what caused the trouble. They gazed down into the depths and soon made out the giant shape struggling frantically. Seizing the lines of the seine they quickly hauled the loggerhead to the surface, where one of them grasped his hind paddle and held it long enough to get a bowline on it. Then they rowed to the shore, towing him ignominiously behind the craft, while the few remaining mullet, who were too small and weak to make the leap for liberty, crowded swiftly through the gap for the open sea. (157–58)

Struggling to subdue the foaming havoc within the closing seine, the fishermen would willingly "lose half a ton of fish fer a fine green turtle." But having identified the loggerhead, an "old fisherman looked up sheepishly and grinned": "He's played it on us fine" (159–60). They give the turtle a rap over the head and return to their torn net. The story ends as the turtle disappears "into the great ocean to the eastward."

Although Hains does not refer directly to *Moby-Dick* in his own whaling story, "A Tragedy of the South Atlantic," there can be little doubt that he knew Melville's work. Like Melville, he emphasizes the mystic superiority of the whale's consciousness, but the reality he envisions has none of the biblical overtones of Melville's book. The natural theology from which Melville had created his great whale had long since given way to the Darwinian view of life that Hains projects in *The Strife of the Sea*. According to Hains's dream of his great finback, "The experience of a hundred years taught him something. The oily brain learned slowly. The instinct, or feeling, had gradually come upon him that to fight is a great waste of energy" (287); "strife was a useless thing, fit only for the young and unthinking, or those possessed with the killing spirit" (301). But the finback is repeatedly pressed by the whaling schooner *Erin*, a modern, steam-powered vessel that gathers whalebone. Her guns propel harpoons "charged with a heavy load of powder. The explosion would open the huge barbs of the harpoon and drive them deeper" into the whale's flesh (284). At first, the whale outwits the whalers by lying safely below the surface and looking up at them. The captain had "never seen sech a scary whale. Look at him! Blamed if he didn't wink at me. Will you look at that eye?" Hains allows that this "wink" might have only appeared so, from the rippling water, but the whale "seemed to be very much absorbed in profound contemplation of the ship" (291). This encounter ends when the whale evades the *Erin*, knowing that "the sea was wide" and "there was room enough for all" (292). Finally, when the whalers succeed in killing several of the whales, including one of the bull's favorite cows and a calf, the large bull disproves their confident sense that "a sperm will stand" when a companion has been killed, "but a finback, never" (299): this finback destroys a whaleboat and its crew, and after being harpooned himself, rams the *Erin*. The captain "felt the heavy jar . . . and knew what it meant"; he "walked aft as if in a dream" and began to see that the remaining boats were provisioned. It seems that the men will make it safely to the Falkland Islands, but Hains does not follow them. His last images are of the whales' carcasses and the "birds [that] hovered and screamed [above them] as if to mark the grave of the lost ship"—and of the reported sighting, a year later, of a great wounded and wary bull. In this prolonged sinking, which resembles that in the *Essex* incident and a later one in Jack London's *Michael, Brother of Jerry* (London might have had it in mind, for he owned a copy of *The Strife of the Sea*, as well as one of Hains's *The Black Barque*), Hains cannot evoke the instantaneous divine retribution and prophetic possibilities that Melville did in 1851 in the *Pequod's* sinking. The harsh and absolute Darwinian reality that Hains envisions is nevertheless majestic, and he preserves within it a memorably lyric and dreamlike sense of life's beauty. But though he could imagine a remote future state in which life on earth might be less "possessed with the killing spirit," he could promise only continuing struggle for the possibility of survival.

Such is the case for the human characters in his final story in *Strife of the Sea*, "In the Wake of the Weather Cloth." It is a memorable story for the simplicity of its language, vision, and narrative structure, as well as for its nautical realism. The seamen in the story struggle through a desperate night to claw off and clear the lee shore of Diamond Shoal. In their "fight for life" they must confront only the elements and not the voraciousness of life feeding on itself; but their sailors' struggle is hard and absolute, and they survive: "A man that fights to win is no sailor," one of them says; "it's him that fights when he *knows* he will lose—an' then maybe he won't lose after all" (318). This seems to have been the case for Hains himself, when, two weeks after *The Strife of the Sea* had been favorably reviewed by the *New York Times*, the *Times* reported on 16 December 1903 on its front page that he had been shipwrecked in the Atlantic. Hains had sailed in his thirty-foot yacht *Edna* from Ocracoke, North Carolina, for the West Indies. But "she was struck by a hurricane . . . [and] blown several hundred miles out of her course." The *Edna* was lost, but Hains survived when he and his wife and crew were picked up by the schooner *William C. Tanner* ("Author Rescued at Sea").

Hains's other sea stories are more conventional than those in *The Strife of the Sea*; they range from tales of slave ships (*The Black Barque*, 1905) and shipwreck (*The Wreck of the Conemaugh*, 1900), to tales of how the great steamships and the man-crushing corporate powers behind them had transformed life at sea. The seamen in these stories struggle to survive in their conflicts with the elements, with themselves (especially in the traditional conflict between the forecastle and the quarterdeck), or with the corporate powers. In "The Judgment of Men," for example, an old sea captain tells a story that illustrates "the relentless, implacable cruelty of corporations. . . . Their laws are like the laws of Nature—transgress them and you must die" (*White Ghost*, 326). The distinctive quality of these stories, however, is not simply Hains's portrayal of his characters' physical struggles in a Darwinian universe but his simple, humane analyses of the moral and psychological complexities evident in their struggles. This is his emphasis in "The Judgment of Men," as an old captain tells his story at a dinner given by the manager of a shipping company for the captains of his fleet. The captain has been misjudged by others, and his tale of a colleague who had been "smashed" by the corporate powers is a bold and moving refutation of the manager's arrogant insistence that "a thing's either right or wrong . . . and a man is either right or wrong" (322). Similarly, in "The Light Ahead," Hains tells how the first mate of a passenger liner made a fatal but understandable mistake in navigation. In command during the midwatch, "the blackest part of the night," he had seen a distant steamer's running lights, and, "a first-class navigator," he immediately recalled the seaman's "poetry of the night":

> When the lights you see ahead,
> Port your helm and show your red.   (43)

The other ship is twelve miles ahead, and for a moment the mate's mind wanders, preoccupied as he is with having been jilted because he was only a mate. And suddenly, because each ship is making twenty-five miles an hour and therefore closing at the rate of fifty miles an hour, there is a confusion of shifting and fading red and green lights as the ships maneuver but fail to clear. The mate is clearly responsible for the great loss of life, but Hains judges him with compassion that Conrad, for example, would not have extended under similar circumstances. In another story, "The White Ghost of Disaster," even when an arrogant captain brushes aside a mate's warning and drives his great liner, the *Admiral*, to its fatal collision with an iceberg, Hains emphatically condemns the impetuous captain but balances this harshness with a sense of the man's dignity. Awaking as from a dream to the reality of his situation, accepting his complete responsibility, and recognizing with "grim" amusement his own stupidity, Captain Brownson keeps his nerve at the end. In a memorable extended scene, Brownson and the mate he had abused look steadily into each other's eyes—the mate (Smith) from a boat loaded with survivors, Brownson, alone aboard the *Admiral*, from the slanting bridge. Seeing the mate's eyes upon him,

Brownson feels the "immense jolt" of his heart but subdues the panic within him. And in the "eternity" of the ship's last minutes afloat, he strokes a ship's cat that had come to rub against his leg, steps slowly into the chartroom for a revolver he kept there, and returns to the bridge. There, finally,

> Brownson gazed straight at his second officer. Smith saw him raise the pistol, saw a bit of blue smoke, saw his commander sink down to the deck and disappear. A cracking and banging of ice blocks blended with the report, and the ship raised her stern higher. Then she plunged straight downward, straight as a plummet for the bottom of the Atlantic Ocean. (25)

In all these tales Hains's judgments of his characters seem influenced by what his narrator in *The Black Barque* refers to as the "strange voice of the sea" that perpetuates the brotherhood of shipmates. Hearing it, perhaps from "away offshore, in the middle of the southern ocean," the sailor

> realizes the vast world of rest and peace of the countless crews who have gone before, and wonders as though the cry came from some mighty invisible host, calling through the void of air and sunshine. He thinks of the men he once knew, and wonders. They were good. They were bad. They were a mixture of the two. But they were all human. And who shall say where they have gone? (322–23)

This attitude is embodied in Hains's most successful novel, *The Voyage of the Arrow*. Mr. Gore, Hains's main character and narrator in *The Voyage of the Arrow*, cannot rival Wolf Larsen's heroic stature or his rhetorical intensity, but he is one of the memorable characters in American sea fiction of this period, and many readers will find his story both more believable and, as a whole, more successful than Humphrey Van Weyden's in *The Sea-Wolf*. In its presentation of the woman's role, Hains's story is certainly more successful than London's. Hains does not force his simple woman, Miss Waters, to represent anything like the "etherealized essence of life" that Maud Brewster represents in London's allegory of racial evolution; thus she can come naturally to life in a way that Maud cannot (*Sea-Wolf*, 190). Similarly, Hains did not aspire to have his Mr. Gore assume a place with Ahab or Wolf Larsen as "a mighty pageant creature, formed for noble tragedies" (*MD*, "The Ship"). No "sea-king," whose "bold and nervous lofty language" can glow with diabolic power, Gore is like the recollected shipmates in *The Black Barque*—a merely human mixture of good and bad. Insisting that he is "only a sailorman, and rough," and expressing his awareness that his "sailor's tale" may be rejected because other "sailors have been known to enlarge their yarns," Gore speaks a plain and simple language (2–3). Gore is an interesting character because he is at the out-set fully aware of his own fallibility. Already, at age twenty-nine, he had had a command and lost it. As captain of the *Southern Cross*, he had "tried to break the record from Hongkong to Liverpool" and would have done so by "five days" had he "held off shore until the weather moderated" (2–3). Instead, he overran his "distance during a foggy, driving gale and left the whitening ribs of the *Southern Cross* to mark the success of his" endeavor (2–3). And now, as he prepares to tell the present story of his subsequent voyage as mate of the *Arrow*, he is aware that his part in it has caused him to fall even lower in the eyes of "many honest folk [who] hold away from [him] because of it" (1). With his gift of self-awareness Gore can often catch himself in embarrassing moments and confess them with disarming candor. For example, when the ship's agent asks if he had ever been in love, he answers firmly, "never in my life." Then, realizing that "I never knew until that moment that I could lie so easily," he stumbles on to con-fess that he had "made several voyages to China and Japan, and as it is always the custom out there to purchase a wife . . ." (15–16). Or, later, when overhearing a conversation from another table at dinner, he sud-denly realizes that he "had made great progress in listening to matters that were none of [his] business." And even then, a moment later, when the couple had kissed, he "gave a deep grunt of satisfaction before [he] realized what [he] was about" (18).

Gore does go on to distinguish himself as a seaman, earning his cap-tain's respect, as well as Miss Waters's, whose life he saves after the *Arrow* is taken by prisoners from an English convict ship they encountered in a calm. By centering his book in the reality of his hero's human fallibility, Hains is more successful than most writers of his day in plausibly projecting other dimensions of the sea reality as he knew it. With Gore as his nar-rator, he can include Miss Waters in his story and still criticize the popular sea romances of the day as tales "of gentleness and desire" produced by "sweet-scented sea lawyers who fancy they have a taste for description" (1). Moreover, he can portray the rough reality of modern ships and sea-men and thereby deny the popular view that "seamen are no longer what they used to be"; and he can contain all this within the larger biological view of life that he had projected in *The Strife of the Sea*.

When visiting the English convict ship the *Countess of Warwick*, Gore sees, with Miss Waters, a "scene of strife" when her sailors have their "savage play" with a hog they chase and butcher; he sees the butchery of men by men when the *Arrow* is taken; he is aware of the "necessity of [man's] getting married and propagating his species," as the captain ex-presses it in view of Gore's attraction to Miss Waters (87); and he under-stands that the *Arrow's* small crew and its being overloaded are necessary if it is to survive the competition of modern shipping (33, 40). Aware of all these aspects of life, aware also of his own fallibility and of his own willing "reliance" on the "strong" rather than the "weak," Gore "wondered if there really were an intelligent power governing the universe" (207).

In surviving the voyage of the *Arrow*, Gore joins Hains's larger group of survivors, who together constitute a considerable contribution to the tradition of American sea fiction. If one of his characters could stand for them all, it would be Mr. Garnett, one of Hains's favorite characters. Garnett appears in several of Hains's tales, first in 1894 in "Mr. Garnett's Narrative," where Hains compares him to "Cooper's 'Long Tom,' the harpooner" (*Tales of the South Seas*, 112). Portraying Garnett as a representative American seaman at the turn of the century, Hains clearly suggests that the greatest ordeal Garnett had survived was, like Gore's, chiefly that of the mind: "Garnett had removed his cap and was hard at work mopping the dent in the top of his shining, bald cranium, where he had been 'stove down' by a handspike in the hands of a sailor on one of his earlier voyages" (285–86). Garnett is in his own words a "windjammer from the shade o' night, that's what I am" (298). The genius of Thornton Jenkins Hains is in his affectionate admiration for such a family of survivors as those he gave us in *The Strife of the Sea*; or those he gathered in *The Voyage of the Arrow*: Captain Crojack, the "old shellback"; Miss Waters; and the mates Garnett, O'Toole, and Gore, whose rugged powers to survive are written in their names.

James Brendan Connolly (1868–1957)

James Brendan Connolly had little direct experience as a working seaman (he shipped as a hand on a cattle boat to England and back in 1899), but he accumulated an extraordinary amount and variety of sea experience as a keen observer, which he made the basis of an impressive collection of sea stories over a long career. Another true representative of the Strenuous Age, he earned a small place in history by becoming the first Olympic champion of modern times when he won the hop-step-and-jump in the Olympic Games at Athens in 1896. He drew on this experience later in his short novel *An Olympic Victor* (1908), but before that he capitalized on his fame as an athletic hero by becoming a journalist, in particular a sportswriter, and by serving with distinction in the U.S. Army at Santiago. He later served briefly in the U.S. Navy and was given authority by President Theodore Roosevelt to go aboard any American navy ship anytime anywhere and stay as long as it suited him (Romig 76). Accordingly, he accompanied the American battle fleet through the Straits of Magellan, at that time "the greatest of all fleet passages in maritime history," and eventually "had battleship, cruiser, destroyer, airplane, collier, dirigible balloon, submarine and hospital ship experience" (76). But his chief distinction as an American sea writer derives from his experience on Gloucester fishing boats. This, his most valued sea experience, grew out of his work as physical director of the Gloucester Athletic Club after the Spanish-American War. While there, he met several captains of Gloucester fishing boats whom he later accompanied on fishing trips. From these experiences he produced his first collection of sea stories, *Out of Gloucester* (1902), followed by several other volumes of stories and novels of Gloucester fishermen that won him the recognition of various critics, among them Blanche Colton Williams, in *Our Short Story Writers* (1929), F. L. Pattee, in *The Development of the American Short Story* (1923), and fellow sea writers, including Jack London (who owned two of Connolly's books) and Arthur Mason. His stories of Gloucester fishermen were so successful that "*Scribner* and *Harper* magazines both commissioned" him to make other fishing trips with Finnish, Lapp, English, and German fishermen from the White Sea to the Baltic. He also sailed with "the famous Norwegian captain Morgan Ingrebrystken" on "a whaling voyage to seventy-six degrees north" (Romig 76).

As one would expect from the extent of Connolly's experience, his sea fiction is unquestionably authentic; his tales of Gloucester fishermen are certainly superior to Kipling's far more famous *Captains Courageous* in their truthful recording of the fishermen's language and in the nautical verisimilitude with which they present the fishermen at work. Connolly sometimes sentimentalizes the hard lives of his fishermen (as in "A Fisherman of Costla"), and, as Edward J. O'Brien remarked in *The Advance of the American Short Story*, some will doubt whether his work will endure "as literature." Yet O'Brien found Connolly's tales "exceedingly vivid" and "faithful to the life which they describe" (228). Certainly, Connolly is unsurpassed in his dramatizations of fishermen telling the tales their experiences compel them to tell. At their best, these tales give the impression that Connolly heard them himself, "aboard ship in the night-watches when men become holy as little children, revealing their souls simply."[3] One of his best stories, "The Trawler," he heard one winter night on Georges Bank in the fo'c'sle of the *Arthur Binney*. In this tale, which he told again and again, he celebrates the quiet and tragic heroism of two dory mates who were separated from their schooner, the *Grace L. Fears*, in February 1881.[4] But more often Connolly's tales of Gloucester fishermen celebrate their cheerful toughness and superb seamanship as, for example, when loaded with fish, they raced to market:

> There were Gloucester skippers who could truthfully say they never
> hove to their vessel once they swung her off on a market passage. Take
> it in wintertime and a living gale, a frequent happening on the winter
> North Atlantic; take it then, and two rival skippers coming home to-

gether. It would be men at the wheel to their waists in solid water, and now and then to their necks; the vessel rolled down with the windward hatch combings well buried; a wide belt of water white as milk sliding past the lee quarter to a cable length astern. (*Port of Gloucester*, 251)

They raced not only for the best price for their fish but for the "Pride of Vessel" (248, 257). Connolly was aboard the Gloucester schooner *Esperanto* when she won the International Fisherman Championship in 1932, and his pride in that feat (described in chapter 24 of *The Port of Gloucester*) resembles that which he celebrates in three of his stories in *Out of Gloucester*, "A Chase Overnight," "Tommie Ohlsen's Western Passage," and "From Reykjavik to Gloucester." In this last story, in which the heavily laden Gloucester fishing schooner *Lucy Foster* outruns an English yacht in an Atlantic crossing, Connolly shares the impulse of other writers in the tradition from Robertson to Hemingway who celebrate the simple working seaman at the expense of yachtsmen, whose seamanship is always suspect.

Arthur Mason (1876–?)

Arthur Mason was born in Ireland and lived there until he went to sea at the age of seventeen. For most of the next twenty-four years, he worked as a seaman, first as a sailor before the mast, then, after he became a naturalized citizen of the United States in 1899, as mate, and, for a short time, as captain of various merchant sailing ships. He spent most of his career as a seaman working in the lumber trade out of various ports in the Pacific Northwest, from San Francisco to Vancouver, British Columbia. In the summer of 1899 he leased and operated a small gill-netter, a double-ended open boat of twenty-four by six feet, from which he fished for salmon outside the mouth of the Fraser River in the Strait of Georgia. That experience ended after a sudden storm one night that gave his little double-ender "all the motion of a canoe adrift in a waterfall" (*Ocean Echoes*, 176). Seventy-two fishermen drowned that night, including his own boat-puller, who was washed out of the boat. Years later, Mason would remember the "dying screams" from the dark as the drowning Japanese, Indian, and white fishermen called—"louder than the elements of the night"—to their various gods (176–77).

Mason retired from the sea at the outbreak of World War I, when he left the Pacific Coast and took a position as "Superintendent of Deck Rigging in the Port Newark Shipyard" (*Ocean Echoes*, 283). After the war he had an idle period during which he read, and in his reading of sea stories he found himself, like Cooper, feeling that many of the writers "did not know the sea" and "took awful chances with the truth." Then he read Connolly's *The Trawler*, which "got hold" of him, and, thinking that he had something to say and that "no one would sneer at the simplicity of an old sailor," he began his career as a sea writer (*Ocean Echoes*, 284). In his first novel, *The Flying Bo'sun* (1920), which is loosely autobiographical, he emphasizes his awareness that his story is from a former time and clearly demonstrates his authority in handling nautical materials. He gently puts down Dana's mere two years of sea experience, remarking that in this present day of steam, when "there are no yards to square, no topsails, no tiller ropes to steer with," the seaman "doesn't have to sail four years before the mast to learn how to become a sailor" (139). Mason continued writing about the sea for the next thirteen years, but today the date and circumstances of his death are unknown.

Mason's best sea fiction is contained in his novel *The Flying Bo'sun* and the later collection of stories, *The Cook and the Captain Bold* (1924). These worthy contributions to the tradition of American sea fiction are memorable not only for their authentic portrayal of sea life at the end of the nineteenth and the beginning of the twentieth centuries but for the unaffected simplicity of Mason's style and vision. His best work, like that of Thornton Jenkins Hains, is more readable today than much of the work from this period because he managed to free his plots and style from the excess of ideas that ended in sinking many a sea tale. The main ideas of the times are present in his work—his awareness of the new biological reality and its effect on Christian faith; his sympathy with, as well as his reservations about, the socialist movement; his constant awareness that the days of sail had given way to steam. But he never allows these ideas to overshadow the quiet reverence and wit with which he presents his seamen's lives. As a reviewer of *The Cook and the Captain Bold* remarked in the *New York Times* (13 April 1924), "Mr. Mason writes with a humor that remains intensely human and that rubs shoulders time and time again with an unstressed and unmistakable pathos" (19, 25).

The Flying Bo'sun, subtitled *A Mystery of the Sea*, is narrated by the first mate of the schooner *Wampa*, bound with a load of lumber from Puget Sound to Suva Harbor. The mystery involves the captain's death and his later brief reappearance at the wheel of his ship when it is nearly destroyed in a hurricane on the homeward voyage, and it develops out of an old sailor's superstition that the beautiful "tropical bird [the flying bo'sun] snow-white with an exquisite tail . . . is the embodiment of the souls of drowned sailors" (36). Mason presents the mystery in a gentle, refreshing way, without forcing it, as, later, in telling of his disastrous night in the Strait of Georgia, he told of the dream that troubled him before he set out that night: he had watched himself being buried and was amused to see

It is a common tradition among sailors that
[the flying bo'sun] is the embodiment of the souls of
drowned sailors.　　—Arthur Mason, *The Flying Bo'sun*

that the mourners dumped pails full of water into his open grave. "When it was full to the top, the water-carriers disappeared" (*Ocean Echoes*, 174–75).

In his handling of the captain's sea burial we can see something of Mason's simple style and the charm of his gentle humor and "unmistakable pathos":

> While the second mate was back-filling the foresail and hauling the main-jib to windward, to stop the ship for sea-burial, I fell to thinking of our Captain. Here he was, in the prime of life, about to be cast into the sea. No one to love him, no one to care, none but the rough if kindly hands of sailors to guide him to his resting-place. As I glanced around the horizon, and the broad expanse of the Pacific, I was overcome by loneliness. Ships might come and ships might go, and still there would be no sign of his last resting-place, no chance to pay respects to the upright seaman, the devoted husband and father. The silent ocean currents, responsible to no one, would be drifting him hither and thither. (86)

Then, suddenly "astonished" to find himself "alone with the dead" and to realize that he must preside, he calls the crew, who "came aft, everyone of them, in their best clothes, with shined and squeaky shoes, looking very solemn." When a reverent old seaman objects to his having nothing to say except "I commit this body to the deep," he allows him to fetch his prayer book from the forecastle. But the old seaman, Riley, returns "cursing and swearing": "'Howly Mother av Moses,'" he complains, "'they [the rats] have ate the Litany out av me prayer-book, and the poor sowl about to be throwed overboard'" (88). This provokes a heated dispute and near fight between old Riley and the socialist cook (a main figure in the book), who seizes the occasion to preach about such primitive superstitions and the inevitability of the men's future belief "in a Creative Power of Organization." But the new captain restores order by reminding the men that they are in the presence of the dead and by telling them that "'we will raise the plank. While we are doing it let us sing, "Nearer, my God, to Thee"'":

> While we were singing the beautiful hymn, the old ship we loved so well seemed to feel this solemn occasion. Although held in irons by having her sails aback, she did salute to her former captain by some strange freak of the sea, coming up in the wind, and shaking her sails.
>
> Before we finished the singing the cook was leading in a rich tenor voice, and by the time that the last sound had died away, our Captain had slid off into the deep.
>
> .   .   .   .
>
> "Let go your main jib to windward, haul in the fore-boom sheet."
> To the man at the wheel, "Let her go off to her course again." (89–90)

Felix Riesenberg (1879–1939)

Following the example of his father (who, prior to settling in Chicago, had gone to sea as a German sailor before the mast at age thirteen), Felix Riesenberg went to sea at age sixteen. In 1898 he sailed around Cape Horn as an ordinary seaman under Captain Charles M. Nichols on the *A. J. Fuller*, a wooden, bath-built, three skysail yard ship. Then, as a cadet aboard the ocean liner *St. Louis*, he began a career in steam during which he logged many Atlantic crossings and eight passages through the Strait of Magellan. His autobiography records two experiences in his transition from sail to steam that are especially representative of maritime experience during this period as it is reflected in the sea fiction by several authors. In one incident, as the *St. Louis* was racing the *Majestic* in an eastward crossing of the Atlantic, a heat-maddened fireman from the boiler room leaped to his death: "The heat in front of the fires broiled the poor devils with its intensity. Tough assistant engineers seemed to have taken the place of the bucko mates of sail"; and this unfortunate individual, "his face and hairy torso glistening black with sweat and coal dust, red-eyed and insane, sprang over the side" and disappeared (*Living Again*, 82–83). In another incident, a steamship ran down a sailing vessel. After the *St. Louis* had raced at full speed through a night of thick fog, day broke to reveal "the rigging and part of a topmast lying across the windlass on the forecastle head. Some small craft, never again reported, had left her card" (84). The debris was quickly thrown overboard and the incident left unrecorded in the log.

Later in his career, Riesenberg navigated the airship *America* in the Wellman Polar Expedition of 1906–7, and he twice commanded the USS *Newport*, the New York State schoolship, in 1917–19 and 1923–24. In 1918 he began his career as author of maritime books with the publication of *Under Sail*, an autobiographical account of his voyage around the Horn on the *A. J. Fuller*. In it he intended to inform "the seamen and landsmen of today" of "that phase of our sea life that formed and forged the link between the old and the new, between the last days of sail and the great new present of the America of steam and steel" (11–12). He then published two technical books that were widely used at sea, *The Men on Deck* (1918) and *Standard Seamanship for the Merchant Service* (1922); he served as associate editor and wrote a regular column for the *Nautical Gazette*; and he wrote several volumes of sea fiction, informal maritime history, and autobiography. One of his early novels, *East Side, West Side* (1927), not a sea story, was widely read and became famous as a silent film. But on the basis of his single novel, *Mother Sea* (1933), Riesenberg deserves a permanent place in the tradition of American sea fiction.

Mother Sea is an ambitious book in which Riesenberg dramatizes the forces at work in the sea life of his own day, as he had explained them in

Under Sail—the forces that "formed and forged the link between the old and the new," the last days of sail and the new age of "steam and steel." During the years it encompasses, the central character, Clyde Nicholson, becomes captain of the three skysail ship *Cleopatra*; he sails her around the Cape of Good Hope to Hong Kong, then to Hawaii for a cargo of sugar that was especially prized because of the crisis in Cuba, and on to Cape Horn, before losing her in a storm. Rescued by a steamship, Nicholson eventually works his way into steam as captain of the SS *Osprey*. But despite its historical orientation, *Mother Sea* is not merely a historical novel; nor is it simply Captain Riesenberg's occasion for displaying his technical mastery of the lost art of seamanship. As William McFee remarked in his review of the novel, there is in it "an ease in handling all that technical terminology, a robust enjoyment of paring the sentences down to the bone so that the narrative becomes alive, which would gratify Richard Henry Dana himself" (8). Others before McFee had written in appreciation of Riesenberg's style, notably in reference to his earlier innovative novel, *Endless River* (1931). To one complimentary reviewer, that book had seemed "a conjunction of John Dos Passos' method and Ernest Hemingway's style, with a small dash of what might be termed 'philosophical stream of consciousness' thrown in for good measure" (Review, 1). But the general point I wish to make here about *Mother Sea* is not only that it is a work of considerable literary quality in which the sea life of its time is truthfully portrayed but also that it is, more broadly, a tribute to the sea itself, an expression of faith that draws on the tradition's greatest work and promises that the tradition will survive and evolve.

Despite the novel's movement in time from the days of sail to the days of steam, and despite the ambiguous title of its last part, "There Go the Ships," *Mother Sea* offers the promise of renewal. For Riesenberg's title, "There Go the Ships," does not suggest the final sense of "gone," but rather the eternal order of Psalms, from which it is taken. The promise is that "there," on the sea, "go the ships: *there* is that leviathan, whom thou hast made to play therein" (Psalms 104:26). Riesenberg never quotes this full verse from Psalms, but that he intends to perpetuate a Melvillian sense of ocean is clear from what he does with old Captain Glade, the book's guiding spirit. Captain Glade "had been whaling, commanding the *Grampus*" (69). As the marine superintendent of a shipping company, Glade, "the old spouter" (who often appears with his faithful old dog, "Specksnyder") gives Clyde Nicholson command of the *Cleopatra* and survives the changing times by eventually establishing the world-famous Glade Line of steam freighters. He got his start in this enterprise after having salvaged an abandoned ship with Nicholson's help: "Glade, the old spouter, had his harpoon in her," as Riesenberg says. And Nicholson salvages his own career largely because "he always had ahead of him the picture of the old spouter" (361). Toward the end of the book, as Glade nears his natural and peaceful death, Riesenberg specifies that the sea is the source of the old man's vital spirit: "Captain John Glade, grown out of, and loyal to, the mother sea, his years having been many, his old eyes having seen more than was restful to his spirit, romantic, but practical as well, and dauntless, and even devout in his blasphemous sincerity, carried on" (400).

In emphasizing how Glade survived his old friends, how "he survived almost everything, including success," Riesenberg makes it clear that the Darwinian view of struggle and survival that prevailed in his time, and which he fully accepted, need not dispel our sense of hope or wonder. Darwin is heavily present in *Mother Sea*—explicitly, when, approaching Cape Horn and contemplating the "crazy universe" that "seemed epitomized within the *Cleopatra*," Nicholson recalls that "Darwin, who once cruised these waters on the *Beagle*, there evolved his theory of survival" (181). This reality underlies the social and international developments Riesenberg traces in *Mother Sea*, in the competitive struggle whereby steam overcame sail, and in the suggestions of Mahanesque sea power that appear in references to Dewey, Manila, and the *Maine*. Most important, it serves the "mother sea," who, through tests of "fitness and survival," "harden[s] those it [does] not kill" (237, 267). Thus at the end of *Mother Sea*, Nicholson carries on and Captain Glade, with his "devout" but "blasphemous sincerity," dies according to Father Mapple's prophecy—as another Jonah. Nicholson finds "the old spouter, square on his back as if in sleep, his stubby fingers gripping the worn ship's Bible, open at the text—*All thy waves and thy billows are gone over me*" (404). In ending his book with this line from Jonah 2:3, Riesenberg preserves the hope that Melville in one of his darkest times held for Clarel, who might, if he could keep his heart, "Emerge . . . from the last whelming sea, / And prove that death but routs life into victory" ("Epilogue," *Clarel*).

But if he turned to Melville for inspiration, Riesenberg could also return—from far into the twentieth century—to the mystic sense of ocean that he had known himself. He expresses this feeling memorably through Nicholson, who found that "the world had returned to its simplicities" just hours after he had begun his outbound voyage toward the Pacific:

> The *Cleopatra*, close hauled, on starboard tack, the wind having headed her, with a stiff breeze, everything drawing, slipped through the water at better than twelve knots, singing bubbles breaking into a veil of fire, streaming in her wake. It was ominous, as Clyde thought of it, this combination of brilliant flame, flashing in the impenetrable blue cover of the ocean; of fire and water. Life was contrast, full of terrific searing, thought-provoking fire, full of bottomless doubts; above him black close clouds rolled across the swaying mastheads of the ship, there were no

stars, for only under covered skies do the fires light their brightest in the sea, and only when the skies are clear do the decks drip wet with dew; is it any wonder sailors believe in miracles? (97–98)

Clearly, *Mother Sea* constitutes a return by Riesenberg to the tradition of American sea fiction and to his own experience in the last days of sail. But he also made of *Mother Sea* a book that projected the tradition into the age of steam and modernist prose. As his sentences in *Mother Sea* had seemed to McFee to be pared down, and as those in *Endless River* had reminded others of Hemingway's, his vision and his presentation of a modernist reality in *Mother Sea* sometimes resemble Hemingway's. For example, he dramatizes Nicholson's virility (an essential part of his and Glade's ability to survive) with imagery and economy that suggest Hemingway: when Ruth, soon to be his wife, visits his quarters aboard ship, she remarks:

> "You *do* have a large bed?" Ruth stopped herself and blushed.
> "Oh, that's a custom, for the master." Clyde was nonchalant and nervous.
> "Look at the guns!" Ruth examined two rifles and a shotgun, in racks over the berth. "Do you do much hunting, that is, when aboard?"
> "Sometimes, in China, after snipe." (16)

Hemingway, of course, would have cut such little dramas to the bare dialogue, but he would have seen what Riesenberg was after. And another of Riesenberg's brief little dramas is memorable both for its presentation of an everyday reality of sea life that no other writer has risked and for its symbolic possibilities. One morning after breakfast as the *Cleopatra* sailed through the South Pacific toward Cape Horn, two able seamen, Shorty Bensen and Joe Craig, "sat out on the back ropes, under the bowsprit":

> They smoked black pipes, jammed with strong plug-cut. The ship was sailing large, ghosting over an oily rippled sea before a warm wind in the S.W. passage belt. Under them, before the shadow of the keel, a pilot fish, its black and white stripes, the mark of penal servitude, led the ship. Behind the pilot, under the hull, was his master, a lordly shark, swimming in the shadow, ready for anything alive, or dead, that might drop into his maw.
> Above the water, also in the shade of a morning rising toward noon, supporting the bowsprit, below the gammoning, reclined the figure of the Egyptian Queen, her face to the oncoming sea, her hard eyes smiling at the straining men.
> "Well, ther's some breakfast fer yer boss." Shorty addressed the pilot fish, as his contribution dropped and sank below the hull.

"Here's more." Joe Craig added to the sea. Both men sat on the hard served stays, the cool wind fanning their bare bottoms, the smoke of their pipes drifting ahead and across the bow. It was quiet there. The pilot fish ignored them. (176)

By comparison, this scene by Riesenberg seems less strained than Hemingway's when Cantwell squats to make his war monument at the site where he had been wounded (in chapter 3 of *Across the River and into the Trees*).

Riesenberg is at his best in such short scenes, and there are many in this book. A last one is worth quoting for the way it captures something of America's maritime past. It is South Street in New York, as viewed by Ruth Nicholson in the novel's opening paragraph. To her it is a frightful,

> amphibious street of heartless and blasphemous departures, a strange street lined on the shore side by ancient houses of brick, lofts and lodgings on the upper floors, and below these, chandlers, slop shops and saloons, with warehouses standing, iron-shuttered, between the blocks. On the river side of this street, smelling of tar, molasses, horse manure and Eastern cargoes, tall ships were berthed, bow-on against the shore, their raked masts rising to dizzy heights, held by a maze of stays and shrouds, their stout bowsprits poked above the street with shark-tailed martingales triced-up, and lanyards cast adrift, so heavy bobstay chains would not fetch hard upon the rotten bulkheads at low tide. And their varnished jibbooms, and flying jibbooms, were rigged-in to clear the dormers of attic rooms across the way. South Street was a leafless arbor, a cobbled, bawdy arbor, as foreign and mysterious as the trade of ships.
>
> Under those reaching spars, against black and vari-colored-clipper stems, lay a row of reclining figures, eyes cast down, as if in shame, most of them the wooden effigies of women, hard-faced, with painted cheeks and enormous swelling breasts. (3–4)

Ruth sees these figureheads as the "battered sisters of the sea" and the sea itself as a "jealous mother" who will take her man. But Riesenberg will go on to develop his Psalmlike tribute to the *Mother Sea*, where the ships still go, and leviathan is.

Bill Adams (1879–?)

Bill Adams, whose real name was Bertram Marten Adams, was born in England in 1879 of American parents. At age seventeen he left Weymouth College to go to sea, and he was a working seaman for the next four or five years, rounding Cape Horn seven times and becoming mate before he was forced to leave the sea. He had developed a serious respiratory illness as a result of exposure and was told by doctors in San Francisco that he could never go to sea again. He settled in the San Francisco Bay area, where he occupied himself as hobo, housepainter, teamster, gardener, wood-chopper, and the like until he began to write for publication in 1921. Beginning that year, he contributed a regular column to the *Outlook* and published in that magazine, the *Saturday Evening Post*, and others the sea stories that he collected in his single volume of short stories, *Fenceless Meadows* (1923). In the late 1920s and 1930s, he published many other sea stories that he never collected; they appeared in such leading magazines as the *Atlantic Monthly*, *Esquire*, *Forum*, *Colliers*, and *Scholastic*, and several were included in volumes of O. Henry prize-winning stories and in Edward J. O'Brien's series the Best American Short Stories. He also published a collection of poems, *Wind in the Topsails* (1931), and an autobiographical account of his sea experiences, *Ships and Women* (1937), that received very high praise from Lincoln Colcord and other reviewers. The date and circumstances of his death are unknown.

Adams wrote to Charles C. Baldwin, who included a chapter on Adams in his *Men Who Make Our Novels* (1924), that his favorite author was Jack London; Baldwin reports that Adams found "more of the actual slap of the waves in London's *Sea Wolf* than in any other sea book" he had read (8). Adams was also attracted to London because of their shared experiences as workingmen who made careers as writers. He was sympathetic with the socialist movement, but he did not devote himself to the cause, and he avoided the bitter disappointment that London came to feel toward the movement. He wrote, for example, of his hope that America could find a way "to lead mankind toward some fuller brotherhood" and avoid turning her "dream . . . into a nightmare" ("In the Other Fellow's Shoes," 456).

But despite Adams's admiration for *The Sea-Wolf*, his own view of the sea resembles Ishmael's far more than London's. His sea stories are, typically, elegiac recollections of the sailor's life he had known. They exhibit "a rare combination of sentiment and realism," as Lincoln Colcord wrote (Review of *Ships and Women*, 6), but they never lapse into sentimentalism or violate the highest standards of nautical realism. As Colcord suggests, Adams's work is "romantic appreciation, old-style stuff, the stuff of devotion and fidelity to the obscure impulses of the heart" (6). In this limited way—that is, in his constant celebration of the sailors' brotherhood and existence and in his mystic sense of the sea's life—Adams preserves more of the spiritual exuberance that Melville expressed through Ishmael in 1851 than did any other writer of his time.

Yet in his celebration of the sailor's life Adams neither attempts to revive a biblical reality nor ignores the new biological reality that had depressed so many others of his time. In a piece titled "Consider the Insect," he suggested that in the insects' industriousness (their constant "work, work, work!") we can see our true "brothers of the red, the scarlet, and the blue." And in another piece titled "The Finger of Evolution," he expressed his hope that evolution might lead us through the darkness of international racism (e.g., "the problem of the Pacific" as viewed in different terms from each side of the Pacific) to a true "religion," the "brotherhood of man." When two sailors in the story "The Petrels" gaze into a "jar within which, amidst a cluster of amber weed, crawled many minute and bright colored creatures of [the] warm sea," one says to the other, "when you're the steamer officer you mean to be you'll have no time to watch the wonders of the sea" (*Fenceless Meadows*, 254). Later in the same story, Adams images a group of sailors as a line of "light-pursuing animalculae of the night" as they follow a shipmate with a lantern (258). Thus if his elegiac sea stories express loss, they also express affirmation and hope: their chief impulse is to sing with intermingled joy and reverence the feeling that he expresses in his introduction to *Fenceless Meadows*: "God—how good life was, and is!" (7).

The most distinctive feature of Adams's sea stories is their incorporation of sailors' songs within the narrative. He makes more of the singing sailor than any writer in the tradition, and in their sea singing his sailors exhibit an innocence like that Melville depicted in his own portrait of a sailor in the time before steamships, Billy Budd, who "could sing . . . like the illiterate nightingale and was sometimes the composer of his own song" (*GSW*, 437). But, impressed from his original ship the *Rights of Man*, Billy cannot sing as Adams's seamen do, whom he depicts at home in their "sea Eden" (*Fenceless Meadows*, 259). Any reader who would question the authenticity of such an Eden of singing sailors should consider Adams's brief piece called "Singers of the Sea," which he begins by asking, "Did you ever hear this sailor chantey?" He then gives the song, only part of which I quote here:

> When whaling Johnie went to sea,
>   *Whaling Johnie, hi-hoh!*
> A randy dandy lad was he,
>   *All bound away to Hilo.*
> But sailing John, when he came back,
>   *Whaling Johnie, Hi-Hoh!*
> He'd shell-fish growing down his back,
>   *All bound away to Hilo.*

Then, after giving all but the last stanza, he explains:

> It was at midnight at 60′ south that I heard it, sung not on my own ship, but on an unseen ship that passed close by.

We were almost becalmed, after a buster, and bound to the westward. The other ship, eastbound, was setting her topgallantsails. We
could hear the rattle of her sheaves and the squeal of her brace blocks.
As she passed away, and we saw for a moment the glim of her binnacle
light, the last stanza came over the rollers—

> And still he wanders there and back,
>   *Whaling Johnie, hi-hoh!*
> With shell-fish growing down his back,
>   *All bound away to Hilo.*   (168)

Had Adams given us nothing but this single moment from distant
times and latitudes, it would have been enough. But again and again in his
sea stories we can experience this lost reality of sea life that no other writer
has preserved so well. The sailors in his stories sing not only to entertain
themselves or to express their longing for home but to assist themselves in
their work and to contend with their fears: "Sing—someone sing, so's we
can pull together," one sailor shouts in the story "Way for a Sailor!" And
again, "Keeping time together . . . all hands haul[ed] to the long song of
it, water to their knees" (in Tomlinson, ed., *Great Sea Stories,* 604). At
other times they retain their courage through "the song of a man shouting back to the song of the howling storm wind, to the rage of the thun-
derous sea." [5]

And of course the sea songs he incorporates in his stories intensify the
notes of elegy and celebration that characterize his work. The sense of loss
he expresses centers on the sailing ships that had yielded to steam, but as
the following lines from one of his poems suggest, that loss always corresponds with his view that the age of steam and sea power had violated the
sea's life, especially the whales. He wrote the poem "Glory of the Seas" in
commemoration of Donald McKay's last clipper ship, which was "burned
for her copper at Seattle in 1922." She was

> At home upon her sea as were the whales
> Or porpoises that sported in the foam,
> Or albatross that hovered o'er her rails.

And "her seamen loved her" (*Wind in the Topsails,* 105). Adams could contend with such loss in a practical way, by calling for "a close season for
whales" and a "fuller brotherhood" for man ("Politics vs. Whales"). But
his gift was for recalling and celebrating in his fiction the Edenic "watery
world" he had known (*Fenceless Meadows,* 261). For this reason, it would
seem, he did not produce a novel. His longest story ("Fenceless Meadows") is as long as a short novel, but though it has several memorable

scenes and some repeated lines that serve as refrains to unify the narrative, it is not his best work. He will be remembered for such scenes as the following, which I quote at some length to convey the quality of language and vision that characterizes his celebrations of the sea and "the brotherhood of the sea" (*Fenceless Meadows*, 47). The first is a scene from "The Petrels," in which the sailors, some naked or half-naked, rush from the forecastle to a command of "all hands on deck." Their ship has been hit by a sudden gale in the Sargasso Sea. Toward the end of a night of magnificent storm, two sailors are together aloft as new sails are set:

> When pallor overspread the eastern sea rim the tall apprentice, two hundred feet above the sea, lashed robands in a new main skysail. At his side toiled the square-shouldered sailor who, the robands all fast and the sail ready to set, rose upright on the foot-rope and rested a huge hand upon the shoulder of the naked lad beside him.
>
> Thus, together, they gazed toward the breaking of the day.
>
> Suddenly, waving an arm, the sailor encircled an arc of the watery waste.
>
> "*The sea—the sea!*" he shouted.
>
> The apprentice's lips moved. Though with the close of that long night his young body was now grown chill, his wide eyes shone.
>
> "Ours, Manus!" he cried.
>
> The moon paled. The stars paled. The ship, tremulous and beautiful, was become the day star of the sea. Men's cheery songs rose all about her. Lengths of yellow rope trailed in white waters beside her.
>
> Petrels, their cries faint on the wind, circled her wake. (260)

In another story, "Calm" (*Atlantic*, December 1931), the ship, bound from Oregon to Falmouth with a load of grain, is becalmed just "north of the line in the Atlantic." At first, the crew enjoy the peace between their stints of work, painting, chipping rust, and scrubbing the decks. They watch schools of dolphin, "long, blunt-nosed, tapering beauties"; "swimming in the sunlit water" they were "of scintillant emerald," in the "ship's shadow . . . scintillant purple and violet." At sunset, the "twenty sailors danced, barefoot," as another played the concertina. The "mate leaned on the taffrail and softly whistled for a wind." But as the calm stretched into the third week, they "no longer danced in the daywatch . . . no longer sang." Tempers were short; the supply of fresh water dwindled. There was "No motion. No birds. No fish since the dolphin. Thirst. Salt food." The ship seemed "forgotten of God, on an unremembered ocean, sun-dazzled by day, lightning-dazzled 'neath the stars and moon." Then,

> At dawn of the twenty-second day a jet cloud appeared low along the western horizon. While it slowly rose we fetched up the rain sail

Thus, together, they gazed toward the breaking of the day. —Bill Adams, "The Petrels"

and, stretching it from side to side of the deck, made it fast in the mizzen rigging, its long canvas spout pushed down into the now all but dry tank.

We stripped off our clothes and gathered at the railing—twenty naked sailors, dry-mouthed and voiceless.

Hanging from sky to sea, the black curtain advanced slowly. Rain in a well-nigh solid sheet—a wall of rain, straight-falling. Flying fish leaped in myriads at its foot. Dolphin, albacore, skipjack, bonito, barracouta, leaped to catch them on the wing. Sea birds dropped from above, wheeling and screaming.

The skipper spoke two words to the mate. The mate's voice rang along the deck. "*Sheet home!*"

We grasped the long-idle sheets and sheeted sail after sail home. We hoisted staysails and jibs—twenty naked sailors, running and shouting hoarsely.

We lay outstretched on the decks, on our backs, our mouths wide open. Having drunk deep, we fetched bars of soap and soaped one another. Rain stood two inches deep on the uncanted deck. Streaming from the scupper holes, fresh water spouted to the salt gray sea. We shouted, we laughed, we jested. We played leapfrog, and slapped one another's glistening bodies, flat-handed.

A light puff of wind came. Block, sheet, brace, and halyard creaked as the sails jerked full. The ship heeled over. Bubbles burst at her bow. Bubbles raced once more along her sides. Sailor's weather again! (793–94)

8

From Sail to Steam: Sailor-Writers of the 1880s and 1890s

William McFee (1881–1966)

According to some accounts of his life, William McFee was born at sea on his father's three-masted square-rigger, *Erin's Isle*. His father was the designer, builder, owner, and master of the *Erin's Isle*, which in 1881 was bound from India to London. And five of McFee's uncles were sea captains. But when McFee himself went to sea in 1906, at age twenty-five, he went as an engineer in steam. By the time he retired from the sea in 1923, he had logged sixteen years' experience as an engineer—in the British merchant service (1906–11), the British navy (1914–18), and various assignments aboard American merchant ships (1913, 1919–23). McFee is the only writer to identify himself fully and proudly with steam: he published a collection called "Essays on Life and Letters" under the title *An Engineer's Note Book* (1921). The narrator of several of his novels (e.g., *Family Trouble, Captain Macedoine's Daughter, Derelicts*) is the chief engineer Mr. Spenlove, whom McFee acknowledged as his alter ego, and he jocularly referred to himself as "Lord of Below" and—long after his retirement from the sea—to his bedroom as "The Chief Engineer's Cabin."[1]

Aside from Jack London, McFee is certainly the most famous of all the American writers of sea fiction during his time. He was a fluent and very productive writer of sea fiction. And, more than any other, he deserves credit for having fully embraced the modern reality of steam and shown that sea fiction need not attempt to revive the sailing life. But whether he should be counted as a "brother" within the tradition of American sea fiction is questionable. He lived and worked in America for most of his writing career, and he became a citizen of the United States in 1925.

But he is outside the tradition in a number of ways—in the unusual extent to which he identified with the engineer's role and the age of steam; in the characters and settings for most of his novels and stories, which are not predominantly American; and, most significantly, in the writers of sea fiction he most admired. Although he was a notable critic and reviewer of sea fiction, he ignored Melville during the years of the Melville revival, and most of his fairly extensive remarks about Dana seem intended to undercut Dana's authority and reputation and elevate his own. In his introduction to *Swallowing the Anchor,* he remarks that if his "notes of a seagoing engineer have any significance in literature, it depends upon the fact that they are the actual productions of a man born of seafaring people and bred to engines and the sea, and not written, like 'Two Years Before the Mast,' by a young college gentleman who took a sea voyage for his health, and discovered, not only his health, but a genius for narration" (xii–xiii). He saw Jack London's fiction as "only a violent motion picture, a mechanical rapidity of action and much noise"; and though he saw Richard Matthews Hallet and Lincoln Colcord as the best contemporary American writers of sea fiction, capable of "first-class work," he thought the merits of their work were "concealed by the meretricious slickness and glitter" that the "popular magazines" prefer over originality (91, 309). His general complaint about American sea fiction was that it "fails to provide us with any sea characters save the grotesque monstrosities accepted by the editors of cheap magazines as representatives of the much-advertised merchant marine." His favorite example of such characters was O'Neill's Yank in *The Hairy Ape* (305). "Notice is served upon intellectual persons," he wrote, "that ships are manned by human beings and not by Hairy Apes." Charging that O'Neill was "misinformed" about Yank and the "injustice" he represents, McFee thought that "if all the hairy apes in every coal-burning vessel were brought ashore and shot at sunrise it would be a distinct benefit to shipping" (xiii, 307).

McFee's negative remarks about American sea fiction might be construed as a lover's quarrel with his newly adopted country; a suggestion of this appears in his introduction (subtitled *The Apology of an Immigrant*) to *Swallowing the Anchor,* which he wrote toward the end of the "five years' probation" the Immigration Department had imposed before granting him citizenship (ix). But contrary even to his assertion in *Swallowing the Anchor* that his remarks there are those "of a man . . . without a country" (ix), his work is clearly in the British tradition. He was drawn to Robert Louis Stevenson and Rudyard Kipling, and he wrote frequently and with obvious admiration of Joseph Conrad, with whom he is often compared.[2] In the introduction to his own anthology *Great Sea Stories of Modern Times* (1953) he emphasized his opinion that Conrad is the "greatest sea writer of all," that his work is the "supreme achievement" in sea literature (9, 11).

The kinship he felt with Conrad is evident in his remarks about Conrad and himself. In "A Wayfarer from Britain," the wayfarer (who is obviously himself) remarks that Conrad took "a dark pleasure in the tragedy played by Fate and Folly" (*Swallowing the Anchor*, 232); and in his preface to *Aliens*, he confesses his own obsession "with the problem of human folly": "I find" in "men and their ships . . . a never-ending panorama which illustrates my theme, the problems of human folly!" (vii, xii). Certainly it is this view of life that he projects in his best and most famous book, *Casuals of the Sea*, which he dedicated "To those who live and toil and lowly die," the "poor Casuals of the way-worn earth" who "leave no lasting trace." He sees such lives (exemplified in the novel's main character, Gooderich) as "frail craft upon the restless sea / of Human Life," or "the feckless wastage of our cunning schemes." As the dedication indicates, the sea itself is far less prominent in *Casuals of the Sea* than the title suggests. It is a rather depressing study of the Gooderich family, which seems destined to "leave no lasting trace," and only about half of Book Three, "The Sea," describes Hannibal Gooderich's sea experiences on the steamer *Caryatid*. Hannibal's chief folly is that he imagines that by going to sea he will become "a man," that he will "experience" life and be in touch with "the heart of things" (337, 399, 324–25). He would follow the advice of his old friend Mr. Grober—"Be master of yourself"—but he cannot avoid the reality that Grober had described: "The world is not an oyster to be opened, but a quicksand to be passed" (304). Like the other characters in the book, even Captain Briscoe of the *Caryatid* is destined to be a "casual of the sea" of life. He is caught in a web of social, biological, and economic forces that McFee suggests in his references to George Bernard Shaw, Herbert Spencer, and theories of social struggle whereby the efficient classes dominate the inefficients: the male, Hannibal, is caught by the female; Captain Briscoe displays a Spencerian "nervous tension"; helpless sea birds ("tiny casuals of the sea") are preyed upon by the "yellow death-hawks," the "efficients"; and rusted old steamers (also viewed as "casuals of the sea") go "blindly on as the markets [bid] them up and down, across and across" (357, 410, 434, 358).

In McFee's analysis of Hannibal's life there is a peculiarly British emphasis that is also prominent in his essay on *Two Years Before the Mast*, in which his main point is that "Dana had nothing of the proletarian about him" (xii). Focusing on Dana's reference to seamen as "that class of beings," McFee describes Dana's "aristocratic temperament" and charges that his protests about the sailors' brutal treatment developed not out of any "solidarity with working men" but out of "his conviction that a gentleman was bound to defend the lower orders" (xii). Although there is a good deal of truth in McFee's observation, his own work is more conscious of class and social order than is Dana's. McFee and his character Hannibal seem driven to escape an oppressive sense of fixed social order; the day Hannibal runs "away to sea" is "the day of his emancipation" from the social and economic restrictions of his English life (317, 455). But his exhilaration in being "away" is dampened somewhat when he comes to understand "the infinitely subtle sense of caste that runs up through the ranks of the Merchant Service" and when he sees Captain Briscoe's helplessness against the superior powers that control his career (416). In turn, Briscoe looks upon the common seamen as "scum" (396, 405). Despite his charge that Dana felt "no solidarity with working men," McFee's own sea fiction expresses a sense of racial superiority that is far more British and Conradian than it is American: "The ultimate good to be derived from the sea by those who dwell in the hot, unhealthy huddle of towns," he writes in *Casuals of the Sea,* is that "at sea, you behold the ignoble rabble in perspective, the black many-headed swarm lie on the fair earth like a blight; you perceive the contemptible insignificance of their passions in comparison with the terrible passion of the sea" (382–83). At sea, free of the rabble, he can "see the lights of eternity" and "harken to the voice of the storm" (383). To some extent, this compels him to honor the sea, but what he honors most is the power by which he can free himself from the social and economic forces that would entrap him ashore. He is like Hannibal, whose first sensation "at sea" is that "he could feel the beat of the engines down below him" (317). Certainly he shares Hannibal's "awe at the great silent engines"; and when he turns, with Hannibal, to watch "the shining little engine that drove the dynamo," we see him most clearly as a writer outside the tradition of American sea fiction. For McFee, "the heart of things" is not so much in a mysterious sea as in "the blue fire that snapped now and again from the [dynamo's] brushes" (325).

Lincoln Ross Colcord (1883–1947)

Lincoln Colcord was born in a gale off Cape Horn aboard the bark *Charlotte A. Littlefield.* His father, captain of the *Littlefield,* was engaged in the China trade and took his family with him. Thus, for the first fourteen years of his life, Colcord "was brought up on the quarter-deck of a sailing ship" (preface, *An Instrument of the Gods,* viii). He had no professional sea experience beyond these years with his father, but they shaped one of the memorable careers in American literature of the sea. Colcord became a critic of sea fiction, a historian of maritime affairs, and, most notably, a writer of sea fiction, with one novel, *The Drifting Diamond* (1912), and two collections of stories, *The Game of Life and Death* (1914) and *an Instrument of the Gods* (1922). His critical work appeared in the

Nation, the *Bookman, Freeman*, the *New York Herald-Tribune*, and the *American Mercury*, and his contributions to maritime history include his "Record of Vessels Built on Penobscot River and Bay" in George S. Wasson's *Sailing Days on the Penobscot* (1932) and his service as a founding editor of the *American Neptune*.[3]

Like his fellow writers in the tradition, Colcord based his fiction on his own sea experience—the fourteen years with his father. As he explained in his preface to *An Instrument of the Gods*, "We live in manhood to explore and circumnavigate our boyhood; it is the only world we ever know" (viii). Accordingly, the chief characteristics of his own "explorations" in fiction are that his tales are often set in the Chinese waters he knew as a lad, that they return to the last years of sailing ships, and—invariably and most important—that they are presented from the captain's point of view. In writing from this position, Colcord differs from most writers in the tradition of American sea fiction: he is far less interested in the able-bodied seaman than in the master mariner, whose conduct and character (or "spiritual integrity") he measures in terms of his seamanship. His constant theme is that "the dominating note of sea experience is that inaccuracy, incompetency, insincerity spell danger, ruin, defeat, and even death"; he scorned the writer who lacked sea experience or who used the sea material simply "as a source of romantic plot material" (preface, *An Instrument of the Gods*, x, ix, xv). Because this is the "dominating note" in his own sea fiction, and because he admired the work of Joseph Conrad, his work was often compared with Conrad's. But despite some obvious similarities between his work and Conrad's (their Asiatic settings; their analyses of sea captains' competence or incompetence in maintaining discipline and running their ships; and their narrators, Colcord's Captain Nichols and Conrad's Marlowe), it is not true that Colcord was simply a disciple of Conrad. It is clear that he learned something about narrative structure from Conrad—particularly in his stories that are narrated by Captain Nichols. But for his Asiatic settings and his sense of the sea he drew on his own impressions. And in his understanding of the "dominating note of sea experience," the chief influence was certainly not Conrad but his own father: "At my father's knee" (he tells us in his preface to *An Instrument of the Gods*, xvi), he developed the values and vision that shaped his fiction.

Colcord was justifiably proud of the "nautical verisimilitude" he achieved in his fiction; and by this standard, as a critic, he judged other writers and their work. In his view, an author's nautical verisimilitude corresponded to a sea captain's seamanship. When the noted authority on maritime history Samuel Eliot Morison judged Colcord's fiction by the same standard, he paid him the highest compliment, comparing Colcord's work as "art" with Melville's and Conrad's. In his review of *An Insturment*

of the Gods, Morison praised the "fundamental, not a mere casual," connection "between the sea and personality" that exists in these stories, and
he welcomed Colcord's "economy in sea terms and sailing-ship technique.
It is not with a babbling of buntlines and bowlines, but with such phrases
as 'the horrible gasping of water over rocks awash' that he signals his mem-
bership to the fraternity of seafarers" (196).

In a famous literary incident in 1929, Colcord reviewed Joan Lowell's
Cradle of the Deep and exposed it as a "literary hoax." It had been brought
out as a "work of genuine autobiography" in which she told of her supposed
seventeen years at sea with her father, and it had been highly publicized by
the Book-of-the-Month Club. Colcord noted that "romantic and thrilling
adventures follow each other in quick succession" in *The Cradle of the
Deep,* and he observed ironically that "it would make a superb movie" (5).
But he pointed out some of Lowell's obvious failures at nautical verisimilitude. Referring to a moment when Lowell had her sailors go "aloft to 'reef
down the topsails,'" for example, he noted that "there are no topsails on a
schooner that can be reefed; to 'bend' a sail is to fasten it to its spars, not
to 'set' it. . . . [She] has them 'bend every inch of sail to hurry the ship' to
catch a squall" (5). Later, in "Are Literary Hoaxes Harmful?" he raised
the question "of the integrity of writing, publishing, and criticism." As a
result of Colcord's exposé, the Book-of-the-Month Club offered refunds for
the book, and a year later Lowell published *Kicked Out of the Cradle.*[4]

Exposing Joan Lowell's hoax was an easy task for Colcord, whose actual sea experience was so like that which she had faked. But he had already successfully wrestled with a far more challenging problem as a critic
when in 1922 he wrote "Notes on 'Moby Dick.'" One of the earliest pieces
of criticism in the Melville revival, "Notes on 'Moby Dick'" remains one
of the most durable. Only a critic with the authority of Colcord's sea experience could point out "how little of real nautical substance there is in
'Moby Dick,'" how it "lacks the final touch of nautical verisimilitude"
(176). In pointing out such limitations in our great sea book, Colcord
helped bring its genuine greatness more clearly into view, and he had the
integrity to recognize the limits of his own critical standard: despite the
lack of nautical realism in *Moby-Dick,* he praised its "genius," its "magic
literary power." He could see how much greater this was than the mere
"atmosphere" in Conrad's work. In his judgment, *Moby-Dick's* "divinity"
was "something above atmosphere, the aura of sublime and tragic greatness; not light but illumination, the glance of a brooding and unappeas-
able god" (175).

Because of his own quarterdeck upbringing, and because he wrote
during a period when the simple seaman was no longer idealized to the
extent that he had been in Melville's work, Colcord could balance his
nearly boundless admiration of *Moby-Dick* with his accurate observation

that Melville knew little of "the psychology of the quarterdeck, the psychology of handling a vessel, [which was] foreign to him"; Melville's "nautical psychology," as Colcord accurately assessed it, "was that of the forecastle, the psychology of obeying orders" (178). This is the source, from his point of view, of Melville's failed nautical realism in *Moby-Dick*, one "major instance" of which is "the account of the typhoon off the coast of Japan." Suggesting that "it might have been written by one of your Parisian armchair romanticists," Colcord remarks that no "realization of the behavior of a vessel in a typhoon runs behind the pen" in Melville's account of the storm (179). He knew that Melville "must have seen plenty of storms at sea" and could conclude only that because of his Transcendentalist tendencies, Melville was "divinely inefficient as a seaman," which prevented him from presenting "an adequate or even understanding picture of a ship beset by a heavy circular storm." But Colcord also knew that to dwell on this nautical "inefficiency" in *Moby-Dick* would be to "wish away the book's divinity" (178, 186).

No one, certainly not Colcord, would hold up Colcord's sea novel, *The Drifting Diamond*, to *Moby-Dick*, but the typhoon scene in that novel constitutes a success that even Melville or Conrad would have appreciated. The novel has little else to recommend it. Colcord's apprentice work, it is a romantic tale in which the influence of Robert Louis Stevenson is more evident even than that of Conrad. The main characters in the novel, Captain Nichols and his philosophical Chinese friend Lee Fu Chang, are witnesses over a period of years as a large diamond (for which "a man would almost sell his soul") determines the lives of those who touch it (17). As the plot unfolds, Colcord shows how the diamond distorts "all human and innocent relations" (35). One of the innocent victims is a magnificent native of Butaritari, in the Gilberts, whose natural responsiveness to truth and beauty is destroyed when he finds the diamond. Finally, the drifting diamond is returned to the "well-bred" Briton, Lane, who had originally started the cycle of misfortune when he purchased it as a young man; now, however, his Greek wife has the primitive strength, wisdom, and love to throw it overboard (for the last time) in Hong Kong harbor. The typhoon scene occurs early in the novel, as the "noble old elements" intervene to reveal the "essential nakedness" of man, particularly Lane, who throws the diamond (a kind of Jonah) overboard in the height of the storm.

On the becalmed *Omega*, Nichols first sensed the approaching storm when a "trio of glassy swells caught [her] under the bows. A yard creaked loudly aloft; a low swishing sound followed the wave along the vessel's side"; this was "a message from beyond the horizon, an undulation sent out into the still waters from the very heart of elemental wrath" (64). Colcord is good at building suspense and describing how Nichols prepares the *Omega* for the storm, which, by the next morning was upon them:

> By seven o'clock we had all the day that we were to see. The scene was appalling. Low black clouds swirled above us, almost brushing the tops of the masts as they passed. . . . They arched over us, they made the world seem smaller and the ocean a confined plane; they drove at us suddenly, enveloped us in gloom, and as suddenly were gone. . . . And the sea! Enormous waves lifted us, battered us, shook us. . . . [And] in wind, wave, and sky—there was the threat of latent force, the menace of increasing, swelling, exhaustless power, the clear warning of more to come—more to come! (90)

By noon the storm had built to the extent that Nichols knew it could not "blow any harder!—there isn't any more wind in the sky! And the next minute, '*Whoof!*' would come a squall fiercer than the last, and blow all my convictions, calculations and experiences into a million shreds" (96). Nichols recalls that in these squalls "I couldn't have moved my hand to my face—that it blew the sails out of the gaskets, stripped the yards clean save for a few fag-ends of rope and canvas—that it took all the strength of my neck to keep my head upright" (96). In the wind's "tremendous liquid power" it was as if he were immersed in a terrible river: "My body clove a little space for itself; all around me that rushing intangible medium fitted tight, blotting out the rest of the world" (96–97). Then, suddenly, in the afternoon, the wind was gone, and he realized that they were in "the center of the typhoon." They cut themselves loose from the shrouds where they had lashed themselves behind the mizzen rigging and struggled aft to avoid being caught on the lee side. But they were caught by an enormous sea and buried in "green water," and when it went off Nichols saw that "the rail ended at my hand—beyond, it had been carried away" (100).

Colcord's description of the storm lacks the full force of Conrad's tour de force in *Typhoon*, but most readers will agree, I think, that it is the work of a genuine seaman, that he is sure of his material and in control of his writing:

> All around us, a whirling circumference, we could see the wind tear at the tops of the waves less than a quarter of a mile away. The sea in this area was like a maelstrom, like a pool at the base of a gigantic cataract; it seethed and boiled, it tossed upward, as if impelled from beneath. Waves came at us from every quarter; they reared in tall points, in crests of greenish and oily foam; they stumbled, swashed, subsided into themselves with shocks that quaked the deck; they traveled swiftly and mar-

vellously across the open, like ponderous shifting pyramids. Deep holes yawned in the ocean—holes that the ship could have fallen into. She'd topple on the brink, give way beneath us, drop—when suddenly the hole would vanish, and a mighty arm of water would shoot out of the place where it had been. Or two waves would attack her, bow and stern, in opposite direction—would bend her, buckle her, spin her on a pivot through half a circle. She was no longer a ship, to be steered by a rudder, to be handled by sails; she was a bobbing cork, a wallowing log, a piece of flotsam flung about at the will of the waves. (101)

Even if we can imagine that Jack London or Conrad would have recognized the genuine sea experience behind this scene, it is impossible to suggest that Colcord could stand as a novelist with either of these fellow sea-writers. But he was a talented writer of sea stories, and some of his best stories could stand as worthy companions to London's or Conrad's tales in an anthology of great sea stories. The major themes of his stories are suggested in his dedication to *The Game of Life and Death* and his epigraph to *An Instrument of the Gods.* He dedicated the first volume to "My Father, on a Long Deep-water Voyage," and he chose as an epigraph for his second volume these lines from Captain John Smith:

> Of all fabricks, a ship is the most excellent, requiring more art in building, rigging, sayling, trimming, defending, and mooring, with such a number of severall termes and names in continuall motion, not understood of any landsman, as none would thinke of, but some few that know them.

The best stories in these volumes analyze the captain's integrity and competence in running his ship and exercising his authority. Among these captains, some fail to withstand the stress of command, and the ideal captains exhibit a stern but fatherly love that Colcord seems to have treasured in his own father, who had died aboard his vessel the year before the war.

In writing from the vantage of the quarterdeck, Colcord was sympathizing with his own upbringing, but he was also expressing one of the themes of late nineteenth- and early twentieth-century American sea fiction—that in the fierce competition of shipping and of life in general, only the strong can survive. As Felix Riesenberg noted, the bucko mates and tough captains in the sea fiction of this era were drawn from real life (*Under Sail*, 8). One such captain in Colcord's tales is Captain Bray in "The Final Score." In this story, which is one of his least successful, Colcord sacrifices much of his nautical verisimilitude to make the point he boldly asserts in the beginning: "The sea is a primitive place; and following the sea is a man's business. Power rules on shipboard, through the medium of fear; as it was in the beginning and ever shall be. The failure of this natural law brings death to many, and works harm until the final score is paid" (*Game of Life and Death*, 221). The story begins when Captain Bray is forced to sign on a second mate named Gilfoy, who begins almost immediately to violate the "natural law" by committing the "unpardonable sin" of becoming "familiar with the crew" (221–22). Gilfoy is outraged when Bray, "severe but just," corrects him, and after his hurt festers, he leads a mutiny one night. In the confused fighting "it was kill or be killed," and several are killed, most notably the first mate, a personal favorite of Bray. But Gilfoy is able to lie his way out of it and to bring charges against Captain Bray himself, claiming that he had mistreated the crew and that in the uprising Bray himself accidentally killed the first mate. The case is heard by a Mr. Wingate, the young American consul at Batavia, and here Colcord indicates who the real culprit is—Richard Henry Dana, Jr., whom, within the tradition of American sea fiction, he must confront in expressing his sympathy for the quarterdeck. Wingate has "a pleasurable feeling of excitement and satisfaction" at this unexpected "opportunity to score a sailing-ship captain. Ever since reading a book called 'Two Years Before the Mast' he had deplored the atrocities of the merchant marine" (234). In brief, Wingate refuses to prosecute the mutinous sailors and takes no action even later, when "drink loosened a man's tongue" and "the true story came out" (238–39). But years later the "final score" is settled when Bray has the very unlikely opportunity to save another captain from Gilfoy's abuses: in the "fierce and terrible" battle between them, Bray kills Gilfoy "with his bare hands" (242–44).

"The Final Score" is an ugly and artless story, but, fortunately, it is typical of Colcord's work only in its extreme presentation of the quarterdeck point of view. Although, like Conrad, he never writes with the sympathy traditional in American sea fiction for the sailor before the mast, he is never elsewhere as mean-spirited as here, where he wrenches his material into conformance with a Spencerian sense of justice. Most of his stories develop more naturally out of his characteristic sense not only that the fit shall survive but that life develops positively, by a process like that suggested in Lloyd Morgan's *Emergent Evolution* (1923) or Samuel Alexander's *Space, Time, Diety* (1920). As he wrote in his long Whitmanesque poem *Vision of War* (1915),

> Religion of Valor—Will to Power—
>   the Superman:
> They are nothing but an attempt to
>   apply to the spirit a theory of
>   evolution which can only be
>   applied to the body.   (126)

Colcord awaits the sure rising of the "Waters of spirit, rivers of truth, deluge of perfect love!" that will develop into a true "Brotherhood of Man!" (135, 149). And he projects something of this positive view of life in the best of his stories in *The Game of Life and Death*, "Thirst: An Incident of the Pacific."

Like many of Colcord's stories, "Thirst" is told as the main story within the story, by an old sea captain, Alexander Gordon. He and the unnamed "I" of the enveloping narrative are "rowing along a stretch of our northern home-coast" one summer afternoon and pull in to shore for a drink from a spring there. Gordon discovers that he had visited this spring as a boy and that his memory of it had once helped him cling to life when he had been shipwrecked; he had survived thirteen days in an open boat without water. Captain Gordon is Colcord's ideal experienced seaman: he "had watched the passing of the square-rigged ships . . . sailed uncharted waters . . . been dismasted in a cyclone," and survived more than one mutiny (159–60). "He had lived hard; and emerged finally from years of action bearing a clean record, a reputation for honesty, courage, skill, for discipline without tyranny, for daring without impudence, for decision without arrogance" (160).

At twenty-three Gordon had sailed as mate with Captain Caleb Armstrong on the *Equator*, bound with a cargo of coal from Cardiff to San Francisco. They had "a fast and easy passage" around the horn, but just after having taken the southeast trades, they found themselves "afire, in mid-Pacific" (162–64). They could not smother the fire or put it out by pumping the *Equator* so full that she would stagger, "roll over on one side, and stay down for five minutes at a time. A sickening sensation" (165). Finally, the mast "burned off at the level of the 'tween decks," and, in falling, the butt "pried up bodily a great section of the top of the after house"; the ship burst into flames, and they pushed off in their three boats. With the two mates in command of the whaleboats and the captain of the longboat, they steered west by north for Tahiti, a thousand miles away. As fate had it, there was "a nasty sea running"; the overloaded boats could not keep together, and within hours the captain's longboat had gone under. Gordon "turned for a single instant, and saw against the white crest of a distant wave a row of tiny black arms extended in stiff attitude. . . . Far away, a confused crying arose for a moment, an insignificant murmur on the floor of the great deep. Then the wind and the waters drowned it, and we swept on" (173). Captain Gordon tells how "the tragedy of the longboat stood before my eyes. I saw the Captain, back there on the empty Pacific, gone to rejoin his ship; a fine and honorable old man, my seafather, who'd taught me all that I knew" (175). But during the thirteen-day ordeal, Gordon proved his own fitness to command.

Gordon's most severe test develops after Crowell, an inexperienced sailor of his own age, had carelessly left the water-breaker unstopped. It had been his responsibility, and during the night nearly all the water had leaked into the bottom of the boat. Gordon is "stunned . . . into silence" by this news, but he must deal at once with the crew's angry "muttering chorus" and later with Crowell's despair: "He looked at me with two tears in his eyes" and cried, "'For God's sake, sir, don't be too hard on me!'" During the following days both Crowell and Gordon behave admirably, Crowell refusing his meager ration of water, his eyes "bright with an ideal." Gordon navigated, preserved order in the boat, and struggled with himself. They were all maddened with thirst and tormented by the sweet breeze, the soft clouds, the tender sky: "The world mocked us—a speck upon the waste of a vast sunlit ocean, a company of silent and passive mortals dying of thirst"; the waves "chuckled," the Pacific "laughed" (187). Then in a "flash . . . from the mysterious region beyond the veil," he remembered the spring, and it soothed him even as it tormented him. But on the morning of the thirteenth day he finally lost control:

> [After] I had wound the chronometer and taken the time, I lost myself. The pain left me, the thirst let up its grip upon my bowels. I sank into a blissful state of oblivion. I must have kept on steering, west and by north. Something steered for me now, in truth—something which I would call my navigating angel. At noon it tapped me on the shoulder. "Get a sight—get a sight!" it said. I took my sextant, and screwed down the sun. So much I dimly remember. Beside me on the seat they found a sheet of paper, where I had worked the observation. I had worked it correctly. I had spread the chart, and pricked off our position. I can show you the chart at my house, with its thirteenth dot and circle. (190)

Later that day, "lost in wonder" and through filmed eyes, they saw land, a "white beach,' a "green mountain floating against the sky"—and the other whaleboat, which had reached Tahiti just before them. Except for the several dead in each boat, they were saved; and now, touching again the spring he had once seen in a dream, Captain Gordon thinks about "time, and the slow immeasurable forces, and death. . . . Was I ever as thirsty as that?" he wonders, "or is it all a dream?" (192). "Thirst: An Incident of the Pacific" and another fine story, "A Friend" (in *An Instrument of the Gods*), are among the best American short stories of the sea; and as they transcend the limiting settings and circumstances implied by the term "sea story," they would be worthy pieces in any collection of memorable but neglected American stories.

Most of the stories in *An Instrument of the Gods* develop the theme suggested by Colcord's epigraph from Captain John Smith, concerning the art of handling ships. Two of these, "Servant and Master" and "Moments of Destiny," tell of captains who fall tragically short of Colcord's high standards of the master mariner. In the first, Captain Sheldon, "bustling with arbitrariness," loses his ship, "the very means of authority," when he abuses a faithful old Chinese servant and ignores his advice. In "Moments of Destiny," Captain Chandler loses his grip in two "moments of destiny," the first when he is preoccupied with having been rejected by his lover, the second, in another navigational crisis, when he is paralyzed by the memory of his first blunder. In another tale, "Cape St. Roque," Colcord pursues his interest in maritime history by telling of three sea captains who raced in their passages from New York to Hong Kong. They had disagreed about the validity of Lieutenant Matthew Fontaine Maury's famous theories of ocean winds and currents in his *Sailing Directions;* and the winner, of course, is Captain Forbes, who charted a course in accord with Maury's theory and arrived weeks ahead of his friends. In "Cape St. Roque" and a better story in this volume, "Rescue at Sea," Colcord celebrates the art of handling a ship, and his own handling of nautical technicalities is, as Samuel Eliot Morison noted, precise and economical. "Rescue at Sea" is a rousing story told "in the captain's own words," of how the medium clipper *Pactolus* rescued the crew and passagers of the *Santiago,* "a large three-masted bark-rigged steamer."[5] The *Santiago's* crew had taken to lifeboats in a winter gale after the ship had caught fire. The story's drama and suspense develop naturally from the circumstances as Captain Clark maneuvers the *Pactolus* in several tricky situations. Colcord is at his best here in dramatizing the raw conflict between the sea captain and the elements and between the captain and the circumstances (including his own nerve) he must engage in making his way. Indeed, no sea writer can surpass Colcord at this kind of narrative. But "Rescue at Sea" celebrates not only the handling and "The psychology of handling" a ship that Colcord found lacking in Melville; it also celebrates, as elegy, the lost glory of sail—the days when "the lanes of the sea were crowded with handsome square-rigged sailing vessels" (134).

This was, of course, a frequent theme of American sea fiction between the 1890s and the 1930s, but very few writers pull it off as winningly as Colcord does here, even after he has informed the reader at the outset that this is his purpose. Even if sensing at first that the story will create a poetic justice in which the sailing ship prevails, rescuing the steamer, the reader is swept up in the drama and—because of Colcord's sure hand—is never distracted by an undertow of disbelief. Thus, at the end, the reader can share Captain Clark's pride as the *Pactolus* heads in with her "wonderful reach . . . under the lee of the Long Island shore. She was a trim and lofty vessel, lean and graceful on the water; a cloud of canvas aloft . . . heel[ing] at a constant angle, as if moving through a picture, while the long curl of a wave rolled steadily from her lee quarter, as she swept like a bird over the smooth sea" (161).

The *Pactolus* had not only saved all hands and passengers from the stricken bark-rigged steamer, with the crises of maneuvering that that required, but, making her steady ten knots, she had overtaken and passed another ship, the German steamer *Energie*, which had stopped to offer unneeded assistance when the rescue was nearly completed. Finally, when the *Pactolus* is anchored off the Statue of Liberty, and Clark is preparing to go ashore with his papers, Captain Potter of the *Santiago* offers a salute to Captain Clark and the *Pactolus:* to his mustered crew he calls,

> "Three cheers for Captain Clark! and give them with a will!"
> They gave them.
> "Three cheers, now, for the good ship *Pactolus!* And when we're cast adrift again, pray God she picks us up!"
> You could hear the cheer all over the upper harbor. The Staten Island ferryboat, on her way from the Battery to St. George, changed her course and passed close beside us, to see what all the excitement was. (167)

This is Colcord's tribute not only to Captain Clark but to the other "seafathers" he had known in his life and in his fiction—a tribute to their lost arts of "building, rigging, sayling, [and] trimming" (as Captain John Smith had written), and to the great ships themselves, "of all fabricks . . . the most excellent."

Richard Matthews Hallet (1887–1967)

Richard Matthews Hallet was the last Dana, the last educated young easterner to go to sea before the mast and to transform that experience into a literary career. Hallet had already graduated from Harvard before he went to sea. When he sailed on the bark *Juteopolis* from Boston to Sidney in 1912, he had earned both his B.A. (in 1907) and an LL.B. (1910), and at twenty-five he was six years older than Dana was when he sailed on the *Pilgrim.* Hallet's effort to make a literary career of his sea experience before the mast was both facilitated and complicated by the examples of Dana and Melville. He "shipped on the Windjammer" with his eyes wide open, and his friends knew that he "was in search of material," that "the writing bug had bit" him (*The Rolling World*, 35). But he could hardly aspire to create of this experience another *Two Years Before the Mast* or *Moby-Dick.* It was, after all, 1912, and though it was then "fashionable . . . for young men fresh from college to embark in [cattle ships] for their wanderyear," one could neither learn nor test his "seamanship" aboard a cattle ship (1). So when Hallet discovered that "the Standard Oil company still chartered square-rigged ships," he jumped at the opportunity; he knew that there were far greater literary possibilities in sail and that it was "more adventuresome than steam" (1).

When he was done with the sea, the total of his sea experience would not equal Melville's or, it would seem, even Dana's two years, but in a way it spanned a much greater period of time—from sail to steam. His first and only voyage before the mast on the *Juteopolis* lasted only about four months; then, after having labored for some time in Australia as a stone breaker and sheep shearer, he shipped as a fireman aboard the *Orvieto*, from Melbourne through Ceylon and Port Said to England on a voyage of thirty-five days. Later, after the outbreak of World War I, he returned to Harvard and earned the degree in navigation that got him his position as junior officer aboard the *Wittekind* (soon to be renamed *Iroquois*), a horse ship that ran from Boston and New York to France. A short time later he served as third mate on the U.S. Army transport ship *Westland,* which carried a freight of locomotives from the United States to France, arriving—after sighting and avoiding several submarines—just as the war ended. Finally, he worked for a few months firing the iron ore freighter, *James M. Jenks,* on the Great Lakes. From this experience he produced several good short stories of the sea and, most significantly, two novels, *The Lady Aft* (1915) and *Trial by Fire* (1916).

Because Hallet published a volume of autobiographical reminiscences (*Rolling World,* 1938), we can see more clearly than in most careers how heavily autobiographical his sea fiction is. "'The Lady Aft' was the story of the voyage of the *Juteopolis,*" he tells us in *The Rolling World* (115), and this is evident in the many direct parallels between incidents and characters in the novel and the autobiography. I mention this not to belabor the clouded theoretical distinctions between biography or autobiography and fiction, for no reader would doubt that *The Lady Aft* is fiction, but to emphasize that one of the chief sources of interest in *The Lady Aft* is that in it Hallet follows Dana in his effort to "give [the] life and experiences" of "common seamen" as one who could profess to "know what their life really is" (preface, *Two Years Before the Mast*). Hallet's fictionalized "*voice from the forecastle*" will never overshadow Dana's in the history of maritime writing, but it does provide us with one of the most reliable, interesting, and well-written views of the sailor's existence in the very last years of sail. This is the chief value that Jack London found in *Two Years Before the Mast*—that in it Dana had written "for all time, the picture of the sea-life of his time" (*Human Drift,* 102). That life, from London's point of view in 1911, had "passed utterly away. Gone are the crack clippers, the driving captains, the hard-bitten but efficient foremast hands" (102). Now, obviously, even the sea-life that Hallet experienced in 1912 has "passed utterly away"; and though the *Juteopolis* would have impressed London as only a "sordid type of sailing ship," it is alive in our imaginations today, as it certainly was for Hallet when he became an able-bodied seaman in 1912 (*Human Drift*, 102).

As a realistic sea novel, *The Lady Aft* is noteworthy not only in its portrayal of the seamen and their work but in the way its plot includes the lady who was obliged, according to the current publishing market, to accompany such voyages. Hallet feared that his book did not have enough plot to satisfy a publisher, but the reader who accepted it, Sinclair Lewis, "eyed" him "severely" and let him know that "there was if anything too much plot" (*Rolling World*, 116). Looking back on his novel in *The Rolling World*, Hallet could see this truth; he had "installed" his lady aft because of his notion that "a book without a woman would be like a ship without a sail, and that the wind of fortune could never kiss its cheek" (115). His notion was correct insofar as it helped the book to find a market, and if Lewis's remark about the excess of plot in *The Lady Aft* is also true, it applies more devastatingly to *Moran of the Lady Letty*, *The Sea-Wolf*, and *The Mutiny of the Elsinore*. Both Thornton Jenkins Hains in *The Voyage of the Arrow* and Hallet are far more believable in their decisions of "what to do with" their women once they had them aboard than were Norris, London, or a number of other writers of that period (*Rolling World*, 115). Hallet knew that his woman "couldn't, in those days, very well pull on ropes or climb ships' rigging. I didn't even trust her with the navigating, celestial or terrestrial" (115). So he made Mary Ellen the captain's daughter in *The Lady Aft* (there was no lady aboard the *Juteopolis*), giving her ship's duties and a role in the plot as a disruptive flirt that save her from the grandiose theatrics that London, for example, forced upon Maud Brewster as race mother.

Two simple and predictable themes develop in parallel in *The Lady Aft*; the "stiff," as the young hero is called, becomes an able seaman, and he wins the woman. But Hallet manages to salvage this overworked plot by creating an array of interesting characters, the bo'sun, for example; by enlivening the romantic attraction between the stiff and Mary Ellen with the suspense he generates in the seamen's superstition that women "poison a ship"; and mainly by the impress of his style. Much of the book's charm derives from Hallet's comic perspective of himself as the self-conscious stiff who sailed before the mast in 1912. He capitalizes on this comic potential and places it within the larger context of life's absurdity—the kind of thing he had already learned "at the feet of the philosopher, George Santayana," at Harvard. Santayana had taught him that "'even what we call invention or fancy is generated not by thought itself, but the chance fertility of nebulous objects, floating and breeding in the primeval chaos'" (*Rolling World*, 64–65). Hallet saw the stiff embarked on such a voyage as, later, he would see himself in 1912 from the perspective of 1938: his mind was carried along by the "material world . . . as a ship carries a curious passenger. . . . [He was] afloat in the primeval chaos," hearing but failing to "interpret these promptings of nature" (65). In this way the stiff lives a largely passive existence in a willy-nilly universe and suffers a variety of embarrassments. He resembles some of Stephen Crane's "little men" who suffer similar comic defeats in their mock-heroic confrontations with an indifferent universe. And as Crane saw the possibility of a genuine or "mysterious" heroism in the chaos of war, Hallet sees that his stiff *can* get his sea experience and become an able seaman, but only after he is stripped of his romantic illusions as to what that entails. When the stiff finally wins his prize by fighting another sailor and serving the lady aft—with a cup of tea—the battle is realistic, brutal, and bloody; yet the outcome is determined partly by the ship's sudden rolls, and Hallet emphasizes that the incident was perhaps a necessary "trifle . . . so small a matter as to seem ridiculous, and yet there was nothing larger in life" (*Lady Aft*, 209).

The stiff is first drawn to the sea when, as a young lawyer, he delivers marine affidavits along the waterfront. The sea is "in [his] blood," and it offers an escape from "that steady thing, his job" (41, 13). He sees himself "going into the subway, fumbling for change, jamming himself into a car, watching all those wrists, fat and lean, smooth and hairy, sway together as the car lurched. That mass of pallid faces, full of sodden resignation, of a craven acceptance of that nauseating fact of mere existence" (13–14). Feeling the disparity between himself as measured by his A.B. degree and what he might be as an A.B., an able-bodied seaman, he fantasizes about the affidavit's wording, "Competent by sail or steam for all oceans":

> For all oceans! That phrase, rolling on and on, tidal, in his head, had set his brain awash. It was this being competent for all oceans, no doubt, that gave the fellow that sweeping insolence, and the look he had of rocking the earth gently under him with his two feet, as if he used the planets for stepping stones. There was independence for a man. There was the iron showing through. That fellow had ribs, bulwarks. Competent for all oceans! (2—3)

After a series of embarrassing incidents—notably, for example, when he is soundly whipped in his first fight by the testy bo'sun as the tug takes them out to the ship—the voyage begins. Hallet was well aware that the steel bark *Juteopolis* was "not a ship to love" (352). Unnamed in the novel and referred to only as the "old hooker," it is one of the "sordid type of sailing ships" that London deplored but could not resist, as when he rounded Cape Horn on the *Dirigo* this same year. But like any young man on his first voyage, the stiff—with his eye "for all oceans!"—thrills to his first sight of the ship under sail:

The late sun glowed and sparkled on her gray sides; and she rolled to a long swell, a swell felt and not seen, like a faint sigh checked in a stilled bosom. Dirty and disheveled she shambled forward over a brilliant sea; and her great walls of canvas, spread and full of yellow light, waxed and waned, rippling, and tugging at the leeches. She seemed both beautiful and odd. Something in the acreage, or in the mere fact, of sail, was unbelievable, was magic. . . . In that moment, he wanted this voyage to prove eventful. He wanted storms to rack her, and disease and muti-nies to foul her ports and stain her decks. He wanted to be washed over-board by one wave, and washed back by another, in imitation of one of his great-uncles. He wanted to be hanged to a yard-arm. (54)

When the stiff first came aboard, he told a fellow sailor that the sea was in his "'blood. My great grandfather built ships'" (41). But the sailor replied, "'It's no a good line, lad. There's nothing in the blood but blood, I'm thinking'" (41). And Hallet further undercuts the stiff's romantic flight toward mutinies and stormy seas with the remark that "this was because he had the sea in his blood, instead of in his experience" (55).

The experience the stiff does acquire in "these black times of incom-petence and nautical darkness" will lead him to a manhood that is also a childhood, to an immersion in reality that is stern and admirable yet ridicu-lous and absurd (116). He will prove himself an equal among the rough "crew of men unwept, unshaven; uniformly drunk, and uniformly nothing else"; he will learn to "swing [their] bludgeon or raw speech" as well as the bludgeon ("one of the sailmaker's fids") he uses in his decisive battle with the cook (72, 205). Yet he will come to see these men as "bulky children," "children of the high seas" (7, 156). In short, this voyage into "nautical darkness" will bring him into touch with the "primeval chaos" that most sea-writers of his time envisioned at sea, where man's role in the biological drama is most clearly felt. The stiff is "a monkey that has lost confidence in his tail," a "mule-head," a "jelly-fish" (86, 32, 152, 330), and with the rest of the crew he will survive a storm by "sticking to [the] ship with the unconscious tenacity of barnacles" (326). The oldest of these able seamen, Old Tom, is "like an aged gorilla," and the tough little bo'sun, who seems to be all hands, "became master of the ship" (47, 73).

Ultimately, the "nautical darkness" Hallet projects in *The Lady Aft* involves much more than his sense that the age of sail had passed, the sense he images in the tattoo on a dying sailor's chest: "His opened shirt showed the brig which had stood out boldly once on his big chest in red and blue, now shrunk and fallen in between his ribs. As he breathed slowly, the faint sails seemed to waver" (321). A deeper, yet comic, black-ness derives from Hallet's sense of what man lost during the last years of sail when he began to grasp the implications of the *Origin of Species* and

The Descent of Man. This realization requires a far deeper sense of time than the sailor's tattoo suggests, and Hallet presents a memorable glimpse of these depths of time in a scene that captures not only an ordinary reality that any seaman of any period would have recognized but also, simultaneously, the primeval reality on which *The Lady Aft* is floated. Dining on infested sea biscuit, the stiff looks

> on weevils for the first time; these mysterious creatures with black bodies, tapering heads, strong haunches, and short, useful horns. Some were alive and some were dead; these last canted on one side like a ship on a beach, their armor shrunk, their feelers crumpled; dead perhaps, aye, they and all their train, these five generations past. The biscuit was indeed a vast necropolis, like the Nile around the Great Pyramids. As he gazed, the stiff could fancy the last turn of all; a feeble essaying of the granite surface; in vain . . . death closing in . . . that brief inspiring activity concluded. And too often there was a shining something about its iron case, testifying to a perfect opulence of power; the horns un-chipped, the armor bright, the natural vigor unabated. The sea is full of mystery. (57)

Hallet's last ironic sentence in this scene cuts through all the romance of the sea to a twentieth-century reality that would have seemed mysterious, indeed, from Dana's point of view.

Before the stiff can fully comprehend his own place in the sea mystery, he must have his "lesson in sea-buffeting," the inevitable "'soul-and body-lashing'" that the able seaman endures in his storm crises aloft (140, 142). This, emphatically, to Hallet in the last days of sail, is the experience that tells: exposed aloft to the elements' "furious misdemeanors . . . the very soul was likely to be swung away from its moorings, plunged into a shivering remoteness of indifference, in which its only longing was for rest, a cessation . . . peace . . . oblivion" (142). Hallet is clear in the meaning he derives from the sailor's experience aloft, but he is also sure and impressive in his description of the actual work. When the stiff first went aloft one "dirty night," for example, he saw, climbing higher into the rigging, "the pyramid of sail rising out of a pother of spray—blood-full, aching tight, black with rain, without a quiver. . . . The narrow top-gallant mast stays swayed as he went up, seeming as unreliable as floating threads of cobweb. Once his foot caught. Through the fury of the wind and the conflicting motions of the ship he knew only that his grip was solid on the stays as death" (134–35). Then, the "first aloft," he

> laid out on the yard, sliding his feet along the footropes, and gripping the iron jackstays which ran along the top of the yard. But the wet sail was stretched, and drawn down like iron to these stays, so that even

finger-room was denied him. Then the helmsman luffed, and the yard shivered its whole length, buckling like a fishpole. . . . [Two sailors next to him] caved over the end of the yard, and picked up the snapping leech, heels together on the footrope, the rain in their faces a solid front of water. The wind felt savagely under them for holds to pry them off. The sails bulged over them, wet and hard, in rasping folds. Gripping the wire lift, they rammed their elbows into the canvas to no purpose. They couldn't even dent it. The wind sang and moaned inside it. They tore at it with aching fingers; it slipped, bellied again, grew limp, then iron-hard. The wind was steady as a fountain under it then. (136)

In this "first lesson in sea-buffeting," the longer of two extended scenes aloft, the stiff

was learning what it is like to struggle, as if for all time, against a merciless caprice of wind and wave; against those sudden swelling assaults of a mad spirit let loose from original blackness, which strike a man in his helplessness like something funny, something preposterously final and without reason. (140)

When he lets "go the weather rigging" and returns to the slanting deck, he lands with a thump and slides into the hatch with a "stunning force" that seems to "shorten his spine." It was as though whatever "personality" he once had was "affronted" by this jolt and took "flight. . . . He was aware that some organism, to which he had been related once, warmly, was now beating all over with one accumulated tide of pain . . . ; he had lost that lordly correlation of parts which had served him in the mild watches" (142). And after he is "sucked . . . into the scuppers" and pounded by another "solid wall" of water, he struggles to his feet and "wonder[s] at the extraordinary persistence of this wrecked mechanism which would balance itself on its two legs, time after time, when given the least chance" (143).

The essential drama in *The Lady Aft* is the seaman's biological survival in a chaotic universe. The lady's role in the story was "installed," as Hallet remarked in 1938, mainly to help market the book. Yet she has a believable part in the plot; an attractive young woman, she naturally flirts with a number of the sailors, violating her father's understandable wishes to protect her and to maintain the ship's order. She does disrupt that order, for in her role as a simple woman in search of a man, she subjects them "at once to the mightiest and least of all caprices" in this universe of "nebulous objects, floating and breeding in the primeval chaos" (156, 64–65). The stiff's struggle to survive as an able seaman is also an initiation into manhood, as it is for many other young sailors before the mast in the tradition of American sea fiction. And Hallet emphasizes the sexual dimensions of this initiation in the stiff's first going aloft, when he sees the "sail rising out of a pother of spray—blood-full, aching tight, black with rain, without a quiver" (134). But Hallet is most passionate in this autobiographical book about his first voyage when he describes the "superhuman labor" he had experienced (141). He sometimes intrudes to tell us, for example, "You've no idea, man, what a tug it is to get out of your bunk in the watch below"; or "It was cold, man, cruel cold" (304, 249). The sailing ship and his work aboard her had shaped his life. Always, he tells us at the end, he would have the image of her, that "old hooker": "black, bare, ponderous, shaken to the very heart, her thousand ropes trembling, ink-black, against the moon and the cold sky pointed with stars like powdered ice. . . . She was his first ship" (352).

Hallet's voyage on the *Juteopolis*, his first ship, was essentially a voyage into the past. But his next voyage, as a fireman on the steamer *Orvieto* from Melbourne to England in 1913, was a voyage into modern time. Again he would celebrate his own descent into the reality of laboring seamen, but this would be a descent not into the forecastle of a sailing ship but into the firehold of steam. Like his character Slim in *Trial by Fire*, "by force of will he would sink himself among [the firemen] and be lost; and come into the agony, that was good for him" (165). He entered this fiery arena of "the heavy workers of the world" in search of material, self-consciously following the example of Stephen Crane, whose descent into the lower reaches of the social structure in New York City had provided the material for such stories as "An Experiment in Misery" and "The Men in the Storm."[6] In *Trial by Fire*, an experienced fireman tells Slim that he should get out; he does not belong in the firehold: "You will think you are a man in a storm" (292). But by 1915, when Hallet wrote *Trial by Fire*, his interest in "the heavy workers of the world" involved a quarter-century's developments in the international labor movement that Crane could not have known. Without losing his sense of the comic and absurd yet heroic struggle of the individual seaman's confrontation with "the shimmering remoteness of indifference" (*Lady Aft*, 142), he focuses in *Trial by Fire* on the social "paradox of labor and leisure side by side, the illogical subservience of the visible body to a distant brain" (121). The character Slim "is divided in his mind between socialism and anarchy" (66); his father, the exploitive shipping magnate Bartholomew Grant, finds "society ready to my hand" and employs it understanding that he could do "just as well in a state of anarchy—or barbarism" (59); and Grant's associate, Wrenn, agrees that the principle, "the heavier the work the less the pay," is "good economics." But Wrenn sees also that "it will make devilish red history some day" (190). And the main character, the fireman Cagey, exhibits the defiance that comes from "the oppression of bodily torment" (11). His "round enormous arms, with their red hair, and their loose-hanging habits, oddly [suggest] the arms of a gorilla," but the defiance that burns in his eyes "is something more than the unthinking ferocity of an ape" (10). "'Hah,'" he says, "'some guy has got to get the steam,'" and, "like a vast ape he [swings] himself down, down into that whispering blackness" of the firehold (309, 108).

No reader of *Trial by Fire* can escape the conclusion that it is a major and unacknowledged source of Eugene O'Neill's *The Hairy Ape,* which appeared six years after *Trial by Fire.*[7] O'Neill took much more from Hallet than the idea of presenting his seaman Yank as a hairy ape. (Nor can Hallet be credited with creating the ape-like seaman, a commonplace in American sea fiction of this period that was first developed in a meaningful way by Morgan Robertson.) And the similarity between *Trial by Fire* and *The Hairy Ape* exists despite some obvious differences between the two, most notably in that *Trial by Fire* is set not on an Atlantic liner, but on a Great Lakes ore ship, the *Yuly Yinks* (after Hallet's own ship, the *James M. Jenks*). Although the novel seems to draw on Hallet's experience aboard the *Orvieto* as well as that aboard the *James M. Jenks,* his setting in the Great Lakes helped him to emphasize the unnaturalness with which "the mechanism of modern life [deals] with those who had built it" (264). The defiled waterways and industrial waterfronts, as along "the stinking Cuyahoga," reflect the loss that several of the characters know from having been "salt water men" (262, 13). Into the lives of these former seamen, "rails, cinders, rolling stock, [and] red signals" intrude, and the tale as a whole is "set on the immovable, or seemingly immovable roundness of a planet hung in center-most star space. Odd beyond words. Only," he emphasizes with irony, "in the waste of waters was there commonplaceness" (276).

There seems to be no record of O'Neill's ever having mentioned Hallet, but it is hardly possible that he did not know of him. Hallet's stories received much attention during these years. Edward J. O'Brien, for example, selected "Making Port" as the best American short story of 1916 and dedicated his volume for that year to Hallet. In this same year O'Brien praised Hallet's "Quest of London" as one of the year's best, and this story's apelike fireman, its setting on an Atlantic liner, and its expressionistic illustration by Henry Raleigh of the writhing, heat-maddened fireman all prefigure the setting and imagery of *The Hairy Ape.* Nor could O'Neill— who had gone to sea two years before Hallet, who had read the sea stories of Conrad and London with passionate interest, and who claimed that his "real start as a dramatist was when I got out of an academy and among men on the sea"—have failed to notice the attention given *The Lady Aft* and *Trial By Fire* (quoted in Gell and Gell 156). The reviewer of *Trial by Fire* for the *New York Times* (9 July 1916), for example, found "something distinctly American" in the story, which he thought noteworthy "for its vivid pictures and characterizations of the men who get the steam." But *Trial by*

Fire was not as well received as was *The Lady Aft.* Hallet does not even mention it in *The Rolling World,* and it seems likely that its brief notoriety when it first appeared was soon obscured in the traumatic years of World War I. It was perhaps this twist of the times that enabled O'Neill to claim that "some of the atmosphere and dialogue" of the play he wrote in 1921 and 1922 were suggested by his friend James "Slim" Martin, rather than by Hallet and his autobiographical character Slim (Gell and Gell 488).

Since my purpose here is to describe Hallet's place in, and his contributions to, the tradition of American sea fiction, I will specify only the most obvious parallels between his forgotten novel and O'Neill's famous play. Hallet emphasizes the anarchical hairiness of his characters even more than O'Neill does, and his descriptions of his seamen's gorilla and apelike appearances are as frequent and emphatic as are O'Neill's. The name of Hallet's main character, the fireman Cagey, and the many ways in which he dramatizes Cagey's imprisonment are clearly repeated in O'Neill's emphasis on "cage" in his scene directions, his text, and the climactic scene when he leaves Yank where he "at last belongs," in the gorilla's cage. Also, through his character Avis, the shipping magnate's daughter, Hallet juxtaposes the two worlds of leisure and labor, as O'Neill later did in dramatizing Mildred's confrontation with Yank in the stokehole. And as this confrontation in *The Hairy Ape* stirred love (as Paddy says) or hate and outrage in Yank, driving him to his futile end, Cagey, in *Trial by Fire,* is obsessed by the "contrast of use and beauty" he sees in himself and Avis (45). Once, for example, he sees his own "black arm swollen, shaggy, scarred . . . and beyond it the fair slim body of her who brought him life [in a drink of water when he had been dragged on deck, nearly dead from the firehold heat], and yet would walk on his bones" (255). At the end, "alone with his fires," he remembers "the pressure of [her] soft palm against his heart, which beat heavily; and as he stood, gleaming, a smile of ultimate puzzlement touched his lips, relieving their cruelty with a child's wistfulness" (309, 307). The voice of experience and wisdom that O'Neill embodies in Paddy in *The Hairy Ape* is clearly derivative of Hallet's character Shorty (or Riley). Shorty does not express the poetic sense of loss that Paddy does in his lamentation for the days of sail, but like Paddy, he sees how he is exploited and drinks to ease the pain. Taking a shot of the "amber-colored fluid" on his "impty stomach," he refutes Cagey's sense that he needs only strong hands and not his head to survive:

> The wurrld would niver shpin on an impty stomach. No, Cagey, me
> lad, Cagey ye are by name, and cagey by nature, I take it, but niver will
> ye explain into me the pearls on the wan hand, and the swine on the
> ither. Niver will ye tell why I put me honest hand to a shoovel, and see

me frind Shlim here toy wid the nayked shoulder iv a queen. 'Tis not
brains, 'tis circumstance, 'tis not what I can tell you. A strange wurrld it
is; it's all a mix-up and all a complication; that's me sooming up iv the
sum and substance iv ut. (90)

In addition to many other explicit similarities between *Trial By Fire*
and *The Hairy Ape*—references to the wealthy as Frankensteins, for example, and to the laborers' crucifixion (*Trial by Fire*, 263 and 252, respec-
tively, and *The Hairy Ape*, sc. 5)—there is a general similarity between
Hallet's heightened or "mannered" style and O'Neill's expressionistic
drama. Readers of today will undoubtedly see Hallet's style as dated and
perhaps overheated (more in *Trial by Fire* than in *The Lady Aft*), but we
should see also that his style reflects not only his period but his youthful
passion to present his nautical and social realities "against an eternal background," as Edward O'Brien assessed it.[8] This is evident by his setting his
tale on this "planet hung in center-most star space" and in the imagery of
his characters confronting the universe—as in "Thus Slim to the un-
answering stars"; or Cagey "with his slice bar black against the moon"; or,
referring to Shorty's mournful song, "sang the Irishman to the chaste stars"
(252, 53, 303). That this force in Hallet's style influenced O'Neill's ex-
pressionist drama at least as much and perhaps more than did his reading
of Henrik Ibsen and Maurice Maeterlinck, as is often suggested, seems
clear, for example, in the image of Yank turning his "bitter mocking face
up like an ape gibbering at the moon" (sc. 7). And there can be no doubt
that O'Neill's heavy emphasis on the image of Yank in the posture of
Rodin's *Thinker* derives exactly from Hallet's final and far more subtle image of Cagey sunk "forward with his chin on his fist and his elbow on his
knee, staring with hard eyes into the hot blackness between the dusty
boilers" (309).

In Hallet's view, Cagey contributes to his own imprisonment (just as
Yank would) by seeing himself as an independent man of iron, wrestling
"with the great god steam, [bringing] him to his knees . . . turning the
shaft over": he is "the independent slave of a great idea" (18). But Hallet's
view of the workingman's predicament is far more complex than O'Neill's,
who seems to imply that the working American might find his salvation in
the International Workers of the World. Hallet's tale is more deeply rooted
in American literary thought, and it suggests an apocalyptic end to the
labor problem rather than any hope for a negotiated solution. His sense of
the "devilish red history" that might "some day" come of it all reflects not
only his awareness of the revolutionary forces that had disrupted and were
continuing to disrupt the Western world but also his American sense of
evil that he introduces in the imagery of Jonathan Edwards's "Sinners in
the Hands of an Angry God." In the firehold Slim "shrivel[s] . . . like an

unwary spider"; and when an industrial crane's huge magnet dangles great pigs of iron, "not unlike some vast revolting spider," Cagey remarks, "That's us . . . one minute we hold together; but the next minute we are all in pieces" (213, 266). In *Trial by Fire* Hallet transforms this Puritan sense of evil by exposing it to the fires of modern industry and Social Darwinism until it issues as Cagey's cynical "philosophy of flame" and the vision of a modern world "for dark gods to laugh at" (251, 155). There is a "consummate charity" in it all, as Slim sees, "a strange order, a giving of the strong to the weak, without material return, which yet made the strong more strong, although in evil" (273–74). And Hallet insists that the biological struggle among men is not sublimated in a larger, impersonal struggle between the laboring and the leisured. Bartholomew Grant, the shipping magnate, had himself been an able seaman and the secretary of his union, and his arms are just as hairy as Cagey's, who, it turns out, is his dispossessed son.

Sailing before the mast on the *Juteopolis* in 1912, Hallet self-consciously joined the fraternity of writers that Melville had acknowledged in referring to Dana as his "sea-brother." Hallet presented "the life of a common sailor at sea as it really" was in his own day, as Dana had presented that reality as he had known it. But as a writer of serious fiction, Hallet also shared Melville's interest in presenting man's place in the *universe*. His knowledge of Melville is clearly reflected in his brief portrait of the captain in *The Lady Aft* (45) and in an extended "monkey rope" episode in chapter 10 that symbolizes the "dog eat dog, like devour like" reality his modern seamen know in *Trial by Fire* (21)—as distinct from that which Melville had presented in "The Monkey-rope," when Ishmael is "wedded" to Queequeg and regards him as his "dear comrade and twin brother." And it seems likely that Hallet's extensive emphasis on clean-shavenness and his linking of hairiness with anarchy and mutiny derive from the chapters in *White-Jacket*, "Man-of-War Barbers" and "The Great Massacre of the Beards."

The Lady Aft and *Trial by Fire* are interesting and worthy contributions to the tradition of American sea fiction. Neither can withstand comparison with *Moby-Dick*, but Hallet's story of his own first ship is as formidable a work in the tradition as Melville's *Redburn: His First Voyage*.

Archie Binns (1899–1971)

Archie Binns is the last writer in the tradition of American sea fiction who was born in the nineteenth century, went to sea as a working seaman, and wrote self-consciously within the tradition. (Hemingway was born nine days before Binns, but he did not "go to sea" and write about it in the traditional sense.) Born and raised in the Puget Sound area, Binns always knew the sea as part of his environment, as well as part of his family's history (his mother was born on the SS *Atlantic*, commanded by her father, who was killed at sea near the Cape of Good Hope); and he accumulated an indefinite amount of experience as a working seaman. He served for nine months on a lightship near Cape Flattery in 1917 (the experience on which he based his novel *Lightship*, 1934), but the extent and nature of his other sea experiences are unclear. According to the biographical note, "About the Authors," in *The Maiden Voyage* (1931, coauthored with Felix Riesenberg), after his service on the lightship, he "went to sea for six years in various waters, including Atlantic, Pacific, China Sea, Indian Ocean, Hoogli River, and the Arabian Sea."

Few books within the tradition have been so highly acclaimed and quickly forgotten as Binns's *Lightship*.[9] Every reviewer applauded it, and Lincoln Colcord and the English sea novelist and sea captain David W. Bone could hardly contain their admiration for it. Colcord thought it "not only a true nautical work but also a novel of deep insight and profound feelings, of first class technical proficiency and genuine literary power," and he could "not recall having read a finer or more moving account of a shipwreck in any work of fiction" (Review, 1). Similarly, Bone wrote that *Lightship* "is as fine a book about the sea as I have ever read" (65).

Lightship is the story of *Lightship 167*, which is anchored outside a reef off the coast of Washington State. As its unromantic name suggests, *Lightship 167* has seen its day, and so have several of the crew, some of whom are old deep-water sailors retired to this dull duty, and others have had full careers in steam. *Lightship 167* is steam-powered, but she still carries unused riding sails that can be fitted to her two masts. In the crisis at the end of the novel, when the ship, nearly out of coal, is blown off her mooring, it takes both her steam and her sails, her sailors and her donkeymen, to keep her off the reef and maneuver her to safety. The theme behind this scenario is that at sea, despite the darkness of this historical setting, we might still discover an illuminating sense of our origin, identity, and destiny. The story is set in the years just before World War I, when steam had nearly displaced the sail and widespread social and international strife had seemed to confirm a Darwinian view of life that all but extinguished traditional faith. *Lightship 167*'s "first consideration," as Captain Lindstorm tells his men, "is to give light to other ships," but as Binns tells the stories of these men's lives, and as they argue among themselves over the meaning of life and death, we see that *Lightship 167* has "its haven of darkness inside" (145). Although *167* no longer voyages, the novel constitutes a traditional voyage to knowledge in which a very troubled and tentative knowledge is achieved: at the end of the book, "still in the darkness of flying water," driving off the lee shore with both steam and sail and having ordered his crew to chop up all the ship's remaining wood for fuel, including the "boat spars and chocks and the boats themselves," Captain Lindstrom is attracted by the "thought that a man must burn his boats in order to reach port" (345).

It should be clear from what I have already said about *Lightship* that it is a very ambitious book in which the author, like many others in the tradition of American sea fiction, has moved offshore to achieve a view of America and Americans as they exist within time and within the larger community of humankind. Much of Binns's success in accomplishing this difficult task in *Lightship* derives from the life stories the men bring with them to the ship and the way their lives are drawn together under the guidance of Captain Lindstrom. Three of these lives are especially important for what they project about both the American experience in general and the tradition of American sea fiction. Chapter 2, "Backwater Voyage," tells the story of Clark, who had gone to sea at nineteen. In his early twenties he and a shipmate were paid $500 each as their shares of a ship they had helped salvage. With this small fortune they purchased an old cutter they had found shored up in a creek off the Columbia River. The *Galathea* needed lots of work, but her size, forty-eight feet in length, made her suitable for sailing into any waters where their dreams might lead them, "the South Seas or China coast, or anywhere" (33). Shortly after they set about to restore her, they meet two local girls who come under the spell of the *Galathea* and eventually convince the seamen to accept them as partners in the venture. The girl Clark soon falls in love with and eventually marries first articulates the dream:

> "Think of it," she said, "sailing to the islands!" The way she said "islands" was wonderful; like some name you say over and over to yourself when you are a child and are half afraid to say because it is magic. "I hope you see them first at sunrise!" (40)

Binns's description of the developing love between Clark and Virginia is beautiful and memorable, particularly when they swim together in the river, naked under the stars: "The current carried Virginia down toward Clark. She was very lovely, like something floating in a dream—a dream of the islands." In the dark river he saw her "woman's body by its own light, it seemed," and he accounts for their sudden intimacy by offering that everything "was so natural as soon as we were in the water" (50–51). Clearly, with what they had together, "they were living now," and it was as lovely as the vision of Typee that guided them, as in Clark's dream of "Virginia standing beside him on deck, the cutter rising and falling gently with the sea, and the enchanted island of Nukuheva rising out of the sea at dawn" (46).

Soon, however, the dream begins to fade. Out of money, the men are forced to go to work in the nearby sawmill, and before long the work discourages Clark's shipmate, who abandons the project and returns to sea. Clark and Virginia remain, but within a few years their small investment in timber was lost to one of the unscrupulous "big companies." And Virginia died of influenza. Years later,

> Clark saw the Islands from the *Ventura,* on the way to Australia. They were as beautiful as he had imagined them, but something was missing. He wasn't seeing them right. The way to see the Islands is to sail your own boat across the Pacific. That way, you discover them. You and she are on deck; her hand is firm and trusting in yours. The cutter lifts and falls with the sea. It seems to lift more than it falls. Flying fish are bright silver; white pilot birds circle the truck of the mast. The land breeze flows over the two of you like a sudden tide of perfume. And then you see the Island of Nukuheva rising out of the sea at dawn. That is the only way you ever see it. (62)

Chapters 8 and 13, "Daughter of Crazy Horse" and "The Land of the Enemy," give the life story of another crewman, Harry, a pathetic character who had become a sailor when he was shanghaied out of New York, "drugged and robbed and sold into slavery in the year of grace 1905!" (186). He was a pants presser in his former life, with a domineering wife and a four-year-old daughter whom he loved deeply. He had long been obsessed with the plight of the American Indian, and before he was shanghaied, he had given his daughter a play tepee. Now, in his own loss, he identifies more than ever with the Indians, particularly with his hero Crazy Horse, for he knows the story of how Crazy Horse had lost his own four-year-old daughter, Little Brown Rabbit, and how in his mourning her death, he had had a vision. Harry is guilt-ridden by the "terrible story of the cruelty and greed and treachery of [his] white nation" (264), but he sees also that his own shipmates Clark and Ole have suffered from greed and treachery. He can console himself only by recalling Crazy Horse's vision:

> Crazy Horse looked toward the west, and saw that the Sioux Nation had driven out the ancient men who were in the land before them, and they in turn had driven out the giants. He saw that nothing lasts but the earth. And people are like water on the earth, driven in waves beyond the Great Wind. He saw that the past and present are the same, and time is only an illusion. (273)

Harry's hope is that "when all is said and done maybe the white, confident race of people wouldn't last any longer than a cigarette poster on a billboard" 188). But he is afraid that the new race will be machines.

Harry's story constitutes an important part of Binns's vision of lost innocence in America during the period when steam power came to dominate the sea, and it is constantly and naturally a part of the larger story of *Lightship 167* because, visible from the ship, inside the reef, there is an "Indian village on the shore . . . sleeping in darkness" (11).

Ole's story is told in chapter 4, "The 'Stadsholmen,'" which begins, "'Praise be unto God in Heaven,' Ole Hanson had become a sailor and a man" (77). A sixteen-year-old Swedish boy, he prepares to sail on his Uncle Olaf's bark *Stadsholmen* to Galveston, where Ole and his friend John plan to leave the ship, "to run away and hunt buffaloes. After that, they might go to the gold fields in California. In a few years they would return to Sweden, rich men" (78). His friend John is "as beautiful as his sister and of much more importance because he was a man and a member of the *Stadsholmen's* crew" (78). From the boys' point of view, the ship and her enterprise had nothing to do with "necessity or profit"; rather, they see their "splendid adventure" as "part of the beautiful and mysterious purpose behind this life" (84). And Ole thinks that "God must be something like Uncle Olaf . . . immense and bearded and ageless, but ever so much more powerful" (84).

As the ship makes its way toward America, the young shipmates practice their English:

> "*Many buffaloes roam the plains of America,*" John would sometimes say in English. The sentence enchanted him.
> "*Allow us yump on our rapid horses and give them a pursuit.*" Ole would answer solemnly.
> "*Where is the way to California? There is much gold in America.*"
> "*Allow us try and get some.*"
> "*The day is fine on the sea, is it not?*"
> "*Yes, is it not?*"
> "*The sails make shadows on the deck and the winds blow freely.*"
> (81–82)

But their lovely dream is shattered one day when John falls from the weather yardarm and breaks his back. Ole was at the wheel and saw his chum turn on the footrope and wave to him: "His hair, which had grown long on the voyage, rippled like a clear flame in the wind as he tossed his head" (85). Then there was "a great thunder on the loosened sail" and Ole "glimpsed something falling. . . . A wave raced away toward the setting sun with an evil glitter" (85). John, alive but unconscious, is taken to the captain's cabin, where Ole watches over him for days, thinking that in Galveston "the American people would be touched by the sight of a beautiful foreign boy brought in from a ship"; they would "rush him to a hospital" (91). "God was good. There was plenty of wind," he tells himself, but the wind becomes a hurricane, the *Stadsholmen* is driven onto a bar, and the crew are forced to lash themselves high in the rigging. This is the shipwreck scene that Lincoln Colcord thought "finer and more moving" than any he could recall in fiction; I quote only part of it here to emphasize how the wreck changes Ole:

> The darkness about him caught fire and burned with a flickering blue light under the low scud. He looked down and had a clear, brief view of the poop, with the skylight and companionway gone, and square black holes, like open graves, where they had been. Then the sea rose and buried the deck.
>
> John was down there, drowning or drowned already! (100)

"He began screaming" and at that moment became the man we know aboard *Lightship 167*: "There is no God!" he screams into the wind, and when at last he is able to hear his own voice, it "gave him courage": "He moistened his split lips and shouted into the darkness, across the frenzied sea, above the grave of his shipmate, 'There is no God! There is no God!'" (102). Later, in Galveston, he watches at John's funeral, as "the coffin was lowered into a hole partly filled with water. The Grave was near a young palm tree, uprooted in the gale" (104). Then, wandering in despair along the waterfront, Ole is assisted by "an affable little man," a crimp, who gives him money and ships him off to Peru aboard a ship with "a remarkably brutal lot of officers": "Ole had become an American seaman. The only comfort he got from his new berth was the circumstance that no one on board mentioned the name of God except in blasphemy" (106).

The several stories of disillusionment in *Lightship* give rise to versions of evolutionary thought, for example Harry's (i.e., Crazy Horse's) sense that "people are like water on the earth, driven in waves before the Great Wind." On the other hand, Ole, believing that there is no God, has faith in the "power for good in the hearts of people doing their duty" (309), like Robert La Follette, who was responsible for passage of the Seamen's Act (255). And he envisions a time when science might lead us beyond the limited view of traditional evolutionary thought:

> The world was like a ship. Things could not be right while there was disease and ignorance and superstition on board. Until now, people had only played at being alive. It had all been dress-up and foolery. People had tried to make themselves angels, devils, monkeys—anything except men and women. Now men and women were going to have their chance. (205)

Finally, these versions of evolutionary thought are subsumed and articulated in Captain Lindstrom's thoughts about death, after the cook had killed himself by jumping overboard. Lindstrom is a competent and humane captain, and once, when they are being blown off the mooring, the autobiographical character Ben sees him "bareheaded . . . with his long black hair and beard setting off his fair, gentle face. If Christ had given up everything and followed the fishermen, instead of the other way about, he would have looked like that, the boy thought" (312). It is therefore fitting that in his efforts to make sense of the cook's death, Lindstrom expresses his tentative faith in "the sea, which was our mother and our first home." Clark cannot understand the captain's nervous speculation on evolution, "but he saw his captain's need for talking." So he listens with the others as Lindstrom is carried away with ideas about how "our blood is nothing but an ebbing and flowing tide of sea water, with one-celled animals—the first life—swimming in it." And in his "need," he wonders how our minds might change: "We are too new to our present conditions—fish just pulled out of the deep sea. We only know that we are not what we were, nor yet what we will be. In enough millions of years, we will have immortal souls. Not all of us, of course. One or two at first, the more. That will be the final change" (303–4).

Binns's attitude toward the captain's promising speculation is wonderfully ambiguous. Lindstrom's speculations have a certain scientific legitimacy, and as a man and captain he is exemplary. But there is also something of Binns in Clark's response to the captain's need: "He listened faithfully," but "he took out his knife, secretly, cut some of the dark drug from the heel of his pipe and put it in his mouth—as he had seen old seamen do in great extremities" (304). It is fitting that *Lightship*, the last sea novel by a nineteenth-century American seaman, should end as it does, in a crisis offshore with the captain's recognition that "neither sail nor steam alone could do them any good" (342). Drawing on the tradition of American sea fiction and projecting it into the future, Binns shares something of Crazy Horse's vision that "people are like water on the earth, driven in waves before the Great Wind. He saw that the past and the present are the same, and time is only an illusion" (273).

9

Hemingway: Coming to the Stream

> I wanted to live deep and suck out the marrow of
> life . . . to drive life into a corner, and reduce it to
> its lowest terms, and, if it proved to be mean, why
> get the whole and genuine meanness of it, and
> publish its meanness to the world; or if it were
> sublime, to know it by experience.
> —Henry David Thoreau, *Walden*

Hemingway was never a working seaman in the tradition of
Dana, but he created for himself—on his own terms—a working relationship with the sea that provided the basis for his contribution to the tradition of American sea fiction. At an age when the typical writer within the
tradition would have gone to sea (e.g., Dana and Melville at nineteen,
London at seventeen), Hemingway was off to the war, writing home to his
family from "Somewhere on les briny," aboard the French liner *Chicago*
(*Letters*, 9–10). The ship was "the rottenest tub in the world," but before
it entered the "submarine zone" and the excitement of war, the young
Hemingway had gone through a "regular storm" aboard her, suffered from
seasickness, and known how "very good" it was "to look upon [the Atlan-
tic] at night when the phosphorescent waves break out from the bow." He
had seen "several porpoises and flying fish" but was skeptical of others' reports that they had seen a whale.

By the time he arrived at Key West, ten years later, in 1928, twice
married and a father, he had established himself as a brilliant professional
writer with an international reputation. But as suggested in his letter to
Maxwell Perkins from Key West in 1929, he was proud that "nobody believes me when I say I'm a writer," and he had begun to imagine himself as
a simple seaman: "We sell the fish we get in the market (the edible ones)
and get enough to buy gas and bait. Have been living on fish too" (277).

He could almost believe, as he wrote to Dos Passos in 1932, that he "could make a living here catching marlin—really believe. Maybe not" (360). And in "Out in the Stream" (1934) he projected himself as a kind of working seaman, a semiprofessional marine biologist catching and classifying the Atlantic marlin. He was not earning his living at it, but he thought his work important enough to be "subsidized." "By the time you buy gas in Havana at thirty cents a gallon to run twelve hours a day for a hundred days a year, get up at daylight every morning . . . pay a man to gaff—another to be at the wheel, buy bait," and so on, it was "physically and financially" exhausting (158). And in his more famous *Esquire* piece of 1936, "On the Blue Water," he could imagine the satisfaction that comes from the fisherman's simple economy: "Then in the morning of the day after you have caught a good fish, when the man who carried him to the market in a handcart brings the long roll of heavy silver dollars wrapped in a newspaper on board it is very satisfactory money. It really feels like money" (185). He could not actually be a simple fisherman, but as a working writer he created for himself a working relationship with the sea from which he could create the simple working seamen in his novels—Harry Morgan or Santiago; or, more clearly in the image of himself, the not-so-simple Thomas Hudson, who saw himself as an artist and a naturalist, "a painter of marine life for the Museum of Natural History" (*Islands*, 316).

Many readers have thought to compare Hemingway with Thoreau: both were drawn to nature and both shared "convictions about the nature of art" that are most apparent in their urgent efforts to achieve "simplicity!" in their lives and in their prose (Baker, *Artist*, 178). But perhaps because of Hemingway's famous remark that Thoreau's "literary" inclinations made him unreadable (*Green Hills*, 21–22), the relationship is seldom traced to the point at which their vital similarity, and also their profound dissimilarity, is most evident: the famous passage from "Economy" in Walden that begins, "I went to the woods because I wished to live deliberately" (from which the epigraph to this chapter is excerpted). Taken by themselves, Thoreau's expressions "suck out the marrow of life," "drive life into a corner," "reduce it to its lowest terms," and "get the whole and genuine meanness of it" could constitute as fine a writer's credo as Hemingway ever articulated for himself. These writers' shared "dusky knowledge" (as Baker refers to it in *Artist*, 178) is as evident here as it is in the opening of "Higher Laws," where Thoreau confesses to the "strange thrill of savage delight" he felt when, returning to his house with a "string of fish," he saw a woodchuck and "was strongly tempted to seize and devour him raw."

But if both writers begin by driving life into a corner and finding a certain meanness there, and savagery, it is at this corner that their paths diverge, for here each must confront the inevitable question: in what way do "men differ from brute beasts?"[1] And Thoreau's answer—that man can "let his mind descend into his body and redeem it," or that "embryo man passes through the hunter stage of development" by a process we might call transcendental evolution—is unacceptable to Hemingway ("Higher Laws," 148, 142). Hemingway rejected this variety of naturalist writing because it is shaped by "economic-religion."[2] And the religious basis for Thoreau's trust that boys taught to hunt and shoot "would soon outgrow it" is perfectly clear: they might become "hunters as well as fishers of men" (141). In reference to these remarks by Thoreau, Philip Young opened his chapter "The Man and the Legend" by wondering what Thoreau would have thought of "an adult"—Hemingway—"who never did outgrow it" (134). The theory Young went on to develop to explain the violence in Hemingway's work—the Freudian "theory of the traumatic neurosis" Hemingway experienced as a result of the wounds he received in World War I— became a landmark in Hemingway studies (169).

Hemingway's war wounds certainly influenced his life and writing, but by now it seems clear that their influence was scarcely as monolithically Freudian as Young thought in the 1950s. I would suggest here that, among the many other shaping forces in his life and career (e.g., the Waste Land view of modern life, his conscious as well as his unconscious use of Freudian and Jungian concepts, other people, especially his father, and other writers), a crucial force that underlies them all is rarely if ever acknowledged: his sense as an amateur naturalist as well as a self-consciously modern writer that we had scarcely begun to grasp the extent to which modern biological thought had revolutionized the meaning of "humanity." The simplicity of his style and his subject (which was "violence and pain," as Young remarked [208]) derived from his seemingly innate grasp of the basic, violent biological realities. As a child his eye was drawn naturally to the violent life-and-death exchange in nature, as we see in the earliest of his extant writings: "Dear Papa: Last Friday in our aquarium in school the water was all riley. I looked in a clam that I had brought to school from the [Des Plaines] river. Had shut down on one of our big Japanese fantail gold fishes tales" (*Letters*, xiii). But if the young Hemingway was attracted to such scenes, we should not call it a childish attraction, any more than we would term childish Thoreau's fascination with the warring ants. Hemingway never completely "outgrew" his boy's love of hunting—the spell of violence—because as he matured, he saw quite clearly that *mankind* had never outgrown it, and he could imagine no possibility for such "growth."

As naturalists, Hemingway and Thoreau are profoundly separated by the biological revolution that began in 1859. Thoreau's religion of transcendental evolution had been displaced by the theory of evolution by natural selection, and Hemingway found himself without even Darwin's faith in the Creator, his consolation in the "full belief, that the war of nature is not incessant, that no fear is felt, that death is generally prompt, and that the vigorous, the healthy, and the happy survive and multiply" (quoted in Russett 88). Indeed, the thrust of Hemingway's career is to deny such transcendent or "happy" assessments of the biological reality—to insist that the war in nature *is* incessant and that fear very certainly *is* felt. His great talent was his power "to understand fear and to realize its importance in life," as he wrote from Key West in 1936 (*Letters*, 432). The "biological trap" he envisioned was not simply that "the limits . . . as circumscribed by life" are that "death is the end of life," as some have concluded, but that the "genuine meanness" of life—all life—is its necessary violence.[3]

It is important to remember that during the years when Hemingway became a writer, Darwin's ideas were passé. An earlier generation of writers, the "naturalists" Crane, London, Norris, Theodore Dreiser, had registered the impact of Darwinian thought in American writing, especially as it centered around Social Darwinism and what Thorstein Veblen described as the "Evolution of Institutions" (part of his subtitle to *The Theory of the Leisure Class*). But in the early stages of Hemingway's career, the disillusionment caused by World War I, the possibility of a Marxist solution to social injustice, the Waste Land view of modern life, the intensifying interest in Freud and Jung (both of whom were heavily influenced by Darwinian thought), and the beginnings of New Critical thought in the aesthetics of Ezra Pound and T. S. Eliot: these were the prevailing currents in American literary thought. And evolution had "become one of those topics so well founded as not really to be exciting to educated people any more, and consequently direct references to evolution in literature [became] almost as rare as direct references to the law of gravity" (Appleman 549). Of course, Hemingway had followed the Scopes trial and parodied William Jennings Bryan's religious conservatism in *The Sun Also Rises*, when Bill and Jake mockingly debate the chicken and egg question: "Let us not doubt, brother. Let us not pry into the holy mysteries of the hencoop with simian fingers" (121–22). But his references to evolution are usually submerged, surfacing mainly as images of the constant hunt in nature, as when Thomas Hudson "saw the shadow of a very big barracuda that was stalking the mullet and then he saw the lines of fish, long, pale, and gray. . . . [Then] he could not see the predatory fish; only the wild leaping of the frightened mullet" (*Islands*, 377). Only occasionally do his references to Darwinian evolution surface more prominently, as when he asked, "What use is the sailfish's tail to that fish? Why should this fish which seems to be an unsuccessful model, an earlier and more fantastic model for the marlin, thin where the marlin is rounded, weak where the marlin is strong, provided with insufficient pectoral fins and too small a tail for its size, have survived?" ("Out in the Stream," 19). This observation was written just weeks before Hemingway spent a month aboard the *Pilar* with the ichthyologist Henry V. Fowler, whose studies, "helped by

Ernest's 'excellent knowledge of the marlin and their habits,'" enabled him to "revise the classification for marlin for the whole North Atlantic" (*Baker, Life Story*, 264).

For all his keen observations of nature, however, it would be misleading to represent Hemingway as much more than a devoted amateur naturalist. There is no concrete record even of his having read Darwin, as there is in John Steinbeck's case (DeMott). But it is clear that his settling in Key West in 1928 constituted a return to the intense intimacy with nature and natural settings that he had experienced as a boy in Michigan, that he had apparently developed as a high school student of biology and zoology in Oak Park,[4] and that had frequently burst into view in the journalism and fiction he wrote while living in Toronto and Paris.

It is no wonder that the Gulf Stream would provide both material and inspiration for a major part of his next quarter-century's work. For in "The Great Blue River" (the title of his piece in *Holiday*, July 1949), he could draw on both the great watery sources of many American masterpieces, the river and the sea. Corresponding to the natural force that draws the great rivers seaward, washing with them literal landscapes of the continental heartland, "rivers and oceans" have always attracted the American imagination, as Melville noted in "Loomings," his incomparable lyric meditation on water. As Thoreau had responded to the Concord and the Merrimack, Melville and then Twain to the Mississippi, Hemingway responded to the Gulf Stream.[5] Both river and ocean, it gave him access not only to the wilderness, to an intense participation in the hunt of life as he could know it in fishing, but also to the literary heritage of American sea fiction. This, too, he had recognized in his youth, when, after a month's excursion to the seaside at Nantucket, he launched his literary career in a traditional way with his first story, "My First Sea Vouge."[6] In this simple piece he found a natural form in which to express his fascination with animal life, his love of fishing, and his hunger for adventure—that of the Cape Horn voyage. By the time he arrived at Key West, of course, he was far too sophisticated a writer to fall back on the traditional adventurism of the Cape Horn voyage. In his own unique sea stories he would join Ishmael in pursuing the "ungraspable phantom of life," but he would seek constantly to drive this life into a corner. What he grasped finally was a very dark image of life—violent and voracious—in its essential biological exchange with death.

From this biological reality or "trap," Hemingway could imagine no escape for man, nor any basis for transcendent belief. But in accepting the hunter-and-hunted reality of human existence, he had the consolation of having sucked the very marrow of life. His most courageous act as a writer was to insist that a sufficient basis for affirming life exists in its "genuine meanness." He could not only accept, but celebrate, the bloody brotherhood in which all life is joined. And this vision of life came to him from a traditional source, his own sea journey onto the Gulf Stream. The famous passage in which he expresses this view most fully and memorably is not part of a sea story, but it is crucial to any understanding of what Hemingway came to see in the stream—that which he would develop as the underlying structure of his three sea novels, and which would constitute his chief contribution to the tradition of American sea fiction:

> If you serve time for society, democracy, and the other things while young, and declining any further enlistment make yourself responsible only to yourself, you exchange the pleasant, comforting stench of comrades for something you can never feel in any other way than by yourself. That something I cannot yet define completely but the feeling comes when you write well and truly of something and know impersonally you have written in that way . . . ; or when you do something which people do not consider a serious occupation and yet you know, truly, that it is . . . important . . . and when, on the sea, you are alone with it and know that this Gulf Stream you are living with, knowing, learning about, and loving, has moved, as it moves, since before man, and that it has gone by the shoreline of that long, beautiful, unhappy island since before Columbus sighted it and that the things you find out about it, and those that have always lived in it are permanent and of value because that stream will flow, as it has flowed, after the Indians, after the Spaniards, after the British, after the Americans and after all the Cubans and all the systems of governments, the richness, the poverty, the martyrdom, the sacrifice and the venality and the cruelty are all gone as the high-piled scow of garbage, bright-colored, white-flecked, ill-smelling, now tilted on its side, spills off its load into the blue water, turning it a pale green to a depth of four or five fathoms as the load spreads across the surface, the sinkable part going down and the floatsam of palm fronds, corks, bottles, and used electric light globes, seasoned with an occasional condom or a deep floating corset, the torn leaves of a student's exercise book, a well-inflated dog, the occasional rat, the no-longer-distinguished cat; all this well shepherded by the boats of the garbage pickers who pluck their prizes with long poles, as interested, as intelligent, and as accurate as historians; they have viewpoint; the stream, with no visible flow, takes five loads of this a day when things are going well in La Habana and in ten miles along the coast it is as clear and blue and unimpressed as it was ever before the tug hauled out the scow; and the palm fronds of our victories, the worn light bulbs of our discoveries and the empty condoms of our great loves float with no significance against one single, lasting thing—the stream. (*Green Hills*, 149–50)

Many readers have admired this passage for its cresting symbolic and lyric intensity. We should also acknowledge at once that as a tribute to life and the sea, it is sadly dated, in view of our growing ecological sense of the delicate and tenuous balance in which life exists on earth. Downstream in time from Hemingway, the tradition would grasp this truth, too, in Peter Matthiessen's *Far Tortuga*. But I would emphasize first that the passage is a miniature of the traditional sea journey to knowledge: "when, on the sea, you are alone with it and know." More significantly, we should see that the knowledge acquired is very simple—a recognition of the enduring majesty of the stream itself and of the life in it: "The things you find out about it, and those that have always lived in it are permanent and of value." Finally, I would emphasize that the simplicity of these values and the circumstances out of which they were formulated not only characterize the author but provide a clear view of his relationship with the single piece of American sea fiction that most influenced him—"The Open Boat." In both this passage from *Green Hills of Africa* and part 6 of "The Open Boat," the authors acquire their simple values through feelings generated in a kind of mystical experience that I described in Chapter 5 as essentially "religious," in the sense of William James's *Varieties of Religious Experience*. In "The Open Boat" "a verse mysteriously entered the correspondent's head," and then "he plainly saw the soldier"—the "blood [that] came between his fingers" and the "slow and slower movements of [his] lips." In Hemingway's piece, too, the lyric articulation of his ultimate values, the stream and the life in it, is generated by the vision of mystic proportions that immediately precedes it. He recalls how, having been wounded once, he lay "alone with the pain in the night in the fifth week of not sleeping [and] thought suddenly how a bull elk must feel if you break a shoulder and he gets away and in that night I lay and felt it all, the whole thing as it would happen from the shock of the bullet to the end of the business and, being a little out of my head, thought perhaps what I was going through was a punishment for all hunters." My point is not that Hemingway was consciously influenced by Crane as he wrote this passage but that, in proximity with the sea, both writers were moved by mystical experiences to express the highest values they could envision in prose of remarkable lyric intensity. The difference in values they articulated is inherent in the original visions: Crane's mystic empathy with the dying soldier and Hemingway's equally mystic identification with the wounded animal. Hemingway goes on to tell us that as he got well, he concluded that if his vision had been a punishment, "at least I knew what I was doing. I did nothing that had not been done to me. I had been shot and I had been crippled and gotten away. I expected, always, to be killed by one thing or another and I, truly, did not mind that any more." Then came his long lyric tribute to the clear, blue, "single lasting thing—the stream."

Once again, in this passage, the significance of Hemingway's war wounds rises into view, but rather than seeing them as the source of a "traumatic neurosis," a "repetition compulsion," or a "'primitivation' of personality" (Young 170), we might see them as a step on his path first to a felt recognition of the biological fact that there is an incessant war in nature; then to an acceptance of his brotherhood in life, not just with man but with all life forms; and finally to his sense of the individual's insignificance in relation to the stream and life itself. Without denying his great respect for Stephen Crane, Hemingway had by 1935 reduced life to lower terms than even Crane, once "cynical of men," had found in his "subtle brotherhood." Beyond the "comforting stench of comrades," Hemingway had found a darker, deeper, and perhaps more reliable basis for affirming life. On the blue water he could experience the prolonged and repeated ecstasy of engagement in the life-death exchange, the essential struggle transmitted through the connecting line between himself and the pulsing life of a great unseen fish perhaps a quarter of a mile beneath him, the thrill—impossible for the hunter—of "the unknown wild suddenness of a great fish; in his life and death which he lives for you in an hour while your strength is harnessed to his" ("On the Blue Water," 185). And in awe—as intense as that expressed by Gerard Manley Hopkins in "God's Grandeur," for example, despite his inability to share Hopkins's vision of the bright-winged "Holy Ghost"—Hemingway could witness the grandeur of *life,* as when "the calm of the ocean broke open and the great fish rose out of it, rising, shining dark blue and silver, seeming to come endlessly out of the water, unbelievable as his length and bulk rose out of the sea into the air and seemed to hang there until he fell with a splash that drove the water up high and white" (*Islands,* 121).[7]

10

Hemingway's Sea Men

Hemingway worked self-consciously within the tradition of American sea fiction, but, like Jack London, he felt obliged to signal in repeated references to the tradition that his vision of the sea was new. The stories themselves as well as their highly disciplined prose would grasp a reality that had eluded the earlier writers. As London had complained of the "imaginative orgies" in *Moby-Dick*, Hemingway complained that Melville's "knowledge" of how "actual things can be, whales for instance," was "wrapped in . . . rhetoric" (*Human Drift*, 102; *Green Hills*, 20). He had had his own experience with sperm whales, which he reported comically in "There She Breaches! or Moby Dick off the Morro" (1936).[1] Through Thomas Hudson, he ridiculed the romantic adventure of conventional sea stories: "I walk with a rolling gait and carry a parrot on my shoulder and hit people with my wooden leg" (*Islands*, 316). And he rejected—in favor of "simple" pictures—the possibility of seascapes on the grand scale, with conventional, apocalyptic storm scenes (17–19; see also the ironic reference to Roger Davis's supposed novel *The Storm*, when Hudson, his sons, and Roger Davis put on the visiting yachtsmen, 167). Earlier, in *To Have and Have Not*, he had derided the yachtsmen-writers, whose artificial lives he contrasted to Harry Morgan's. One of them sleeps aboard his yacht with a picture of "a clipper ship running before a blow framed above his head" (239); others are depicted as "Our Intrepid Voyagers," authors of popular articles they write while "sailing around in different parts of the world." These "sunburned, salt bleached-headed Esthonians" sail from one "yacht basin" to another, writing and selling one "saga" after another: "It's great to be an Intrepid Voyager" (241).

In his own sea stories, Hemingway denied himself the conventional excitement and adventure of storm scenes, even though, as a seaman of considerable personal experience, he had weathered many. He felt not only that the storm scenes had been overdone in traditional fiction but that they distracted from the reality he would grasp at sea. We can see him sorting these things out for himself in "On the Blue Water," which he published in 1936 while struggling to find a suitable structure for his own first and unconventional sea novel.[2] Explaining why he preferred big game fishing in the Gulf Stream over elephant hunting, he wrote:

> In the first place, the Gulf Stream and the other great ocean currents are the last wild country there is left. Once you are out of sight of land and of the other boats you are more alone than you can ever be hunting and the sea is the same as it has been since before men ever went on it in boats. In a season fishing you will see it oily flat as the becalmed galleons saw it while they drifted to the westward; whitecapped with a fresh breeze as they saw it running with the trades; and in high, rolling blue hills the tops blowing off them like snow as they were punished by it, so that sometimes you will see three great hills of water with your fish jumping from the top of the farthest one and if you tried to make a turn to go with him without picking your chance, one of those breaking crests would roar down in on you with a thousand tons of water and you would hunt no more elephants, Richard, my lad.
>
> There is no danger from the fish, but anyone who goes on the sea the year around in a small power boat does not seek danger. You may be absolutely sure that in a year you will have it without seeking, so you try always to avoid it all you can. (31)

As this brief passage clearly demonstrates, Hemingway might have been a master of the stormy seascape in fiction had he been so inclined. But his fiction contains no rough-water scenes of even these small dimensions. What always interested him most in the sea, as he explains in "On the Blue Water," is the life in it: "Because the Gulf Stream is . . . unexploited . . . no one knows what fish live in it, or how great size they reach or what age, or even what kinds of fish and animals live in it at different depths. . . . Who can say what you will hook sometime when drifting in a hundred and fifty fathoms in the Gulf Stream?" (31). It is never simply the romance or danger of being at sea that interests Hemingway. No "Intrepid Voyager," he would study *life* at sea, as he could know it in the great marlin and in such men of the sea as Harry Morgan, Santiago, and Thomas Hudson.

Harry Morgan

"He's alive," said the doctor.
"That's all you can say."

Hemingway's strategy in presenting Harry Morgan was like Stephen Crane's in presenting Maggie. Both characters are unlikely candidates for praise; but in Maggie's case—when we consider the oppressive environmental forces at work in her life, particularly the brown haze of American industry, as well as the hypocrisy of those who judge her—we willingly agree with Crane that she deserves the place in heaven that is promised in her name. But what of Harry Morgan, whose name (a famous pirate's) and time preclude even the tentative and ironic Christian possibilities that the nineteen-year-old Crane had developed? His case seems as simple as Alfred Kazin imagined in his 1937 review: "The essential point about [Harry Morgan] is that he earns a living by primitive means in a world rotten with waste" (in Meyers 231). But the "waste" in Kazin's formulation suggests specific economic theories such as Veblen's theory of the leisure class or, as other reviewers emphasized, one that "Hemingway carried back from Spain, his own free translation of Marx and Engels" (Malcolm Cowley, in Meyers 235).[3] Actually, Hemingway's economic perspective on Harry is more like Thoreau's in "Economy"; his purpose is to reduce the life in Harry to the lowest possible terms and then to present it—juxtaposed to the hollow, half-lives of the Key West Waste Land—as admirable in itself. His portrait of Harry is a response to both the "economic-religion" that he deplored in Thoreau and the "cult of tiresome defeatism" that he found in The Waste Land and "The Hollow Men" (Meyers 232).

The essential questions about Harry are religious, as they were in Maggie, Walden, and The Waste Land. The first is asked by Harry, himself, in the first paragraph of "Part Two," "(Fall)," when—referred to only as "he" or "the man"—he asks, "Where the hell are we?" The black man Wesley asks the other questions, and his suggestive name and Hemingway's remark about him (he was "becoming religious because he was hurt") signal the author's intent: "You [to Harry] ain't hardly human. . . . Ain't a man's life worth more than a load of liquor?" From his conventional religious point of view, Wesley judges that Harry "ain't human": "You ain't got human feelings" (86). But from Hemingway's point of view, the questions about Harry's being human are best answered by the doctor who examines him after he is brought in to Key West: "He's alive. . . . That's all you can say" (To Have and Have Not, 247).

It is not fair to conclude that all you can say about Harry is that "he's alive," for he has other qualities that are more conventionally admirable.[4] But there can be no doubt that Hemingway's chief point about him is his raw, animal vitality; nor should we doubt that this point was calculated, in Hemingway's characteristically combative manner, to irritate readers like Bernard De Voto or T. S. Eliot. De Voto certainly took the bait in his review of To Have and Have Not, complaining that Hemingway's characters were simply "physiological systems organized around abdomens, suprarenal glands, and genitals. They are sacs of basic instinct" who, along with similar characters in D. H. Lawrence, are part of the abominable "cult of blood-consciousness and holy violence" (Meyers 223–26). Eliot did not review the novel, but it seems clear that in shaping his main character and designing his book, Hemingway at once accepted the Waste Land view of modern life and—with a formidable counterpunch—denied the impotence and despair of Eliot's endings to "Prufrock," *The Waste Land*, and "The Hollow Men." That the book as a whole acknowledges a Waste Land reality is clear in its three-part structure, the parts being subtitled "(*Spring*)," "(*Fall*)," and "(*Winter*)." "(*Winter*)" is by far the longest, and a "summer" section is conspicuously missing. Also, many images throughout the novel reflect the artificiality and impotence of modern man (not merely the wealthy yachtsmen) that Eliot had emphasized since 1917. On the first page of "(*Winter*)," for example, an "old man with long gray hair over the back of his collar" appears. A dealer in "rubber goods specialties," he comes to Freddy's bar for a pint and then "scuttles back across the street," a reflection, it seems, of Prufrock and his pathetic sense: "I should have been a pair of ragged claws, / Scuttling across the floors of silent seas" (Eliot 5). But Hemingway's most obvious reference to Eliot's work is his repeated emphasis on the hollowness of his characters. Eliot's epigraph to "The Hollow Men" (1925, a year after Hemingway's famous tribute to Conrad and his attack on Eliot[5]) is "Mistah Kurtz—he dead," and in the poem he seems to identify Kurtz as perhaps the last of those who had crossed "with direct eyes, to death's other Kingdom," and who

> Remember us—if at all—not as lost
> Violent souls, but only
> As the hollow men.   (Eliot 56)

"Between the desire / And the spasm," he continues,

> Between the potency
> And the existence
> . . . Falls the Shadow."   (59)

But in the room where Marie Morgan views Harry's body for the last time, "the light was very bright and cast no shadows"; and if the doctor is blinded in this light ("He didn't suffer at all, Mrs. Morgan"), Marie is not: "Oh, Christ. . . . Look at his goddamned face" (256). Hemingway would bestow upon Harry the dignity of having suffered and having taken his suffering "quietly" (175), in recognition not of an ambiguous, loving God, but of a force more visibly apparent on the face of the waters, as when, awaiting his death, Harry sees "nothing else in sight across the surface of the Gulf Stream but the gulf weed, a few pink, inflated, membranous bubbles of Portuguese men-of-war cocked jauntily on the surface, and the distant smoke of a loaded tanker bound north from Tampico" (181).

Again and again in the novel, Hemingway derides the hollowness and artificiality of modern life, as when "a hollow had come in [Richard Gordon] where his heart had been," or when his wife Helen defines "love [as] that dirty aborting horror that you took me to" (185–86). But alongside such images of neurotic and artificial emptiness—the grain merchant's "bloated little belly," the yachtsmen's impotence, Dorothy Hollis's masturbation (236, 229, 245–46)—are images of emptiness or hollowness in nature; and these Hemingway accepts. Harry Morgan's chief motive is to fill the empty stomachs of his family: "My kids ain't going to have their bellies hurt," he says in one of many repeated references to natural hunger (96). His almost constant awareness that "I better get something to eat" (107), his occupation as a fisherman, and his eventual death from a stomach wound—all emphasize his natural voraciousness as well as his superiority to such characters as Frederick Harrison, the government official who turns him in. "Fishing is nonsense," Harrison complains: even "if you catch a sailfish . . . you can't eat it" (82). Through Captain Willie, Hemingway's defense of Harry is explicit: "He's got a family and he's got to eat and feed them"; and when Captain Willie corrects Harrison on what one can and cannot eat, Hemingway's play on the Waste Land symbolism is clear: "Listen, sailfish is just as good eating as kingfish" (84). Hemingway's point is that emptiness and hunger are inherent in the violent biological order and that we may justifiably celebrate this order, as others would celebrate the Eucharist.

The ultimate source of Harry Morgan's power is his ability not merely to survive in the life struggle but to engage it willingly, for all its "genuine meanness," and even, instinctively, to celebrate it. Hemingway emphasizes this mystic organic power in Harry at two crucial moments. First, at the conclusion of part two, when he is headed home: "Above the roar of the motors and the high, slapping rush of the boat through the water he felt a strange, hollow singing in his heart. He always felt this coming home at the end of a trip" (87). And again, after he has shot the four Cubans and—he thinks—survived intact: "All the cold was gone from around his heart now and he had the old hollow, singing feeling" (171). In both instances, Harry's "singing" feeling celebrates his survival in a deadly struggle. This primitive celebration is, emphatically, "hollow," for Hemingway envisions no transcendent victory. But, urgent and natural, it stands in stark contrast to Richard Gordon's hollowness, the yachtsmen's impotence, and even the simple man Albert's fear of going "home to see [his] old woman" (144). Harry's virtue is his willingness to take life on its own terms, even if its violent order is as hollow as the "pink, inflated, membranous bubbles of

Portuguese men-of-war," or, most horribly, the "noise like hitting a pump-kin with a club" that his gun makes when he touches the muzzle to the head of the "big-faced man" and fires (172–73). The life's lesson he finally stammers out is at least whole and complete, unlike that toward which Eliot's speaker lurches in "The Hollow Men":

> For Thine is
> Life is
> For Thine is the . . .   (59)

Harry's last sentence—"No matter how a man alone ain't got no bloody fucking chance"—is wonderfully ambiguous, but one simple meaning is certain: no individual survives in life.

In the tradition of American sea fiction Harry Morgan is most clearly related to Wolf Larsen, a far more educated and articulate man but one in whom the primordial life force is embodied, as in a "shapeless lump of turtle meat [that] recoils and quivers from the prod of a finger" (*Sea-Wolf*, 14). Harry, too, is identified with the reptilian life force he exhibits most impressively in his lovemaking, which Hemingway compares to that of a loggerhead turtle (112–15). The "strange, hollow singing in [Harry's] heart" after his crises of survival suggests the sound a wolf like Larsen (or at least White Fang) might howl in victory, and his final words grasp a bloody truth as grim as Larsen's recognition that "the body shall be cast into the sea" (*Sea-Wolf*, 26). Both London and Hemingway envision the individ-ual's ultimate fate, when, in Wolf's terms, his own flesh will "be acrawl with the corruption of the sea," his strength finally part of the "fin and scale and the guts of the fishes" (54). In Hemingway's version, "a school of small fish, about two inches long, oval-shaped, golden-colored, with faint purple stripes" gather under the fingers of one of the dead Cubans aboard the *Queen Conch:* he "seemed to be leaning over to dip his hand into the sea," and "each time anything dripped down into the sea, these fish rushed at the drop and pushed and milled until it was gone. . . . They had long since pulled away the ropy, carmine clots and threads that trailed in the water" (*To Have and Have Not*, 179). Hemingway's long scene has a cold, detailed serenity not to be found in London's version; and that this is so seems attributable to Hemingway's having lost so much during the bloody years between 1904 and 1937 and his having accepted an even harsher view of the Darwinian reality than London imagined in 1904. Hemingway could not cling, for example, to the thread of hope that London saw early in his career in the evolution of race that could be perpetuated through Maud and Humphrey. But in *To Have and Have Not*, the great marlin sur-vives: "'Look at him,' I said. 'He's still jumping.' You could see him out a half a mile, still throwing spouts of water." And Harry Morgan is "alive."

Despite the "winter people" and the squawking peacock that appear at the end of *To Have and Have Not*, Hemingway affirmed that "through the window" of his book "you could see the sea looking hard and new and blue in the winter light" (262).

Thomas Hudson and the Sea

I am a painter of marine life for the Museum of
Natural history. Not even war must interfere with
our studies.
    —Thomas Hudson

CONTINUE SEARCHING CAREFULLY WESTWARD.
    —Hudson's orders from Guantanamo
    (Hemingway, *Islands*)

In an effort to explain the thrill he found in marlin fishing in the Gulf Stream, Hemingway began darkly by contrasting it with the thrill in the hunt of war: "Certainly there is no hunting like the hunting of man and those who have hunted armed men long enough and liked it, never really care for anything else thereafter" ("On the Blue Water," 31). It is like having "the taste buds . . . burned off your tongue" after drinking lye water by mistake. The burned taste buds, however, "will begin to function again after about a week," and one does not know "at what rate other things regenerate" (31). Unquestionably, his experience of being alone on the blue water and feeling "the unknown wild suddenness of a great fish" generated excitement. But even in 1936—and certainly during the years between 1945 and 1951, when he wrote his "sea book"—the deeper question was whether the sea experience could bring about anything like spiritual regeneration. That it might is suggested by the first appearance in "On the Blue Water" of the old fisherman who would eventually become Santiago. And Hemingway's conclusion to "On the Blue Water" suggests a long-range program whereby even he might achieve something of the old fisherman's spiritual vitality. When the Cuban mate Carlos returns from the market where he sold the fish that Hemingway had caught, Hemingway tells him that it will provide "the bread of your children." But he denies Carlos's observation that he is "rich": "Like hell," Hemingway responds. "And the longer I fish the poorer I'll be. I'll end up fishing with you for the market in a dinghy" (185). Carlos finds this unbelievable, as we all must who have lived to see Hemingway's "only aim in life" ("to be a wise old man") elude him (*Letters*, 780). But the course he charted in 1936 would lead him eventually to describe more fully the simple, natural economy that underlies Santiago's dignity and spiritual vitality. Hemingway's remark about fishing longer and longer and becoming poorer and simpler resembles the ancient way, like Lear's, of regeneration through loss and suffering. His four-part sea book would trace a progression of loss and suffering through time. As he explained to Charles Scribner in 1951, "The first part is Idyllic until the Idyll is destroyed by violence. . . . The same people are in books 1, 2, 3. In the end there is only the old man and the boy" (*Letters*, 739). But in this progression, there is no transcendental end to the suffering, and the ultimate humility comes only when, through a series of sea experiences, Hudson and Santiago accept their true place in the biological order of life.[6]

In the first book, "Bimini" (originally titled "The Sea When Young"), we see Thomas Hudson in a far more promising state than Henry Morgan enjoyed even in his "Spring." Although he has failed in two attempts at marriage, he has three sons instead of the three daughters to whom Morgan was grudgingly devoted. He manages to free himself from the Waste Land yachtsmen who appear early in the book; and, wanting never to "miss any spring, nor summer, nor fall or winter," he *has* (unlike Morgan) at least this brief summer with his sons. He has a successful career painting "simple pictures" (18), and he has the wisdom to see that violence among humans is not only natural but perhaps necessary in the individual's effort to contend with evil. The "evil" his friend Roger felt "coming in [to himself] just like a tide" (47) when he fought the decadent yachtsman is quite like the shadows cast by sharks on the "white sand" of the beach, an image Hemingway emphasizes in the first two paragraphs of "Bimini." The sharks usually come in only at night, "but if they did come in [during the day] you could see their shadows a long way off" (3). In response to Roger's confession of the evil that came into him like a tide, Hudson says, "All fights are bad," but "you have to win them when they start" (47).[7] Because he knows "about good and evil," Hudson can correct Roger's mistaken sense that "times aren't good" (as had been the case in Harry Morgan's life, which had no "summer"): "When did you ever see them good?" Hudson replies. In fact, during this idyllic summer with his sons, Hudson comes closer than he ever has to grasping a simple vision of life—one that might bring peace of mind and greater stature as an artist; and he accomplishes this by lowering himself and looking at things more closely—an unconscious variation, it would seem, of his need to keep things straight and simple. Once, lying on the floor in front of his fireplace, "his eyes were even with the line of the burning" driftwood, and he could see "the color that the sea salt and the sand in the wood made in the flame as they burned." Later, he followed the boys into the water, and, "with his head on the same level theirs were on," he corrected his earlier illusion of them

Each time anything dripped down into the sea, these
fish rushed at the drop and pushed and milled until
it was gone.　　　—Hemingway, *To Have and Have Not*

as "being at home in the water" like "sea animals." And still later he comes down off the flying bridge to where David is struggling with his fish: "It was strange to be on the same level as the action. . . . They were all taller and not foreshortened. He could see David's bloody hands . . . [and] the sea looked different to him now that he was so close to it" (5, 69, 136). Hemingway gives to David—a "saint and a martyr" because of his suffering and his ability to love and identify with his fish—the power not only to fill his father with "pity and love" for his son but to instruct him in his art. When Hudson shows David a sketch of the jumping marlin, David asks, "Doesn't water come up with him when he comes out?" "It must," his father agrees, and when he corrects the sketch, David pronounces it "fine": "'Now I see what you were after. It's when he hangs in the air just before he falls'" (160–63). David's saintliness and watery wisdom will emerge in more believable dimensions and circumstances in the later story of Santiago, as many critics have noted. But before Thomas Hudson can find his own tentative measure of inner peace that comes to him at the end of "At Sea," he must lose not only his sons, but—by examining in a confessional mode his own meanness and participation in the ultimate evil, war—considerable self-respect.

"Cuba" (originally thought of as "The Sea When Absent") opens some years later, during the war, as Thomas Hudson has returned home from his mission of hunting German submarines in the waters off Cuba. He will be ashore for several days to resupply and to wait out a spell of bad weather that makes it too difficult for the submarines to surface. Before his last cruise he had received news that his third and oldest son, a fighter pilot, had been shot down. Absent from the sea for the duration of "Cuba," Thomas Hudson reveals in a long series of recollectons and conversations the full nature of his despair and his inability to contend with it satisfactorily. In "Bimini," before his sons' deaths, he had managed with difficulty to stay "in the carapace of work that he had built for his protection" from loneliness (190); it seemed possible for him to achieve in his painting the ideal he had suggested to his friend Roger: "Write straight and simple and good," and even if you aren't straight, simple, and good, "make it straight" (156). With David's help he had successfully sketched the jumping fish, and he faced the challenging problem of painting "the fish in the water." In "Cuba," however, his trust in work is pierced, as we see in his thoughts about Paul Klee's painting *Monument in Arbeit*: its color is as "corrupt" and "indecent" as those in the illustrations of "venereal ulcers" he had seen in his father's medical books (237–38). By the end of "Cuba," having lost all three of his sons and recognized various aspects of his own complex "meanness," he can retreat only into "duty": "Get it straight," he tells himself as he rushes to sea. "Your boy you lose. Love you lose. Honor has been gone for a long time. Duty you do" (326).

It is not possible to define the exact causes of Hudson's despair.[8] The book is, after all, unfinished, and we owe it to Hemingway to assume that he would have tightened it up a good deal before publishing it. And it was clearly part of his plan to emphasize Hudson's bewilderment. In general, Hudson's problem is his complexity as a sensitive man in a very troubled time. Aside from the loss of his sons and the breakup of his marriages, his complex consciousness as an artist is enormously troubling in a way that life could never be troubling for a simple spirit like Santiago. This is the point, I think, of his attempt at self-analysis: "What the hell is wrong with you? Plenty is wrong with me, he thought. Plenty. The land of plenty. The sea of plenty. The air of plenty" (237). This plenitude of troubles is particularly maddening to a sensibility like Hudson's that is devoted to the aesthetics of keeping things straight and simple.

It is possible, however, to identify the chief complication that troubles Hudson in "Cuba": his sense of the knotted violence and tenderness that is love. Hemingway emphasizes this in long scenes that are easily mistaken as being pointless. In the opening pages of "Cuba," for example, Hudson is alone in his home with his cat, Boise, with whom he talks, sleeps, and makes a kind of "love." The obvious effect of Hudson's love for Boise is to emphasize his pathetic aloneness. Although Hudson knows it is probably "a very comic situation," he does not "find it comic at all" (212). But the cat, an expert hunter who was named after the warship *Boise,* is also Hudson's "brother" (218). The point of the episode becomes clear when we are told how Boise came into Hudson's life: he had been given to Hudson and his son Tom on the first Christmas of the war. With his emphasis on Christmas and the war, Hemingway suggests that the gift of love in our time might be more truthfully represented in the image of an affectionate kitten who becomes, naturally, an efficient killer than in the image of a meek savior. And he suggests that the simple Cuban fishermen who are present when the gift is made might realize this instinctively: these "cheerful, self-confident men," with hands "deeply scarred" and hair "bleached by the sun and the salt," never "went to church even on Christmas" (209).

In another scene of over ten pages, Hudson recalls an affair he once had aboard ship with a princess. The scene should and, we trust, would have been cut had Hemingway returned to the novel, but even as it is it functions in a way that resembles the confessional poetry of more recent writers such as Robert Lowell. Hudson's cuckolding of the prince at sea, like the guide Wilson's of Francis Macomber on safari, is mean, but it is undeniably a part of the competition in nature for sexual domination. And the entire scene ends in a startling confession that reveals more than Hudson's vanity and nostalgia for past loves: it resounds also with the man's almost genetic urge, as an individual organism in the stream of evolution, to survive by perpetuating his bloodline: "Why go on with" recalling the affair, Hudson asks himself: "The Baron was dead and the Krauts had Paris and the Princess did not have a baby. There would be no blood of his in any royal house, he thought, unless he had a nosebleed sometime in Buckingham Palace" (232).

Finally, the long scenes with the whore Honest Lil and Hudson's former wife develop the sense that Hudson's despair derives largely from his awareness of his own "meanness" as a participant in the complex violence and tenderness of love (291). Commenting on *Islands in the Stream*, John Updike complained that Hemingway "never formulated the laws that bind" love and death or "achieved the step of irony away from himself"— as though there *is* a formula (in Meyers 565). But Hemingway's constant insistence that love is both violent and regenerative is sound not only in the biological sense but also in the way that it reflects the transcendent, Christian view of love as figured in the crucifix. Hemingway's point in emphasizing Hudson's acceptance of Honest Lil is to reveal his own acceptance of Hudson's human but "mean" sexual hunger: Hudson's tenderness toward Honest Lil is generated from his acceptance or confession of his own meanness. Similarly, the disfigured ex-marine Willie confesses to Lil that he is "horrible," and he is cruel to her; yet he is also tender to her, and he expresses his love to Hudson. And when Hudson and his former wife are together, we see in their past and present behavior how the bond of love between them is also a bond of aggression and violence: when she asks Hudson why he married his present wife, he answers, "Because you were in love" (315). He knows "it wasn't a very good reason." And their interchange, even in the shared grief over their son's death, is as willfully hurtful as those between the sexes in Robert Frost's "Home Burial" or Hemingway's "Hills Like White Elephants": "Would you like to stop it?" "No. It makes me feel better" (134). The violence that destroyed the "Idyll" of "The Sea When Young" is largely that which is reflected in the men's need (in "Cuba" and "At Sea") to get their "ashes dragged" or, as Hudson says, "to clean the shotgun" (*"Variano's a limpiar la es copeta"*) (241, 356).

In "At Sea" (Hemingway's original title was "The Sea Chase") Thomas Hudson earns his place in the brotherhood of memorable sea captains in the American tradition. Like Ahab, Vere, the unnamed captain in "The Open Boat," Wolf Larsen, and Captain Raib in *Far Tortuga*, his exercise of authority is complicated by his burden of knowledge, but he is unique and of his own time in the knowledge he carries with him to sea and in that which he newly acquires in "At Sea." His knowledge of good and evil that first appeared in "Bimini" as the shadows of sharks on his white sandy beach and that became complexly involved in his bruised consciousness with the sense of his own meanness and his loss: all this accompanies him as he prepares, in the first moments of "At Sea," to close in on the escaped crew of the sunken German submarine: "He looked down into the green water and saw the size of the shadow of his ship on the bottom" (331). As the chase intensifies, he will become more painfully aware of his own "shadow," but by the end of the novel—through a sequence of encounters with himself in dreams, with the enemy, and with other participants in the biological brotherhood of life—he will have achieved a measure of inner peace and understanding.

An early step in this process comes in chapter 3, when Hudson takes the opportunity to rest on the beach while some of his men follow the "lovely scent" they had found in the burned village. There also they had found the first German, a sailor who was apparently killed because of "family trouble" by his own group. Hudson is puzzled by the Germans: "They're all brave and some . . . damned admirable. Then they have mean ones like this" (342). But he encounters an even more disturbing "family trouble" in the erotic dream in which his lovemaking to his former wife is interrupted first by his pistol, which is "in the way of everything," and then—after he has promised her to "give up everything" and pleaded with her to "hold me so tight it kills me"—by his awakening to find that his pistol is his penis (343–45). Later, frustrated that they have not closed with the enemy, Hudson imagines that all there is "is this ship and the people on her and the sea and the bastards you are hunting. Afterwards you will see your animals and go into town and get drunk as you can and your ashes dragged and then get ready to go out and do it again" (356). Then, feeling driven to escape this vicious cycle and do something useful, he wonders,

> Why don't you think of them as murderers and have the righteous feeling that you should have? Why do you just pound and pound on after it like a riderless horse. . . ? Because we are all murderers, he told himself—We all are on both sides, if we are any good, and no good will come of any of it.
>
> But you have to do it. Sure, he said. But I don't have to be proud of it. I only have to do it well. (356)

Hudson's predicament is that, despite his inability to feel righteous, he cannot free himself from the puritanic sense that good and evil contend within us or that his "duty" to hunt his fellow murderers is somehow a form of predestiny in a fallen world, as Hemingway suggests in Ara's remark that "this is a bad life for good children." ("Children" here refers to the men's term for their weapons, *ninos*, but Hemingway's meaning is clear.) It is therefore Hudson's fate to suffer, but also to hope, desperately, that in doing his duty he is not "insane" or a "fanatic" (376, 464). Dark, bloody, and desperate as it is, his hope is nevertheless "saving" in that,

*And ahead of him he saw a tall white heron standing
looking down in the shallow water with his head, neck,
and beak poised.* —Hemingway, *Islands in the Stream*

grasping it, he avoids the bleak suicidal end that overtakes so many others in *Islands in the Stream*.[9] More important, it gives him at least the grace of vision. He sees that the captured German sailor, a fellow "murderer," is also a "saint": "The German was thin and there was a blond beard on his chin and on his sunken cheeks. His hair was long and uncombed and in the late afternoon light, with the sun almost down, he looked like a saint" (362). Meekly renouncing life—"nothing is important"; "it doesn't hurt"; "*nein*"—the suffering sailor evokes "loving" responses from Peters and tenderness from Hudson. In fact, the sailor affects Hudson—"I admire him," he says—in almost precisely the way that the "dying soldier of Algiers" affected Stephen Crane's correspondent. Both responses are essentially religious: the correspondent's sorrow and Hudson's "admiration," with the archaic sense of *wonder* that Hemingway surely intended. And in each case the vision of innocence and suffering gives rise to the concepts of brotherhood that constitute these writers' ultimate values. But though it may seem clear that Hemingway acknowledges his debt to the younger writer in this scene, the brotherhood he envisions is much darker and older than Crane's; it rests finally on Hemingway's effort to affirm the violent biological order in life that Crane had not confronted so baldly. The elements from which Hemingway creates his sense of brotherhood emerge most clearly in the crucial chapter 10, shortly after Hudson's encounter with the "saint."

In chapter 10, Hemingway again emphasizes that the greatest obstacle Hudson must overcome before achieving his limited inner peace is the conflict between his duty to hunt and kill the enemy and his sense of brotherhood with the enemy: "It is my duty and I want to get them and I will. But I have a sort of fellow death-house feeling about them. Do people who are in the death-house hate each other? I don't believe they do unless they are insane." And "just then," Hudson witnesses a sequence of events in nature and in himself that will eventually lead him to his understanding. He sees first a "white heron standing looking down in the shallow water with his hand, neck and beak poised"; then he sees the tracks a female turtle had made "to the sea and back and a wallowing depression where she had laid"; then, in the water, "he saw the grayness that a school of mullet made and their shadow on the sand bottom as they moved. He saw the shadow of a very big barracuda that was stalking the mullet," and later he saw "the wild leaping of the frightened mullet. Then he saw that the school was reformed . . . [and then] he saw [the heron] flying with his white wings over the green water and ahead was the yellow sand and the line of the trees along the point." As the clouds began to darken, he walked faster along the beach, and "walking faster gave him an erection and he thought there can't be any Krauts around" (376–78). Together, these scenes—compacted within the space of three pages as Hudson walks the beach in a conscious effort "not to think at all but only to notice things"—constitute a symphony of images that testifies to the essential violent yet regenerative processes of life. The significance of these images is not immediately clear to Hudson, but they prepare for his later encounter with other natural hunters, the flamingoes he sees and seems comforted by as he enters the final stages of his own hunt. And by the end of chapter 10, the things he has noticed on the beach develop into a picture of his own men's innocence as warriors. The rain has come and the men have covered their "*niños*" (their weapons); they bathe, naked, "bending against the lashing of the rain and leaning back into it . . . [looking] white in this strange light. Thomas Hudson . . . thought he would like to have Eakins paint it." He sees the "sun breaking through momentarily to make the driving rain silver and to shine on the bathers in the stern" (382–83).

Hudson's later remark that "it isn't bad to be half saint and half desperate man" derives from his admiration of the German "saint" and from this picture of innocence. Finally, Hudson can accept his own "half saint and half desperate man" reality because he sees it reflected in nature as he prepares for the final onslaught: in the "pink and black" flamingoes that swerve in flight, indicating the German position within the mangroves. These great birds, with their "dreadful, hunger-ridden impersonality," are nevertheless "lovely to see in the sunlight" (399, 418). Moments after reflecting to himself that duty is "wonderful" and "simple" and that he has "chased . . . very well," they appear in flight, "their pink and black wings beat, carrying them toward" Hudson, who "watched them and marvelled at their down-swept black and white bills and the rose color they made in the sky" (418). In "The Sea Chase," the image of these great hunting birds is as revealing as that of the leaping, nearly transcendent marlin in "Bimini" ("The Sea When Young") and *The Old Man and the Sea* ("The Sea in Being"). They appear here to warn Hudson of his enemy's presence but also to console him with the sense that his hunter's duty has a basis in nature: "It's not just the black on that rose pink. It is their size and that they are ugly in detail and yet perversely beautiful. They must be a very old bird from the earliest times" (420).[10] Their brilliant pink suggests the union of antiquity and innocence in the primal order, as did the pink men-of-war in *To Have and Have Not*. Hudson appreciates seeing "the roseate mass on the gray brown flat" and thinks, "It is nice to see flamingoes before you make this trip" (420). Feeling that, until now, they have "chased pretty" and that, "for better or worse," this will be a natural union, he is prepared to close with the enemy in an encounter that will bring his own fatal wounds (451, 427). Entering the battle, he feels "as naked as a man can feel"; then he receives the three wounds that ache in his bones, chest, bowels, testicles. "It hurts," he admits to Willie, but "it doesn't hurt any worse than things that you and I have shot together" (455, 457, 462). He recognizes, as Hemingway had recognized in *The Green Hills of Africa,* that there is a bloody justice in the biological brotherhood of life.

Before he dies, Hudson hears from Willie, "I love you, you son of a bitch, and don't die. . . . Try and understand if it isn't too hard." Like the wounded German "saint," he feels "far away now and there were no problems at all," and his last words, "I think I understand, Willie," echo the tentative knowledge that Stephen Crane's men had gathered from the sea: "They felt that they could then be interpreters." But the limited understanding Hemingway allows Hudson is complicated by a dark half-century's accumulation of knowledge and sea experience that Crane's men could not have known. Whereas Crane left his men confronting the natural elements of the "moonlight," the "wind," and the "great sea's voice," Hemingway leaves Hudson on the deck of his boat: it was "gathering . . . speed," and "he felt . . . the lovely throb of her engines" as they "came through the deck and into him" (466). Hudson, like Crane's correspondent, has found and affirmed a kind of brotherhood, but the closing image of the engines entering him and the novel's last words, Willie's "Oh shit. . . . You never understood anybody that loves you," resound with the complexities in modern life that impinge upon Hudson's hope that he is not insane.

As a traditional voyager to knowledge, Hudson began by feeling that he was safe in his house, which "was built solid as a ship" (3), and in his protective routine of discipline and work. Shortly afterward he hears a parable of civilized life that will characterize his journey: the black boy Louis appears and tells Hudson of the troublesome drunken "Gentleman off'n a yacht" he had seen at the "Ponce de Leon" (the favorite drinking spot, where, of course, there is no fountain of youth). The yachtsman had been outraged when Louis wanted to sing one of the "old songs such as the loss of John Jacob Astor on the *Titanic* when sunk by an iceberg." Louis tells Hudson that the yachtsman (who claimed to be richer than John Jacob Astor) was "difficulter than a diesel engine is to a newborn tree monkey out of its mother's womb" (14). At the end of his long voyage (through "Bimini," "Cuba," and "At Sea"), Hudson will recall his son Tom's boyhood fear that the "ice age" will come again (447); he will have seen the flamingoes and himself, "naked as a man can feel"; and finally, knowing that he is entering his last battle, he will accept his identity: "All right, jungle man" (460). In the next sentence (the first of chapter 21), he receives his fatal wounds. Like the "newborn tree monkey," he has known the difficulties, not only of his engines but of the related complexities of civilized life in the twentieth century—including his awareness of the biological mechanisms of life: his sense that even his son, the "martyr" David performed "as a machine," his sense of his own "carapace" of work, and his sense of his own organic aggression, especially in love.[11] Similar complications seem to define the modern sickness that killed the gentleman from New York in "Bimini." He had planned to kill himself by jumping "off of the highest part of [New York] city straight into oblivion," but, too desperate to wait, he dived "off of Johnny Black's dock into the channel with the tide going out," a clear case of "Mechanics Depressive" (157–58). Toward the end of his life, Thomas Hudson thought to himself that there had been plenty of happy times in his life, but "they were all . . . in the time of innocence and still being able to work and eat" (448). If he could have returned even to the summer days of "The Sea When Young" and painted only simple pictures like the one of the fish in the water; or if, like Santiago, he could have fished for the market from a wind-driven skiff on the blue water. . . .

Santiago and "the prisms in the deep dark water"

The punishment of hunger is everything.
  —Hemingway, *The Old Man and the Sea*

For all his vital simplicity, even Harry Morgan could not survive the complications of modern time that Hemingway heaped upon him. For, if he was almost organically different from the Waste Land yachtsmen, writers, and revolutionaries, he was also of them. As an American seaman he is a hybrid of the authoritative captain and the innocent common sailor. He is an independent operator, but nevertheless a businessman and an employer of men. He regrets that "there's no honest money going in boats any more," and the single alternative he can imagine is to have worked in "a filling station" (*To Have and Have Not*, 174). "In the Gulf you got time" (106), he thinks, but he cannot enter the Gulf in his twin-engined boat without packing a heavy load of gasoline—a modern reality that Hemingway emphasizes with his closing image of a small tanker on the horizon, "hugging the reef as she made to the westward to keep from wasting fuel against the stream" (262). And it is no accident that Harry's death results from his having shot into his own gas tank: two of his shots had passed through one of the Cubans and into the tank; when he stood up to cut the engines to avoid an explosion, the wounded Cuban "shot him in the belly" (172).

In the story of Santiago, however, Hemingway could dream a radical simplicity in his character's life and history whereby *that* man alone on the sea could have a chance to claim a dignified and harmonious existence in nature. The qualities that make Santiago "too simple to wonder when he had attained humility" seem reflected in "his sunburned, confident loving eyes": "They were the same color as the sea and were cheerful and unde-feated." Bathing Santiago in "the dark water of the true gulf [which] is the greatest healer there is" (109), Hemingway freed him from the Waste Land complications that afflicted Harry Morgan's existence and from the com-plexities of warfare and sexual aggression that haunted Thomas Hudson. He also frees Santiago from the debilitating sense that had been reflected in Wolf Larsen's sea-colored eyes. A "protean," "greenish-gray," Wolf's eyes reflected the "cruel," biological struggle of "the sea itself," the fright-ening primordial reality that Humphrey and Maud could hope to tran-scend through the evolutionary regeneration of race (*Sea-Wolf*, 18–24). Santiago's fate, however—like Jack London's simple old fisherman in "The Water Baby"—is not to evolve, but fully to *be* a fisherman. "The Sea in Being," Hemingway's working title for *The Old Man and the Sea*, rests on this simple principle—that Santiago need "think of only one thing. That which I was born for," that is, to be "a fisherman" (*Old Man*, 44). Thus he can exist in natural harmony with all creatures, both "our friends and our enemies" (132), in the simple order whereby each must hunt and eat to live. Repeatedly, this natural order is displayed before his eyes:

> As he watched the bird dipped again slanting his wings for the dive and then swinging them wildly and ineffectually as he followed the flying fish. The old man could see the slight bulge in the water that the big dolphin raised as they followed the escaping fish. The dolphin were cut-ting through the water below the flight of the fish and would be in the water, driving at speed, when the fish dropped. It is a big school of dol-phin, he thought. They are wide spread and the flying fish have little chance. The bird has no chance. The flying fish are too big for him and they go too fast. (37–38)

Hemingway emphasizes that Santiago, gentle as he is, participates with deadly effectiveness in this order. His "cheerful," sea-colored eyes, for example, resemble the "man-of-war" that floats "cheerfully as a bubble with its long deadly purple filaments" (39). To Santiago the man-of-war is a natural enemy, "the falsest thing in the sea," but Hemingway also em-phasizes Santiago's expert falseness as a fisherman when he coaxes the mar-lin to take his baited hooks: "Just smell them. Aren't they lovely?" (46). The men-of-war exist in the cycle, too, and Santiago "loved to see the big sea turtles eating them" (40). This cycle of the hunt is the necessary driv-ing force in life—"that which I was born for," as Santiago understands. Had Melville written in the twentieth century, he might have seen it as the "fate" that ordered life as he could grasp it in "The Mat-Maker," rather than the biblical fate suggested as that scene ends with Tashtego's prophetic cry, "There she blows!": "Thus we were weaving and weaving away when I started at a sound so strange, long drawn, and musically wild and unearthly, that the ball of free will dropped from my hand, and I stood gazing up, at the clouds whence that voice dropped like a wing." Certainly, Hemingway's emphasis on Santiago's fated birth, his emphasis on "chance" in the passage quoted above, and his emphasis on Santiago's and his marlin's "choice" (55) constitute his own effort to weave from the same three forces that Melville interwove in "The Mat-Maker"—"chance, free will, and necessity"—a twentieth-century reality that might represent our existence more truthfully than Melville could in 1851.

Both Melville and Hemingway (in *The Old Man and the Sea*) can accept the necessity of death and suffering—Melville through Ishmael's faith in the Christian mystery, Hemingway through Santiago's affirmation of his fate. And the structuring principle in *The Old Man and the Sea* that corresponds to the doubt over which Ishmael's faith prevails (Ahab's fiery anger that must be extinguished in the sea) is Santiago's reluctance to participate fully in the cycle by killing and eating his "brother" creatures. Santiago's story is made from the language of religious paradox. But in place of the traditional Christian sense that we must surrender our lives in order to win them, that Christ suffered because of God's love for man, is Santiago's sense that he must kill and eat, that "he [the marlin] is my brother. But I must kill him" (65). "'Fish,' he said, 'I love you and respect you very much. But I will kill you dead before this day ends'" (60); "'Blessed Virgin, pray for the death of this fish. Wonderful though he is'" (72). The "but," "though," and "although" constructions that prevail in this story issue from the same source as Santiago's inner physical and spiritual conflict—the "treachery of [his] own body" (as in his thoughts about Joe Di-Maggio's bone spur) when his left hand cramps, and, emphatically, his sense of natural guilt—a post-Darwinian awareness, not that he is innately depraved but that he is inescapably a participant in the innate voraciousness of life. Knowing that he was born to be a fisherman and that "the punishment of hunger . . . is everything," he can only accept his condition and express his sorrow: "I'm sorry fish" (84, 121). Nothing can "save" Santiago, but he can endure his suffering and survive in life by means that are more substantial than Ishmael's meditative wonder and his life-buoy coffin.

Because of the cataclysmic developments in Western thought between 1851 and 1952, Santiago's sea sense is radically different from Ishmael's. Yet because of his age, he is also Ishmael's sea-brother: much of his power to survive derives from his recollection of his own past—his traditional experience as a sailor "before the mast on a square rigged ship" (24). Hemingway emphasizes this experience repeatedly, for it is a key to Santiago's simple existence and his power to affirm life in ways unimaginable for either Harry Morgan or Thomas Hudson. As his life is orderd simply around the knowledge of his fate to be a fisherman, his dreams now return to the single experience of his youth when, off the coast of Africa, he saw "the lions on the beach" (27). ("He no longer dreamed of storms, nor of women, nor of great occurrences.") "Why," Santiago asks, with the interpreters who would understand him, "why are the lions the main thing that is left?" The answer is simpler than that the lions "carry associations of youth, strength, and even immortality" in "a parable of youth and old age," as Carlos Baker has suggested (*Artist*, 309). Unquestionably, as many interpreters have felt, *The Old Man and the Sea* goes "far outside" the limits of realistic fiction to grasp its truths. But Hemingway will not go beyond the severe strictures of his own aesthetics. The significance of the lions conforms to the story's unity and derives from Santiago's recollection of his earliest experience as a fisherman, his recognition of the biological brotherhood, and his knowledge that he was born to be a fisherman. That the fabled king of beasts should *play* on the beach in Santiago's dreams suggests the innocence of their participation in the necessary order, the brotherhood that includes the cheerful Santiago and the cheerfully floating man-of-war. The lions exist in Santiago's dreams to remind him of the lesson Hemingway presented in his fable "The Good Lion" (1951, a year before *The Old Man and the Sea* appeared in *Life*). "This lion, that we love because he was so good," wrote Hemingway, "had wings on his back." All the other lions, "wicked lions indeed," ate not only zebras and antelope but also people, especially fat "Hindu traders," because they are "delicious to a lion." But the "good lion" is a puzzling "pasta-eating lion," who is frightened by the others' roaring laughter, their bad breath, and the "old pieces of Hindu trader" that remained in their claws; so he flies away to his original home in Venice. Safely back in St. Mark's Square, where nothing has changed, however, he realizes that "Africa had changed him." He makes his way to Harry's bar and there meekly asks, "Do you have any Hindu trader sandwiches?" First he would drink "a very dry martini," but he "was very happy" (50–51).

Like the good lion, Santiago has come to resist participating fully in the voracious process of life: "For a long time now eating had bored him and he never carried a lunch" (30). Ashore, he ate the "white eggs" of turtles "to give himself strength" (as well as to draw, perhaps, on the strength of his youthful experience as a turtler), and he drank "shark liver oil" for "colds and grippes" and because "it was good for the eyes" (41). Once, innocent as the lions, he "could see quite well in the dark. Not in the absolute dark. But almost as a cat sees" (74). But now, in addition to his troubled vision, he has difficulty in eating the small tuna he had caught and hit "on the head for kindness" (42). Hemingway develops his point in a passage that clearly echoes Whitman's "Out of the Cradle Endlessly Rocking," when Santiago recalls the pathetic male marlin whose mate he had caught (54). He contemplates his "treachery" and his "choice" in hooking the fish. And because he is fully immersed in the sea life as Hemingway knew it, he cannot console himself as Whitman could in 1859, when he published "Out of the Cradle," with the sense that the sea whispers "the low and delicious word death." Reflecting Hemingway's dark, post-Darwinian sense of the biological order, Santiago falters, thinking, "Perhaps I should not have been a fisherman." And he can overcome his doubt only by recalling, "that was what I was born for," and by resolving: "I must surely remember to eat the tuna after it gets light" (56). Later, he must force himself to eat: "Eat the bonito now," he says; then, "'I'll eat some more. . . . It is a strong full-blooded fish. . . . I will eat it all and then I will be ready. . . . [The marlin] is my brother. But I must kill him and keep strong to do it.' Slowly and conscientiously he ate all of the wedge-shaped strips of fish." Later still, having eaten more of the dolphin and a flying fish, he admonishes himself, as "the sun was rising for the third time," "You're stupid. . . . Eat the other flying fish" (94). Finally, the long ordeal of hunting, killing, and eating comes to an appropriate ritualistic end when, the sharks having taken half his marlin, he is swept into an agony of false thought in an effort to account for his sin ("I killed him in self-defense," [117]). But he realizes, "I must not deceive myself too much. He leaned over the side and pulled loose a piece of the meat of the fish where the shark had cut him. He chewed it and noted its quality and its good taste." Then, sailing homeward with a steady breeze and "chewing a bit of the meat from the marlin," he sees the other sharks and says aloud, "'Ay,'" as if "involuntarily, feeling the nail go through his hands and into the wood" (118). The voracious order will proceed, bringing with it the simple knowledge of loss that Santiago gathers from the Gulf Stream: "He knew he was beaten now" (131). Yet in his ritual of eating the flesh of his "brothers" he can survive and affirm his fate, "The Sea in Being." He must will himself to partake in this strange ritual, for it is as hard a truth to swallow as was no doubt the "raw tidbit of meat" that Hemingway took "to chew on" from the lion he killed in 1953 (Baker, *Life Story*, 516). Such gestures seek more than good luck in shooting; in *The Old Man and the Sea* they honor the sea reality that Hemingway illuminates by refracting the Light promised in the Eucharist. Far from transcendent, this light seems wrestled from the heavens into the stream, where Hemingway captures it in the watery prisms that Santiago sees: "The sea was very dark and the light made prisms in the water. The myriad flecks of the plankton were annuled now by the high sun and it was only the great deep prisms in the blue water that the old man saw now with his lines going straight down into the water that was a mile deep" (44).

For Hemingway, this sea-light illuminates the absolute reality—the sea in being, our violent existence in the stream of life. This is the light that leads Santiago through his dark time:

He came out unendingly and water poured from his sides.
—Hemingway, *The Old Man and the Sea*

He looked across the sea and knew how alone he was now. But he could
see the prisms in the deep dark water and the line stretching ahead and
the strange undulation of the calm. The clouds were building up now
for the trade wind and he looked ahead and saw a flight of wild ducks
etching themselves against the sky over the water, then blurring, then
etching again and he knew no man was ever alone on the sea.[12] (67)

Moments later, Santiago sees signs of "better weather," and then his great
fish bursts into view: "He came out unendingly and water poured from his
sides. He was bright in the sun and his head and back were dark purple and
in the sun the stripes on his sides showed wide and a light lavender" (69).
Later, jumping again, "He seemed to hang in the air above the old man in
the skiff" (104). Finally, the great marlin is alongside and dead, and Santiago sees the mirrored, detached saintliness in his eye (107).

Looking forward to the publication of this story, Hemingway wrote
that it could be "the epilogue to my long book" (his "sea" book, the first
three parts of which we now have as *Islands in the Stream*) or "the epilogue
to all my writing and what I have learned, or tried to learn, while writing
and trying to live" (*Letters*, 757). Perhaps the strangest thing about this
story of a strange old man that had a "very strange effect" on Hemingway
himself and on all the readers who had seen his manuscript is that—despite its being a parable of acceptance in which the gentle Santiago affirms
his place in the violent biological brotherhood of life and accepts his
loss—Hemingway's creation of his parable was as willful and aggressive an
act as anything we associate with his work in general. When, "trying to
live," he wrote *The Old Man and the Sea*, he acted with all the courage and
desperation that is necessary in William James's "Will to Believe" and
that, more than anything, characterizes the tradition of American sea fiction from *Moby-Dick* to the present.

11

Peter Matthiessen and the Tradition in Modern Time

You in de modern time, mon: sailin boat a thing of
de past.
 —Peter Matthiessen, *Far Tortuga*

"It's a great life if you don't weaken."
 —Peter Matthiessen, *Men's Lives*

In the work of Peter Matthiessen, who was born 22 May
1927, the tradition of American sea fiction has survived with renewed vitality late in the twentieth century. Matthiessen has produced several novels and stories that derive their central meanings from the sea, and his
masterpiece, *Far Tortuga* (1975), is one of the greatest sea novels of all
time, in any language. Within the tradition of American sea fiction, only
Moby-Dick is a greater book. Moreover, in his dual experience as a working seaman and as a naturalist, Matthiessen fully exemplifies the brotherhood of American sea writers since 1851. He served as an enlisted man in
the United States Coast Guard Reserve and later the navy between 1944
and 1946 and drew on his experience during these years in his third novel,
Raditzer (1961). But his three years as a commercial fisherman off Long Island were crucial in his development as a sea writer. There, in the falls of
1953, 1954, and 1955, he fished for scallops and clams; during the springs
of 1954–56 he worked with ocean haul-seine crews, fishing mainly for
striped bass; and during the summers of 1954–56 he owned and operated
the thirty-two-foot *Merlin*, chartering parties of sport fishermen in search
of striped bass, bluefish, and tuna.

The money he earned as a seasonal fisherman made it possible for him
to survive as a writer during an early stage of his career, when he produced
his second novel, *Partisans* (1955). But far more important, his work as a

commercial fisherman brought him into direct contact, an immediate and natural involvement with the sea and sea life that provided the basis for his profoundly truthful presentation of the sea life in *Far Tortuga*. Echoing Thoreau's "I went to the woods because," in the chapter "Where I lived, and What I lived for," Matthiessen has explained: "I chartered because it paid for my boat and I made a living out of doors in the season between haul-seining and scalloping; I scalloped and hauled seine because I liked the work, and liked the company of the commercial fishermen, the bay-men" (*Men's Lives*, 97). And having succeeded at the fisherman's life and having been "accepted as a fisherman," he felt that "the three years spent with the commercial [fisher]men were among the most rewarding of my life, and those hard seasons on the water had not been wasted" (123). That those years were not wasted is evident in *Far Tortuga* and in the sense he expresses in *Men's Lives* that man's attraction to the watery life is deeply organic. He resembles the charter fisherman he describes in *Men's Lives* "who believed strongly in the lunar tide tables as a guide to the feeding habits of fish and man; he had noticed, he said, that *Homo sapiens*, wandering the docks with a glazed countenance, would suddenly stir into feeding frenzy, signing up boats with the same ferocity—and at the same stage of the tide—that *Pomatomous saltatrix* would strike into the lures around the point" (93). And describing his own movement from one fishery to another, Matthiessen wrote:

> When pale spring came and the ospreys reappeared, and black-backed flounders nosed along the harbor bottoms, tracing the blood-worms and orange mussel baits on the rusty hooks of old chafed men in rowboats, I slapped copper paint on the *Merlin's* hull at the Three Mile Harbor Boatyard. When the shadblow bloomed and the spring life in the sea brought strong fertile odors to the ocean wind, I got out my black waders once again, my long-billed swordfish cap and dark blue parka with its sweet smell of ancient fish gurry, and went on south across Abraham's Path to Poseyville. "Better try 'em, ain't we, boys?" Cap'n Ted would say, looking up briefly from mending net to squint at us. And I realized that watching those blunt weather-glazed hands slipping that net needle through the twine with such speed and deftness was one of the great many small pleasures of life on the beach that I took for granted. (103)

This imaging of the different species' equal sensitivity to lunar and solar rhythms is characteristic of Matthiessen's essential vision, as a naturalist, that, like fisherman and fish, all the forms of life constitute a single family that is born "of the light" and driven to survive (*Raditzer*, 58). His account of the Long Island fishermen in *Men's Lives* is a story of "their struggle to survive" the harsh economy—biological and social—of their existence. Indeed, their cheerful and tough-minded refrain is expressed by the gill-netter, Richard, who remarks, "shaking his head" and grinning, "'It's a great life if you don't weaken, ain't that right?'" (180, 226).

In addition to his three years of commercial fishing, Matthiessen "sailed on a commercial caymen schooner on a green turtle fishing voyage to the Miskito Cays off Nicaragua" in 1966, and in 1969 served as "writer-diver on an oceanic expedition" to film the great white shark (131). His experience on the turtle fishing voyage gave rise, over a period of nine years, to *Far Tortuga*, and the shark expedition to *Blue Meridian* (1971), a work of nonfiction. On each of these voyages, as during his years of commercial fishing, Matthiessen studied the various species he encountered with a naturalist's eye. And in several other books, his approach is explicitly that of a naturalist. Although he has no formal degree in biology, only university classes in botany and zoology, he has established himself as a prominent contemporary naturalist. Two of his books, *Wildlife in North America* (1959) and *The Shorebirds of North America* (1967), have won especially high praise, and a third, *Oomingmak* (1975, an account of an expedition in 1964 to the Bering Sea area to study and help preserve the musk ox), is also highly valued. Moreover, Matthiessen has successfully extended his interests in the various species, from a naturalist's point of view, into works with broader anthropological and ecological interest, as in *The Cloud Forest* (1961, on South America), *Under the Mountain Wall* (1962, on New Guinea), and *The Tree Where Man Was Born* (1972, on East Africa). For his work as a naturalist, Matthiessen should be recognized as a leading figure in the tradition of major American writers who were also nature writers, from Thoreau to Steinbeck. He is unquestionably the most accomplished naturalist in the tradition of American sea fiction, which, since Melville's cetological explorations in *Moby-Dick*, has emphasized the significance of biological investigations into the meaning of life.

Like Melville, London, and many minor writers in the tradition, Matthiessen served his apprenticeship as a writer by writing of the sea in his first and third novels, *Race Rock* (1954) and *Raditzer*. Although *Race Rock* is not a traditional sea novel (there is no actual voyage in it), it derives its sense of primal order from the sea in repeated scenes of ocean drownings that represent both loss and renewal. The novel opens as its main character, George McConville, contemplates the gravesite of a local legendary figure, Abraham Shipman, who in the year of McConville's birth had found a "path from the world to freedom" by walking into the sea, where "the crabs and snails and sand fleas at the bottom relieved him of age and flesh and brain, returning him to eternity as presentable as any drowned man before or after him" (2). It is a parable of the larger story that unfolds, as George and two friends, Cady and Sam, struggle to mature, to take responsibility for their own lives, and to resolve the conflict that arises among them in their competition for their friend Eve's affection. They live in the Waste Land aftermath of World War II, "whose wretched wake had gelded it of any sense" it might have had for those who died in it. In the shadow of the war, and with the sense of guilt that arises from their sexual competition for Eve, they endure this "era of shame . . . [and] sit around like diseased monkeys" (124). The least promising of the three males contending for Eve is Cady Shipman. Although he is from one of the oldest families on the coast (like the Winthrops and Coffins), he has degenerated into a merely violent man. He is most his "essential" self when he once appears with a "shotgun in one hand and . . . [a] pistol . . . in the other"; and he tells Sam, "I have what they call an animal cunning. I believe in the survival of the fittest. You're not fit to survive. You're a pimple on the ass of society" (231, 222). Sam, a would-be artist, can neither sustain his unproductive marriage with Eve nor find the courage to drown himself in the ocean. His attempted suicide brings about a second drowning, that of a local Indian, Daniel Barleyfield, who drowns searching for Sam. And, in turn, this sea death is instrumental in George's eventual development into full manhood, which is signaled by his returning to Eve at the end of the novel. George is revulsed when he finds Barleyfield's body washed up onto the beach, his "eyes [which] had been open . . . now . . . gone from their sockets, carried into the shadows of the woods in the bellies of the [fish]crows." Then, "listening to the pound and rush and suck of the sea," he finds the strength to confront "the gull scream and the ocean din and the presence of death" (280–81). After retrieving the body, he returns to get the Indian's "heaven-green skiff" and in a scene of ritual launches it through the breaking surf. On the early morning sea, then, he removes his "heavy garments . . . until he was white and naked under the sun. His skin was alive with a clean glory he had not known since a child, a sense of beginnings, of infinite possibilities." Rowing offshore, he falls unthinkingly into "a harmony with the ocean rhythm, the vast invisible world where man had come from and [to] which Daniel Barleyfield" had returned (285).

Race Rock was well received as the first novel by a young man who had already earned a small place in literary history as the founding editor of the Paris Review, but its enduring interest might well be only in what it reveals of Matthiessen's preliminary efforts to create his great sea book. Nevertheless, the ideas with which Race Rock seems overburdened and which reappear, brilliantly purified, in Far Tortuga, are essentially those with which the tradition of American sea fiction has been most concerned over the last hundred years: immersed as we are in the violently competitive biological processes of life, as set forth in the *Origin of Species* and *The Descent of Man,* how can we perpetuate a sense of brotherhood like that which Melville had idealized in "A Squeeze of the Hand"?

The main character in Matthiessen's second novel, *Partisans,* worries about such a question, but in a social setting far from the sea. Involved in the strife of proletarian revolutionary forces in Paris, Barney Sand (whose name suggests a relationship with other characters in Matthiessen's sea stories) wonders where "the world [would find] itself at century's end"; his fear is that the world might awaken too late, that "Richman, poor man, beggarman, thief might find a fellowship at last, strewn side by side beneath that final sun" (174). Six years later, after a divorce and his extended work on *Wildlife in North America,* Matthiessen returned to this problem in settings and situations that were more explicitly relevant to the sea in the story "Horse Latitudes" and his third novel, *Raditzer.* In "Horse Latitudes," two natural enemies must share a stateroom aboard a "freighter that hauled guns, Christmas trees, and small machinery" to South America: Horace, "a Baptist fundamentalist and missionary," and Hassid, "a Lebanese merchant with a Protestant grandmother, a Freemason father and a Catholic past" (7). They fall "immediately" into "competition," each claiming that his recent operation (one's surgery for an abscessed nose, the other's hemorrhoidectomy) had been the greater ordeal. Toward the end of their voyage, at the end of the story, these shipmates "shrieked their strange love song into the wind like a pair of gulls, their small bent figures rising and falling on the swarthy clouds of the vast tropic horizon" (14).

Raditzer more directly addresses the problem of whether we can sustain a brotherhood in this warring world. Set in the last months of World War II, its voyage begins as the USS *General Pendleton* pulls away from the pier at San Francisco, on its way to Pearl Harbor. In the second paragraph, as in the opening paragraphs of *Race Rock,* Matthiessen presents a naturalist's parable that captures the reality his novel will acknowledge:

> The tug blasted its horn, and at the pier end a starved gull with a dragging wing edged out from behind a bollard. Two others, wings spread, beaks wide, swooped in to punish it, and it fell on its dirty breast. It struggled free again, and the two clean gulls, like warders, moved in haughtily and flanked it. The doomed bird huddled where it was, and together the three awaited the next instinct, sitting ceremonially, feathers stirring in the famished wind. (3–4)

By the time he passes beneath the Golden Gate on his return to San Francisco, the novel's main character, Charlie Stark, will have found himself inextricably involved in this harsh reality, this instinctual treachery.

He will recognize the disheartening inaccuracy of his father's assurance, "*We are not animals, after all. . . . We maintain charities and asylums. Among animals, the old, the weak, are driven out or even killed*" (140). He will meet a shipmate, Raditzer, who represents an even darker human possibility than Conrad's secret sharer and who, like the wounded gull, will be set upon by the haughty strong of his own species and driven from the human community into death. Raditzer seems to have "been placed on earth by a disgruntled God as a kind of latter-day Jesus, an immaculate corruption," but in "reality," he "had once been a small child, identical in his innocence with all the rest of them, and . . . after two decades of hand-to-mouth survival, his malnutrition, evident in his weak, rickety body, had spread like a cancer to his mind" (42, 45).

Stark had joined the navy not, as his father had imagined, "*to get in there and do your part,*" but rather because "he had only wanted to go, to get away" (24);[1] and his voyage will make it clear to him that he cannot get away from the human reality against which he had vaguely rebelled. At the end of the novel, the *Pendleton* having brought him under the Golden Gate toward home again, he accepts his share of the responsibility for Raditzer's death and, in the novel's last words, takes "his place in line." He is brought to this place by a series of crucial experiences that involve the sea. The first occurs one night early in the *Pendleton's* outbound voyage, when he is standing fire watch on the foredeck during a night of storm: "A sea breaking across the deck seized him up and swept him violently against the rail cables, nearly washing him over the side" (22). Realizing that the officers on the bridge were "unaffected by the storm" and that no one would have missed him, he thinks, "to hell with you" (22). Later, "exulted in his solitude . . . in the wild isolated realm of wind and water," he senses that "the pulse of blood which filled his heart" is "somehow aligned . . . with the blind, mighty risings and declines of tides and winds and seasons," at one with the whirling earth (23).

These first sea experiences leave Stark with the naive sense that the sea can somehow free and cleanse him. But the disgusting Raditzer attaches himself to Stark and, "a sort of ambulatory bad conscience for mankind," makes Stark feel responsible for him. Raditzer pleads, "You're the only guy understands me, Charlie," and he chastises him for denying that they are "buddies": "You ain't even got the milk of human kindness!" (100–101). Stark begins to recognize the truth of this charge as he seeks to rid himself of Raditzer and as he leaves the Hawaiian girl Raditzer had set up for him. In exploiting and then abandoning the native girl, he recognizes his guilt—his infidelity to his wife at home, his similarity to his former hero, Gauguin, who "replaced the South Sea idyll with syphilis and solitude," and his kinship with "all the joes," as the girl tells him: "All you want me for is making pom-pom" (25, 86–87). Stung by this charge, and filled with "self-disgust," Stark seeks to "refresh" himself in the sea. Instead, however, his early morning plunge into the lagoon brings a frightening vision of his shared guilt for the "innocents [who] had been slaughtered" in Hiroshima and of his own helplessness in the sea-world. "Across the lagoon" he hears his friend Robert, a young Japanese fisherman, calling to him. Previously, Robert had taken him fishing near the "community of Japanese fishermen" at Punaluu, and now Stark sees Robert standing and shouting at him from his skiff: "His silhouette was black against the red rays of the rising sun, imminent as an explosion behind the etched outline of the headland to the eastward, as if the fireball of the atom had carried around the world. '*Kaku!*'" (88). The Japanese boy waves violently, holds up "a long gleaming silver fish," and yells again, "*Kaku!*" (Barracuda!), "Go way!" Stark manages to swim safely to shore, but in his fear, "panic," and "frenzy," he has had his first real taste of the "primordially hostile" world (88). And when he goes fishing again, near the leper colony at Molokai, he sees the biological reality with new eyes: the charter boat he was on

> pursued the frigate birds, which traced in turn the schools of flying fish, pursued from below by other silent hunters. When a dark bird hung above the wake, it was usually a matter of moments before the sea astern would gleam with emerald fire, and the *mahi-mahi* itself, the dorado or dolphin, would crack a white furrow in the dancing chop, flashing toward the bait. The resplendent fish, boated, would gasp away its color with its life, fading from emerald to sapphire, then swift as a rainbow to gold, yellow, silver, and at last a dirty gray. (102)

Still, it is not until the *Pendleton* is carrying its "cargo of men . . . toward the continent of home" that Stark finds himself most horribly implicated in his shipmates' "instinctive" attack on the weak outcast Raditzer, "the dirtiest scum that ever crawled the earth" (119). The scene is a ritual sacrifice: Stark "had a strong sense of a religious tableau." The harsh reality it represents, however, is that engendered not by a god of love but only by the unforgiving "bald sun" (15, 137). Thus, when Raditzer finally dies (Matthiessen is ambiguous as to whether it is a suicide), and his body disappears in the water below the pier in San Francisco, Stark rushes to the ship's side and drops to his knees. But he sees only "a grapefruit rind" revolving in the tidal current near the pier, and "near the submerged posts the minnows poised, quick as thin magnets, and far below an eel swayed in the green sea algaes clinging to the creosoted wood." Stark turns toward the onlooking crowd and stares "in disbelief" (148). He agonizes in his realization that "*we killed him,*" but a fellow sailor grasps him—"with talons"—to bring him to his senses. In his last paragraph Matthiessen returns to the bird imagery with which he had begun the novel: "On the bow of the ship" newly arrived in San Francisco, "a gull stretched its dry leg and wing, then slipped forward and glided out across the harbor." And Stark takes his final place "in line," a brother among sailor-creatures whom St. Francis would not have known.

Again in *Raditzer* Matthiessen worked with the ideas of biology and brotherhood in a way that some readers will find heavy-handed compared with his brilliantly simplified presentation of the same ideas in *Far Tortuga*. Even in his next novel, *At Play in the Fields of the Lord* (1965), which won him far greater critical acclaim than his first three, he worked perhaps too self-consciously with the same idea. Again he attempted to dramatize "the way to innocence" that he refers to in his epigraph from Hermann Hesse: "the way to innocence, to the uncreated and to God leads on, not back, not back to the wolf or to the child, but ever further into sin, ever deeper into human life." And again, in his novel this path leads through renunciation, not of the flesh but of all that is not essentially the flesh. In the end, his main character, Lewis Moon, half-white, half-Indian, feels "bereft, though of what he did not know. He was neither white nor Indian, man nor animal, but some mute, naked strand of protoplasm" (372). *At Play in the Fields of the Lord* is not a sea novel, but in it we can see Matthiessen probing at the same troubling question that had haunted Jack London when he wrote of the "essence of life" that was embodied in Wolf Larsen—"the elemental stuff . . . of life," that "which lingers in a shapeless lump of turtle meat and recoils and quivers from the prod of a finger" (*Sea-Wolf*, 14). Whereas London had hoped that life might evolve beyond Larsen's wolfishness, Matthiessen hopes that in his half-breed's protoplasmic innocence there is something more promising than that which is represented in his friend Wolfie.

Wolfie's presence in *At Play in the Fields of the Lord* seems intended to play on the sense of the epigraph from Hesse rather than to recall *The Sea-Wolf*, but during this period Matthiessen was deeply involved in his long work on *Far Tortuga*, in which the problems of biology and brotherhood are central. And in the following passage from *Blue Meridian* (1971, six years after *At Play* and four years before *Far Tortuga*), it is clear that his thoughts on these matters were exactly relevant to a major theme in American sea fiction after Dana. Near the end of the book, after the crew aboard the *Saori* had successfully captured the great white shark on film, they gathered

> in a cold twilight, drinking rum in the galley-fo'c's'le, [as the *Saori*] rolled downwind across Spencer Gulf, bound for Port Lincoln. Though the sea was rough, the fo'c's'le was warm, and bright, filled with rock

[The boat] pursued the frigate birds, which traced in turn the schools of flying fish, pursued from below by other silent hunters.   —Peter Matthiessen, *Raditzer*

music. Valerie saw to it that the supper was cooked properly, and wine soon banished the slightest doubt that we all liked one another very much. "Is there anything more splendid," Waterman cried, "than the fellowship of good shipmates in the fo'c's'le after a bracing day before the mast?" After three weeks in the fo'c's'le, Stan had embraced the nineteenth century with all his heart. (202–4)

By the time he published *Far Tortuga* in 1975, Matthiessen still had his doubts about a possible "fellowship of good shipmates in the fo'c's'le." The seamen in *Far Tortuga* frequently use the words "brother," "ship-mates," and "friendship," but Matthiessen's very tentative faith in the pos-sibilities of these ideas is suggested by the awful hatred between the half-brothers who are so prominent in the novel, Captain Raib and Captain Desmond. Vemon, the character who first and most frequently uses the word "brother," is one of the least attractive men in the book, a drunken racist; yet Captain Raib, whom Vemon calls his "brother," respects his foolish decision to jump ship and plans, even then, to return for him (379). Although the half-brothers, Raib and Desmond, both use the ex-pression, "Oh, dat sun wild" (these are Raib's last words), Desmond, in his disgusting sexual conduct and his abandonment of their father, is far less than half the man Raib is. And the character Speedy, whose "friendship" another man, Byrum, enjoys, is forced at last to kill this "friend" when his aggressive actions threaten the other survivors in a small boat. Yet, hard as he is when pressed, Speedy is the gentlest of these seamen, as Matthiessen indicates in two scenes when Speedy comforts his two shipmates, Brown and Wodie (321–22, 334).

In the world of half-brothers in *Far Tortuga*, Matthiessen could not affirm the possibility of either an ideal Christian or Marxist brotherhood among his seamen. But he had freed his art of the sense of guilt that had dominated it in his first four novels, as his characters struggled to accept the frightening and disruptive biological reality of their lives. Still, the seamen in *Far Tortuga* are not without consciences. One character espe-cially, Will, struggles poignantly with his constant awareness of the *Ma-jestic* disaster. He and some others had escaped the doomed ship when others had remained aboard her, in loyalty to the captain. Will remembers "de way dem fellas was lookin down at us from de rails of de *Majestic*. . . . Dey looked like children." He "was in friendship" with one of them, in particular, and continues to see him in his "mind's eye," along with the image of another who had waved from the *Majestic*, "like a little boy: I carry dat wave with me to de grave" (222, 246). Will's conscience is en-livened at the exact point of conflict between his need to survive and his need to remain loyal to his shipmates and captain. That he is a central and an exemplary character in *Far Tortuga* is evident very early in the novel when, almost as though Matthiessen intended to dedicate the novel to Will, he reproduces alone, on a single page, the inscription on Will's grave:

SACRED

TO THE MEMORY

OF

WILLIAM PARCHMENT

BORN

16TH DECEMBER 1924

PERISHED

APRIL 1968

ON THE MISKITO BANKS.

It is Matthiessen's testament not only that, in the harsh biological economy of life, the instinct to survive is innocent; but more: that we can be uplifted—perhaps even saved—by those innocent and necessarily short-lived survivors in whom a conscience also lives. There is something promising in Will and the novel's two strongest characters, Captain Raib and Speedy, who honor the larger family of life—from seamen to sea turtles—even as they exist as hardened individual survivors within it. Expert fishermen in life's voracious order, they also recognize their own vulnerability as fellow participants in the same order. They are somehow on speaking terms with their fellow sea creatures, as when Raib "talks softly to [a] wild-eyed fish"; or when his son Buddy "sinks beside [a captured turtle], on his knees," and asks, "You watchin us?"; or when Speedy, the lone survivor, utters the novel's last spoken words: "Don't cry, girl. Swim. Dass very very fine." Nearing shore after nine days in an open boat, he had cut free and released the bound turtle that had been taken into the boat for provisions. Speedy's last gesture arises from his awareness of his relationship with the countless others of all species within the larger struggle for life beneath the sun.

This is the essential view of life toward which Peter Matthiessen's twenty-year voyage as a sea-writer had taken him by 1975. It is embodied in the novel from beginning to end. And in one of the novel's many brilliantly innovative touches, he frequently dramatizes the primordial kinship of these seamen and sea creatures, the hunters and the hunted, by reproducing their shared simple language of "gasps" and "sighs": wondering

*Sea turtles. The mystery and beauty of these primeval
creatures have evoked a sense of wonder in a number of writers from
Hains to Matthiessen, as the whale's had in Melville.*

"what I doin out here on dese reefs, all de days of my life," Raib (*sighs*),"
and he "(*sighs*)" when telling of his dream of retiring to Far Tortuga (225,
331); the netted "turtles thrash and sigh" (204); the "turtles sigh" and "the
men . . . sigh" (252, 211); "Raib turns [a turtle] on its back, [and] it
blinks, gasping its ancient sound," and Raib, telling the men about "*true
sign! Sign of wind!* (*gasps*)" (163, 251).

12

Far Tortuga

A shadow in the eastern distance, under a sunken
sky, like a memory in the ocean emptiness.
   —Peter Matthiessen, *Far Tortuga*

Far Tortuga opens brilliantly, with the penetrating efficiency
of Stephen Crane's famous first sentence in "The Open Boat." Its initial
series of images dramatizes the life-giving, life-shaping ultimate reality in
which its characters will exist and into which they will journey more
deeply. The reader is immediately at sea, cradle of life on earth, as the
earth spins within the solar system. We see the earth rotate into the light
of day, westward from point to point across a seascape of the eastern
Caribbean:

Daybreak.

At Windward Passage, four hundred miles due east, the sun is rising.
Wind east-northeast, thirty-eight knots, with gusts to forty-five: a gale.

Black waves, wind-feathered. White birds, dark birds.

The trade winds freshen at first light, and the sea rises in long ridges,
rolling west.

Sunrise at longitude 76, 19 degrees north latitude.

Sunrise at longitude 77.

Sunrise at the lesser Caymans. . . .

The sun, coming hard around the world: the island [Grand Cayman]
rises from the sea, sinks, rises, holds.

As the three-page dramatic prologue develops, the sun burns, the earth
spins, the wind blows, the sea heaves. And before the first men appear
(then only as "three figures"), the sun touches Grand Cayman from east to

west, finally bringing into view juxtaposed images of human remnants and of elemental life in the timeless sea: "In the graveyard behind the falling church grows oleander and white frangipani. On the ironshore below, incoming seas burst through the black fissures in the rock, and black crabs scutter" (7).

Against this background, Matthiessen projects a simple tale whose stark dimensions lay bare the essential reality he envisions for his characters. Captain Raib Avers, age fifty-four, is the last of the old-time "wind" captains, and his vessel, the *Lillias Eden,* is the last of the old sailing fleet. Already driven to desperation by the natural passing of time and the intensified competition among Caribbean fishermen for the vanishing green turtle, Raib has struggled to keep up with "modern time" by converting the *Eden* to diesel power. Though newly fitted with twin diesel engines, she has retained shortened masts and is still capable of sailing. Now, short of both time and money, and having failed to complete the conversion (notably the job of relocating the wheel to a point from which the helmsman can see to steer), Raib must embark for the turtle grounds late in the season: it is the windy season in an unusually windy year. And the pressure on him is intensified when, nearing the turtle grounds, he learns that Nicaraguan officials will close the turtle fishery next year to Cayman vessels such as his own. Finally, arrived at the mysterious, uncharted Far Tortuga Cay, the *Eden's* last hopes for salvaging the season dissolve when they discover the cay to be overrun by starving Jamaican egg hunters who threaten to overpower the *Eden's* crew. After an ugly, intensely dramatic scene, Raib attempts to escape the Jamaicans by sailing the *Eden* through treacherous reefs at night, only to lose her on the invisible, last "wild rock" that blocked their free passage.

As Matthiessen unfolds his simple plot, he constantly emphasizes the sun's presence: it is the enlivening force, shaping winds and seasons and illuminating a seascape in which the voracious biological drama of life proceeds—as in these fishermen's lives. The image of life feeding on life surfaces everywhere throughout the novel, as, for example, when we see

> bonita crisscross, chasing bait fish; where the bonita chop the surface, the minnows spray into the air in silver showers, all across the sunlit coral. . . . The sprays of baitfish, catching the sun, have drawn the hunting terns, which beat along against the wind, just overhead. Fish and birds chase back and forth across the catboat's bow, the tern shriek lost in the cavernous booming of the reef. (196)

Or, aboard the *Eden,* such imaged dramas as this: "From under the rough slats of the galley side, a cockroach extends its feelers: the feelers twitch, hold still. From under the stove wood the rat watches the big roach"

(280); or, after a crewman has put butchered turtle meat "aside for stew. In the sinking sun, the purple reptile flesh is twitching" (239).

Nature is as sharkish in *Far Tortuga* as it sometimes is in *Moby-Dick*, but without Melville's accompanying sense of devilishness. Moreover, Matthiessen's image of the voracious order in nature emphatically includes his sense of the disturbing yet darkly promising expression of sexual energy. The great green turtles themselves (wonderfully ancient and mysteriously seawise, their watery eyes often fixing on the men, they represent life almost as fully as whales do for Melville) are drawn south to the breeding grounds each April:

> Go to lay dere eggs. De she-turtle haul out on dis long beach, black-lookin sand, y'know, with big seas rollin in, and de he-turtle lay around dere just behind de surf lookin to coot dem as dey come and go. Some dem big old bastard looking to coot so bad dat you can come up alongside and harpoon dem. (80)

This life force is related to the "procreant urge of the world" that Whitman celebrated in "Song of Myself," but in Matthiessen's view, the innocence of regeneration is shaded with frightful, blind violence: "Fall in de water, mon, you in bad trouble. You gets grinded." And Matthiessen is careful here to include the human community: "Dose he-turtle, dey like Athens [one of the *Eden*'s crew] dat way—day coot *anything!*" (81). The image of man's participation in the primitive reality of violent and competitive sexual expression is prominent in *Far Tortuga*, most disturbingly when a fisherman from another boat is shown copulating with a pregnant girl on a sandy beach. He has wounded and driven away another man: "Because of her big belly, the man has mounted her from behind; except for his street hat and a pair of ragged shorts hung on one ankle, he is naked. A knife glints by his hand. His ear is pressed to the girl's back, as if he were listening for the life in her" (162). Elsewhere, Brown, another crewman often seen crooning off-key love songs to himself, brags to the others of having committed necrophilia. Disturbing as such images are, they have their undeniable place in the harsh yet vital reality Matthiessen portrays. Still, we are allowed to share with Captain Raib, hardened to life as he clearly is, at least a fleeting sense that the sea can cleanse: he is repulsed by the copulating man and pregnant girl on the fouled beach, but his eye finds relief "in the sea, [where] a silver light flips back and forth over a round green leaf of sea grape. The playing fish arcs out of the water, flashing its silver side, its eye a bright black spot": "Raib stands transfixed" (163).

Matthiessen's sense of reality and man's place in it is harsher than that envisioned by Stephen Crane from his open boat late in the last century, when he felt nature's answer to his pleas as only "a high cold star on a winter's night." Yet Matthiessen's fisherman captain, having drifted nearly a full dark century into time, has a steadier grasp, a more primal and physical sense of his place in nature than did Crane's hero, as we see when Raib takes his bearings on the stars: "The ship shudders under jolt and buffet of night seas. In the bow, legs spread, Raib keeps his balance, taking bearings on the stars" (79). Repeatedly imaging Raib against the sky, sun, and stars, Matthiessen uses a technique like Edwin Arlington Robinson's in "Man Against the Sky" (1916), but the reality he projects for man is at once darker and more vital than Robinson's. Matthiessen's man has survived the haunting "chaos" and "glare" of World War I that colored Robinson's image of man; but the succeeding half-century has stripped him of human pretense, reduced him to the elemental existence of mere man in nature, and, paradoxically, cleansed him, freed him completely of Robinson's debilitating sense of man as "the last god going home / Unto his last desire." Raib is earthbound, but he has a simple dignity, and he is at home in raw elemental nature, drawing his strength to survive from the sea that finally claims him.

The portrait of Captain Raib is, in fact, the center around which *Far Tortuga* coheres. The novel's full range (and Raib's course—his simple story of survival, struggle, and death) can be charted in three essential images of the captain: (1) as he first appears, from his crew's sea-level point of view in a catboat alongside the *Lillias Eden*: "On the blue morning sky above, a heavy-headed man lays big hands on the rails"; (2) as he is caught midway through the voyage: "The *Eden* is broadside to the seas . . . riding heavily, and Raib's figure, high in the rigging, is black on the veering sun"; and (3) as he is imaged in his final crisis, guiding the *Eden* across the treacherous reefs of Far Tortuga at night: "Black clouds rush past the mast; the sail is ghostly. On the crosstrees, the Captain flings his free arm wide, exalted . . . WE IN DE CLEAR!" And then "the ship strikes" (19, 180, 366–67). As these images suggest, the voyage in *Far Tortuga* is chiefly Captain Raib's. In structuring his novel around the image of Raib against the sky or sun, Matthiessen demonstrates what is perhaps his greatest stylistic contribution to the tradition of American sea fiction: not only has he pursued the traditional questions in a twentieth-century setting, but he has created, through his use of the image and his portraiture of Captain Raib, a medium for telling his tale in which the traditional elements are simultaneously infused.[1] The traditional mode of the sea journey to knowledge; the tradition's emphasis on authentically presenting the everyday reality of sea experience, including the technical matters of seamanship (as Cooper had hoped to present "truer pictures" of the nautical experience in *The Pilot* than Scott managed to do in *The Pirate*); and the tradition's emphasis (after Dana) on portraying the reality of the common sailor's experience, while at the same time assessing the captain's capacity to exercise his authority with wisdom and humanity—all of these are reflected in Matthiessen's imagery of Raib against the sky, engaged in his seaman's work, his simple struggle to survive. In this way Matthiessen can crystallize his full sense of Raib's reality as an individual seaman immersed in his life's work and as a representative man in the sea of life.

The initial image of Raib as a "heavy-headed man" on the "blue morning sky" suggests that this voyage will follow the traditional course, in search of knowledge as well as green turtle. And from the outset, the book's structure emphasizes the quest motif. Repeatedly, for example, Captain Raib tells old sea stories designed to teach his inexperienced crew about the "bleak ocean"; and Matthiessen frequently dramatizes the men's efforts to know about their condition by recording their attempts to read both natural and supernatural signs, ranging from Raib's belief that a horizontally shooting star "is *true* sign! Sign of *wind*!: to the mystic Wodie's ability (he is the crew's "Jonah") to receive and interpret "sign," sometimes verifiably. But the book's structure as a quest for knowledge is most emphatically indicated by Raib's repeated awareness of the *fallibility* of sea knowledge and experience. He often complains that some men "can't learn nothin from the sea," but he is also painfully aware that his own knowledge is incomplete, as when he confides to Speedy, "Dis mornin sea tryin to tell me something, Speedy. It so *old*, mon. Make me wonder what I doing way out here on dese reefs, all de days of my life" (255). And he is often painfully aware that even the very best and most honored of the old sea captains could lose his "sea wits" (117).

The ironic lesson of the *Eden's* last voyage is that knowledge gained from experience is crucial for anyone who would survive on the "bleak ocean" but that, ultimately, it is also useless. Matthiessen conveys this sense in his epigraph from *Everyman*, "Death, Thou comest / When I had thee least in mind," and he emphasizes it by organizing *Far Tortuga* around the telling of its crucial story within the story, Will Parchment's tale of how he survived the sinking of the *Majestic*. Captain Steadman of the *Majestic* was and continues in legend to be the turtle fishery's most experienced and respected captain, and throughout the first half of *Far Tortuga* Will and Captain Raib speak of him frequently. Despite the many references to Steadman and the *Majestic*, however, the tale goes untold, creating a good deal of suspense, until finally, three-fifths of the way into the novel, Will tells the full long story. Its point—how Captain Steadman lost his "sea wits"—can serve only to undermine Raib's efforts to demand his crew's respect for his own considerable experience and knowledge of the sea. Yet Raib insists that the story be told. He must teach the men to respect his experience and seamanship even as he is aware—and makes clear to them—that his own sea sense is fallible. From the outset of *Far Tortuga*

Raib is "heavy-headed" with the knowledge that comes only at last to Everyman, that finally even our knowledge will abandon us.

Raib's story-lessons prepare for the tale of the *Majestic,* and the telling of that story prepares for the ending of *Far Tortuga.* One of his first lessons to the inexperienced crew is that, on watch

> you gots de men's life in your hands. . . . Dis here a empty part of the bleak ocean . . . and dis vessel ain't got no runnin lights and all like dat to let [passing freighters] know dat fools is comin at'm out de dark, you hear me now? . . . You fellas best listen. . . . I gone tell you a old-fashioned story about standin watch. (50)

The story tells of a sailor who fell asleep on watch and lost control of the ship so that the bow was drawn under: "And one of the crew was washed over de side, and drownded. Got a mouthful of sand, as de old people say. . . . A mouthful of sand" (51). The erring seaman's punishment was brutal, but under the circumstances, just: he was made to stand a forty-eight-hour watch, while being constantly beaten with a rope. It is a hard, vital lesson, rousingly told in one of Raib's fine moments. But the captain has a finer moment when, in teaching another lesson, he reveals his painful awareness that his own teachings are fallible. His initial point in this scene is well taken—that experienced seamen "don't sleep very much after bad weather sets down," but it leads to a disagreement with Byrum, who, resisting Raib's authority, brings to the surface the old conflict between sea captains and seamen: "Time is changin, mon," Byrum complains, "Dese days we got unions and all of dat. A man got rights" (225). Raib responds, after a long silence:

> You hear dat rushin out dere, Byrum? De wind and de sea comin to-gether? Dat de sound of *hell,* boy, dat de sound of *hell!* You way out on de edge, boy, you out on de edge of de world. No mon! Ain't no unions on de turtle banks, I tellin you dat! Ain't no rights out here! Ain't nothin out here but de reefs and de wind and de sea, and de mon who know de bleak ocean de best has got to be de coptin, and de men don't listen to de coptin, dey stand a very good chance of losing dere lifes! (226)

But immediately, recalling the story of Captain Steadman and the *Majestic,* "Raib gives an unwilling whimper, [and] begins to laugh":

> Course Copm Steadman Bodden dere, he were an exception to de case. He told dem men dat were abondonin de *Majestic* dat dey had no business tellin him how to do de job . . . bein dat he had fifty-four years of sea experience! . . . And just de day before, dem dat were drowned was

settin dere just like you fellas, just settin dere thinkin about dere belly
and scrotchin dere balls. Never had no idea at all what was comin down
on dem. No idea at all. (226)

(How concisely Raib's remark expresses his grasp of the way man's biological urges—to eat and to reproduce—dominate his powers to know.) And
the scene ends with an image of Raib that reveals the depth of conflict
within him: "Raib laughs for a long time, staring outboard. The two men
watch him wipe the tears out of his eyes."

When, at Raib's insistence, Will finally tells the full story of Captain
Steadman and the *Majestic,* we see that the circumstances were intensely
complicated. Nineteen men violated Steadman's orders and abandoned
the *Majestic*; they survived and the others were lost, but their survival de-
pended as much on chance as on their decision to violate the captain's
authority. Mysteriously, the wind had died down long enough for them to
row ashore, and a sea caught the two boats, throwing them up into the
middle of the cay. (Similar accidental circumstances accounted for the
correspondent's survival and the oiler's death in "The Open Boat.") Still,
following Steadman's orders, twenty-two men remained aboard the *Majestic* and went down with her. Hushed, Raib and the men had listened
intently to Will's story, Raib, particularly, who "sits expressionless, eyes
closed." And finally, in response to a crewman's remark that the *Majestic's*
entire crew might have survived had they all stayed to help Steadman try
to save her, "Raib opens his eyes to study Will's expression." Again, the
scene closes with Raib's grim laughter, revealing his pained ironic sense
that although authority such as his must be based on sea experience, it is
frighteningly fallible: "Nemmine, Will. (*in a different voice*) Yah, mon!
(*laughs*) Copm Steadman told dem men dat mornin dat he had fifty-four
years of sea experience. And by noon he had a sea experience dat were not
much use to him, cause he were dead" (250).

Ultimately, the *Eden's* loss will result far less from errors in Raib's captainship or flaws in his character than from unfortunate circumstances. He
does not exhibit the pride or madness of Ahab. He bears no crippling
wound—sexual, psychological, or spiritual—from life (or the whale): he
has no monstrous quarrel with God or the ambiguity of life. Rather, he has
embraced life with the vitality suggested by his having fathered eighteen
children. He is an "everyman" captain driven onto the rocks of circumstance by the Darwinian biological reality that has sustained him; by the
cutting winds that blow constantly through the novel, filling him with the
haunting sense that "dis goddom wind is blowin my life away!" (202); by
the forces of "progress"; by time—the wild sun itself.

No sea captain in American literature (and certainly none in British literature) is as fully and simply a mere man as Raib, whom we see at work aboard the *Eden* in his "bare feet," who "appears in yellowed undershirt, scratching his crotch," whose past is possibly tainted with stories of gun-running and arson, and who can tell his crew of the "first time I ever got de clap. . . . Well, dass where I done it, right dere on top of de ground dere by dat hut" (21, 90, 316). Nor do fictional sea captains often exhibit the gentleness Raib is capable of at times, as in his relationships with his father and son (both of whom are aboard the *Eden*),[2] or as we see him at work baiting hooks with flying fish that have come aboard the *Eden* and died during the night:

> His thick hard lumpy fisherman's hands move gently, and though it is dead, he talks softly to the wild-eyed fish as if to calm it.
>   Fly too high, darlin, You fly too high.
> He laughs his deep accumulating laugh, and his broad back quakes beneath the weathered shirt. (91)

Traditionally, the sea captain does not dirty his hands in ordinary labor; he is far more civilized than Raib, far more blessed with the mystique of authority and officialdom or the "god-like" stature of Ahab. The remarkable truth about Raib is that despite his often disappointing, merely human, and even gross qualities, he is nevertheless an admirable sea captain with his own strength and dignity—in a tradition that often portrays the captain as crazed with authority. Even though his men sometimes call him "crazy," as Byrum does in the final crisis, Raib constantly demonstrates his competence as a real sea captain. And he is as little crazed by authority as is perhaps imaginable, particularly among sea captains in American fiction. A man among men in the confining circumstances of life under pressure aboard the small *Eden,* Raib is at times understandably irritable, as the men are. No writer has so forcefully dramatized this simple reality of ordinary seamen's lives: the crew's irritability not only with the captain but with themselves. They are oppressed less by brute authority as it is traditionally imagined in sea fiction than by themselves, by their own bad luck (they fish for shares), and by their own inherent aggression as individual creatures in the biological struggle of life. They argue not only about history or communism or their tastes in music but about the space they inhabit together, their racial differences, their possessions, food, and sex.

In this world of elemental men in conflict with themselves and with the other elemental forces of life, Raib's authority has a natural basis: 'De mon who knows de bleak ocean de best has got to be de coptin" (226). And he demonstrates his full natural right to the captainship when, perched barefoot in the crosstrees, he spots four porpoise playing in the *Eden's* bow wake. He "skins down the rigging," runs to the bow, rigs a pole as a harmless harpoon, "and practices harpoon throws at the porpoise":

> The creatures return to be tagged over and over. One glides a moment on its side; its eye regards the playing man.
>
> Raib stops short, smiling: he does not throw.
>
> The creatures go.
>
> Coiling the line, Raib confronts the empty sea; he blinks as if awakening. (98)[3]

Then, walking to the stern, where the men have watched, he remarks, "By God, I still pretty handy with de harpoon . . . pretty good for an old fella!" When a crewman replies, "You de best man aboard *dis* ship, ain't dat right, Copm?" Raib's laughing response is, as he says, "fair": "I is de best mon on dis ship . . . de best, and de quickest, and den de strongest, and den also de smartest, bein I know so much about green turtle and pilotin and de way of de sea!" (99). To this, Byrum sighs, but the others seem to assent, and the scene closes with the crew's remarks degenerating into a dispute over their own individual claims to seamanship, the drunken Vemon claiming respect by virtue of his seaman's papers.

In addition to what Captain Raib demonstrates of his seamanship and knowledge of the "bleak ocean," including the fallibility of even the best men's sea wits, he learns yet another vital lesson from this humble crew on his last voyage into modern time—the idea introduced by the survivor, Speedy: "Keep people down too much, you got to have trouble. Modern time, mon" (320). This is the hardest lesson for any sea captain. But in one of his finest moments, Raib applies it. The *Eden* has had to put in at Nicaragua on its way to the turtle grounds to register with the officials who govern the fishery. Now, having registered, Raib confronts the drunk crewman Vemon, who is about to jump ship:

> Let's go den, darlin, cause we sailin.
>
> You never treats me with respect! A mon gots to have *respect!* Dass why I stayin, Copm Raib!
>
> You a turtler or ain't you! I ain't goin to shanghai you.
>
> I got *papers*, Copm Raib! You show me no respect for dat—dass why I stayin!

Raib contemplates him for so long that Vemon nervously salutes again. Then he extends his hand, which Vemon stares at.

*[Raib's] thick hard lumpy fisherman's hands move
gently, and though it is dead, he talks softly to
the wild-eyed fish as if to calm it.*
                    —Peter Matthiessen, *Far Tortuga*

> Stay den, mon. You gettin de respect you wants: I respectin your deci-
> sion. And I wish you all de luck of it. (324–25)

Clearly, this lesson costs Raib a great deal, for the *Eden* is already danger-
ously undermanned. And Vemon has served him long and loyally. Raib
seems aged and diminished, but he is a greater captain: "Walking away,
lugging his documents, Raib limps a little in his shoes. On the long pier,
he looks small" (325). This is a crucial image of Raib. Willingly burdened
with the documents and dress of civilization (elsewhere throughout the
novel we see him only in his bare feet), he is Matthiessen's way of resolving
the traditional conflict between the authoritative captain and his men.
Without relinquishing his natural authority, Raib earns the dignity that
comes with humility—the old Christian value introduced into the democratic tradition of American sea fiction by Dana and Melville in their decisions to sail before the mast as common seamen.

Far Tortuga is in many ways a traditional voyage to knowledge, but
the knowledge it attains is distinguishable from the traditional knowledge
that is embodied in our literature as a whole. In it, as in *Moby-Dick,* light
and dark contend. But whereas the *Pequod*'s voyage begins in the symbolic
darkness of December and ends in an affirmation of democratic brotherhood and the Christian mystery, *Far Tortuga*'s voyage begins in the full
natural light of April and ends with the sun having "come hard around the
world" again. Its darkness evokes neither the doubt nor the evil that tormented Melville. Rather, its darkness is the natural "chaotic rush of the
dark universe," the darkness that makes the men "avoid looking out to
sea" from aboard the *Eden* at night (223); or that makes it dangerous to
sail at night—the natural reality that keeps the last "wild rock" from view.
And if the *Eden*'s April voyage suggests that *Far Tortuga* is a kind of cruel
April tragedy, it is much more; for a single crewman survives into May,
undefeated even by Matthiessen's Waste Land image of a man-threatened,
depleted sea. Raib's death recalls the Christ story, but the suggestion is
fleeting and certainly unobtrusive, as though the story of the Passion is for
Matthiessen like the image of Far Tortuga Cay itself, but "a shadow in the
eastern distance, under a sunken sky, like a memory in the ocean emptiness" (336). When the *Eden* strikes the rock, the captain's descent from
the crosstrees (where a moment before he had clung "exalted") breaks his
back, but before he is taken into the sea, the sun has come hard around
the world again, and we see that Raib maintains his full awareness of
where he is: "Raib looks straight up at the sun. Tears glisten in his eyes,"
and he utters his last words, "Oh, dat sun wild. Oh, dat sun wild" (379).

This is a natural end of a man who recognizes the source and character of life on earth; and within the tradition of American sea fiction it

stands in stark contrast to Ahab's final moment when, madly pursuing Moby-Dick, he cries, "I turn my body from the sun" (468). To Raib's suffering, Matthiessen cannot respond as Melville had to the death of his ideal democratic seaman, Bulkington, in "The Lee Shore": "Is all this agony in vain? Take heart, take heart, O Bulkington! Bear thee grimly, demigod! Up from the spray of thy ocean-perishing—straight up, leaps thy apotheosis!" (98). Nor does Matthiessen surround his hero with the aura of gentle, saintly suffering that dominates Hemingway's portrait of Santiago in *The Old Man and the Sea*. Raib is capable of gentleness and dignity, and he feels strongly the mystery of life, but these qualities save him only to the extent that they contribute to his stature as a memorable real man. Raib's loss is powerfully felt. But the story of his voyage ends with a natural sense of consolation that Matthiessen retrieves from the seascape itself: "The sun [has come] hard around the world" again, illuminating the "old morning sea," and the novel's last words present the image of "a figure alongshore, and white birds towarding" (without a period). Matthiessen does not reveal whether this figure is Speedy; but Speedy's last gesture of releasing the turtle back into the "old morning sea" and the novel's lovely last word offer a prospect of renewal. In concluding this voyage into "modern time" with the suggestion that man might retain a place in the ambiguous continuity of life on earth, Matthiessen has willed a belief that is far more tentative than that to which Ishmael had clung at the end of *Moby-Dick*. For when the sea birds "flew screaming over the yet yawning gulf" of the sinking *Pequod*, and the "sullen white surf beat against" her sides, still "the great shroud of the sea rolled on as it rolled five thousand years ago" at the time of the Flood. Older by literally millions upon millions of years, Matthiessen's is a "bleak ocean"; yet he will envision it as the "old morning sea."

Like the greatest works of art in any tradition, *Far Tortuga* feeds on and yet renews its heritage, the still vital tradition of American sea fiction. In its constant sensitivity to all elements of the seascape—the light and dark, sun and stars, the green and often wind-whitened water—and especially in its sensitivity to the teeming life in, on, and above the water—it is more purely a *sea* novel than any in our literature.[4] Its vision of life on earth and man's place in it is reflected everywhere in such images as that of Raib "in silhouette against the sun . . . wind curling the frayed edges of his hat" (165); in the many images of life feeding on life; in Raib's remark about the *Majestic*'s men "settin dere thinkin about dere belly and scrotchin dere balls," completely unaware of their fate; or, perhaps most profoundly, in Raib's exchanged glance with the porpoise. And the image of Raib himself—a contemporary representative man at sea, barefoot, gross, unquestionably real, experienced at sea, heavy-headed with an awareness of his own fallibility and final helplessness under the wild sun—this *man* is at the center of it all, reclaiming for us and an old tradition the sense that, still, it is to the timeless sea that we might turn, with Ishmael, to pursue the "ungraspable phantom of life."

Herman Melville.
Painting by Joseph Oriel Eaton Courtesy of the Harvard University Portrait Collection (gift to Houghton Library by Mrs. Henry K. Metcalf).

Arthur Mason.
From the New York Herald Tribune, Books, *29 January 1933.*

Bill Adams.
From the New York Herald Tribune, *11 April 1937.*

Felix Reisenberg.
From the Saturday Review of Literature, *2 December 1939.*

Dirigo, *the ship aboard which Jack London and Charmian London rounded Cape Horn on their voyage from Baltimore to Seattle in 1912–13. London based* The Mutiny of the Elsinore *on this experience. Courtesy of the Huntington Library, San Marino, California.*

Jack London, aboard his Roamer, *1910.*
Courtesy of the Huntington Library,
San Marino, California.

Stephen Crane
aboard the Three Friends, *1898.*
Courtesy of Yale Collection of American
Literature, Beinecke Library, Yale University.

Morgan Robertson.
From Morgan Robertson the Man.

Thornton Jenkins Hains.
From Bookman, *July 1900.*

The steel barque Juteopolis, *aboard which Hallet sailed from New York to Sydney, Australia, in 1912. He based* The Lady Aft *on this experience. Photograph by Richard Matthews Hallet, courtesy of Mrs. Nancy Hallet Woods.*

Richard Matthews Hallet, 1914.
Courtesy of
Mrs. Nancy Hallet Woods.

Lincoln Colcord.
Courtesy of Donald F. Mortland.

James Brendan Connolly.
From The World's Work, 9: 1905.

William McFee.
From the Saturday Review of
Literature, *24 August 1935.*

*Archie Binns at the wheel of his boat on the Columbia
River. Courtesy of Ellen F. (Mrs. Archie) Binns.*

Archie Binns.
Courtesy of
Ellen F. (Mrs. Archie) Binns.

Ernest Hemingway.
Karsh/Woodfin Camp.

Peter Matthiessen.
Barbara Hall Photographs.

Notes

Chapter 1

1. Thomas Philbrick in his Introduction to *Two Years Before the Mast* (1981); here, far more strongly than in his earlier book on Cooper's sea fiction (1961), Philbrick emphasizes Dana's influence on American sea fiction.

2. See W. H. Auden's remarks that, in the literature of Western culture, the sea's timeless appeal is based in "cosmology"—the idea in Genesis that "the Spirit of God moved upon the face of the waters" or the idea "in one of the Greek cosmologies" that everything began when "Eros issued from the egg of Night which floated upon chaos." Tracing this idea from ancient cosmologies through Shakespeare's late plays, Auden describes how the revolutionary change in sensibility that came about during the romantic period is observable in the "treatment of a simple theme, the sea." Perceived as "the symbol of primitive potential power," the sea, according to the romantic attitude, is "the real situation and the voyage is the true condition of man" (Auden 7, 20, 13).

3. Even here, in describing the tradition of "sea-brothers," working seamen who based their fiction on their direct experience with the sea, I cannot deal with the extensive volume of American fiction by other writers in which the sea is of central importance. The list of authors and titles—for example, work by Frank Norris, Joseph C. Lincoln, Ralph D. Paine, Conrad Aiken, Wilbur Daniel Steele, Gore Vidal, James Gould Cozzens, Charles Nordhoff, James Hall, John Barth, and others—would fill a book. Similarly, one could compile an endless list of nonfiction prose and poetry of the sea, including Joshua Slocum's *Sailing Alone Around the World*, John Steinbeck's *The Log of the Sea of Cortez*, Robert Cushman Murphy's *Logbook for Grace*, William Beebe's *Galapagos, World's End*, and volumes of poetry by Walt Whitman, Robinson Jeffers, Charles Olson, T. S. Eliot, and many others. Such lists of American sea fiction and poetry could not begin to measure the sea's remarkable influence on American writers, as in the extensive use of figurative language based on sea imagery and maritime experience in the work of Henry David Thoreau (see Bonner and Springer in the Bibliography), Emily Dickinson, Henry James, and others. The most complete listings of American sea fiction are those in Charles Lee Lewis's *Books of the Sea* and Myron J. Smith, Jr., and Robert C. Weller's *Sea Fiction Guide*.

4. This brief description of American values and qualities is shaped in part by Tony Tanner's *The Reign of Wonder* (11–12); Richard Poirier's *A World Elsewhere* (in describing the American writer's tendency to build "a world elsewhere" with language, Poirier refers to William James's phrase about "inner authority" [14]); and William James's *The Will to Believe*.

5. See also Allan Hunter's recent book *Joseph Conrad and the Ethics of Darwinism*, in which he argues that Conrad's "overall concern is with that favourite problem of the Victorian age after Darwin: where does morality come from? If we have evolved over many millennia, has morality evolved as well?" (6).

6. O'Hanlon emphasizes the parallel between Nordau's sense of degeneration and Conrad's.

7. For Conrad's remarks on Melville, see Parker and Hayford 122–23.

8. For discussions of the "stigmata" of degeneration see Nordau (7–32) and Carlson (127–29).

9. Among those who emphasize the sailor's role, often as an exploited worker, in the American labor movement, are Morgan Robertson, Jack London, Richard Matthews Hallet (particularly in *Trial by Fire*), Eugene O'Neill, and Archie Binns. This is the central theme in B. Traven's *The Death Ship: The Story of an American Sailor* (1934), in which the main character, Pip Pip, an abused able seaman, comments extensively on American sea life and literature from an explicitly proletarian point of view. For examples of nonliterary treatises on seamen and the union movement, see Goldberg, Taylor, Riesenberg ("Communists"), and the International Seamen's Union of America in the Bibliography.

10. This is not to suggest that Martin's discussion of Melville and *tayo* is the last word on the subject. But it seems essentially compatible with James Baird's earlier and, in my view, more illuminating study of *tayo* in relation to Melville's primitivism. See, for example, Baird's definition and discussion of *tayo* in chapter 6 of *Ishmael*; his remark on how the concept of *tayo*, "the fraternal love of innocent and uncorrupted men," provided Melville with one of the "three elements" he "fused in his total structure of symbols" (the other two elements being "primitive and fecund nature" and his "threadbare Protestant sacrament" [78–79]); and his sense of how "in the Pacific journey Melville was confirmed not in hatred, as some may suppose, but in the art of constructing symbols toward the restoration of belief" (94).

11. Richard Slotkin's discussion of *Moby-Dick* as a Western hunting story is similar to Fussell's (538–50).

12. An excellent discussion of the sea in colonial American literature is available in Donald P. Wharton's Introduction to *In the Trough of the Sea*.

Chapter 2

1. Philbrick's "A Literary Leviatian: Epilogue" (*Cooper*, 260); Santraud 77.

2. Merrell R. Davis's conclusion about Melville's discovery in writing *Mardi* applies similarly to *Moby-Dick*: "Thus in *Mardi*, Melville discovered that the racy retelling of his experience (the "vulgar shoals" on which he had floated [in *Typee*

and Omoo]) was incapable of presenting all that he had to say and of exhibiting his ambitions as an author" (194).

3. For another comment on Melville's lapses in nautical realism, see Heflin.

4. As Jill Gidmark notes in *Melville Sea Dictionary*, "whenever *watery* is joined to a noun as an adjective, the resulting modification is strange and wonderful, giving us Melville's perspective of seeing all things through nautical glasses" (39).

5. Robert Greenberg's recent study of the cetological materials in *Moby-Dick* extends Ward's analysis, which he thinks misrepresents the true "diversity" and "plenitude" of the book (12).

6. See F. O. Matthiessen's remark in reference to a similar passage in "The Tail": "The effect of that burlesque is to magnify rather than to lessen his theme, not to blaspheme Jehovah, but to add majesty to the whale" (431).

Chapter 3

1. His three-week sailing voyage to England on the *Southampton* was a highlight of his life. The third day out he "went up to the masthead, by way of gymnastics"—the last time he would do so. On the fourth day out he saw a man kill himself by going overboard. Melville was "struck by the expression of his face in the water. It was merry." The confused passengers saw him "floating off—saw a few bubbles, & never saw him again." That night, he saw "'corpossant balls' on the yard arms & mast heads. . . . the first [he] had ever seen." There was "a terrific gale," "a regular blue devil day," and later a spell of fine weather during which he "vegetated," "talked metaphysics," and, one evening, "went out on the bowsprit—splendid spectacle." On 25 October, a "fine moonlight night," he recorded how the ship "rushed on thro' snowbanks of foam": "The scene was indescribable. I never saw such sailing before." His return voyage in January marks a significant turning point in his career and in the history of sea literature, for he was then as full of books and plans for his own books as he had been of sailing on the passage out (Leyda 1: 318–22).

2. Quoted by Walter E. Bezanson in "Historical Note," *Israel Potter*, Northwestern-Newberry 227.

3. Ibid., 184, 198.

4. In "Bridegroom Dick" Melville briefly imagined a humane captain of heroic proportions in Captain Turret, who, being "a tall captain," can discipline a titanic "true *sailor-man*" without humiliating him (*Collected Poems*, 177–78).

5. Melville re-created this scene in his description of the Pilgrim Nehemiah's burial in *Clarel*, II, xxxix.

Chapter 5

1. Having looked up the weather records for January 1897, this critic, Cyrus Day, argued that, since the wind was blowing *only* "nineteen to twenty-four miles an hour" (which would have been "comparatively harmless, even to men in a ten-foot dinghy"), Crane's account is unreliable (Day 201).

Chapter 6

1. Important scholarly works on London since 1966 include those by Franklin Walker, Earle Labor, James I. McClintock, Andrew Sinclair, Joan D. Hedrick, and Charles N. Watson, Jr., as listed in the Bibliography.

2. Franklin Walker theorizes that London made the last leg of his journey from San Francisco to Dyea, Alaska, in an Indian canoe (52).

3. For complete bibliographical information see the volumes by Walker and Woodbridge.

4. Labor 95. For a discussion of the influence of Melville, Shakespeare, and Milton on *The Sea-Wolf*, see Watson 53–78.

5. Similarly, no sea writer in the 1970s or 1980s could see what Hemingway saw in 1935 in his rhapsody of the garbage scows off Havana: "The stream . . . takes five loads . . . a day . . . and in ten miles along the coast it is as clear and blue and unimpressed as it was ever before the tug hauled out the scow; and the palm fronds of our victories, the worn light bulbs of our discoveries and the empty condoms of our great loves float with no significance against the one single, lasting thing—the stream" (*Green Hills*, 148–50).

6. This sea burial is based on London's experience aboard the *Sophia Sutherland*, when the "bricklayer" was buried at sea. The extent to which London was affected by the scene is clear from his having re-created it in his story "That Dead Men Rise Up Never" and from the emphasis he gives it in his notes for the projected novel, "The Mercy of the Sea" (TS notes numbered 941 in London Collection, Henry E. Huntington Library, San Marino, California).

7. See also London's description of Wolf's wateriness and his power to survive when he climbs back aboard the *Ghost* after having been knocked overboard in the attempted mutiny: "A sinewy hand, dripping with water, was clutching the rail. A second hand took form in the darkness beside it. . . . I saw a head, the hair wet and straight, shape itself, and then the unmistakable eyes and face of Wolf Larsen. . . . The seawater was streaming from him. It made little audible gurgles that distracted me" (93).

8. In his essay on *Two Years Before the Mast*, "A Classic of the Sea," in *The Human Drift* (102). London's remarks on Dana in this essay provide a clear view of his own understanding of the sea. Whereas D. H. Lawrence would credit Dana for "profound mystic vision" (125); London praises Dana for having provided "a document for the future centuries"—"the photograph detail of life before the mast and hide-droghing on the coast of California . . . of the unvarnished, simple psychology and ethics of the forecastle hands who droghed the hides, stood at the wheel, made and took sail, tarred down the rigging, holystoned the decks, turned in allstanding, grumbled as they cut about the kid, [and] criticized the seamanship of their officers" (101, 108).

9. London was not the first to lament the passing of the great sailing ships; Melville did so in *John Marr and Other Sailors*. But he was the first major writer to emphasize the theme that would soon dominate American sea literature, as in O'Neill. See, for example, his remark in "A Classic of the Sea": "The life and conditions described in Dana's book have passed utterly away. Gone are the crack

clippers, the driving captains, the hard-bitten but efficient foremast hands. Remain only crawling cargo tanks, dirty tramps, greyhound liners, and a sombre, sordid type of sailing ship. The only records broken to-day by sailing vessels are those for slowness. They are no longer built for speed, nor are they manned before the mast by as sturdy a sailor stock nor aft are they officered by sail-carrying captains and driving mates" (*Human Drift*, 102–3).

10. The commander of the U.S. brig *Somers* was, of course, Captain Alexander Slidell Mackenzie; Melville's cousin Guert Gansevoort was a lieutenant aboard her.

11. In *Far Tortuga*, Captain Raib's authority as a sea captain is associated with his virility: he has fathered eighteen children.

12. Watson, *The Novels of Jack London*, xiii.

13. London might have known of the famous British torpedo-boat destroyer, HMS *Albatross*, one of the new powerful warships like those that had impressed Stephen Crane. See Crane, *War Dispatches*, 114.

Chapter 7

1. In addition to the ten writers I discuss in this and the following chapter, at least one other deserves mention. John Fleming Wilson (1877–1922) accumulated considerable sea experience in the Pacific Northwest and wrote several successful short stories set in those waters. His most highly regarded work is contained in *Across the Latitudes* (1911) and *Somewhere at Sea and Other Tales* (1923).

2. In *Morgan Robertson the Man*, a collection of memorial pieces by Robertson's friends, the editor thanks the following people for their "hearty and willing commendations [of Robertson] publicly made": Booth Tarkington, Robert W. Chambers, Irwin S. Cobb, George Horace Lorrimer, Richard Harding Davis, Joseph Conrad, Robert H. Davis, Rex Beach, Finley Peter Dunne, Henry Reuterdahl, William Dean Howells, Bozeman Bulger, J. O'Neill, Charles Somerville, John Kendrick Bangs, and Arthur T. Vance.

3. Mrs. J. H. Temple, Jr., in her chapter on Connolly in Williams (102).

4. Connolly, *The Port of Gloucester* 194, 196. "The Trawler" was published originally as a prize-winning story by *Collier's* in 1914, then separately as a short novel in that year, then in the collectin of stories *Head Winds* (1916).

5. Quoted by the editor of *Scholastic* in "Bill Adams," accompanying Adams's story "The Lubber" (5).

Chapter 8

1. Elder 60; McFee's obituary, *New York Times*, 4 July 1966, p. 15.

2. See, for example, his three pieces on Conrad in *Swallowing the Anchor*, "Great Tales of a Great Victorian," "Joseph Conrad in a New Edition," and "Rolling Home."

3. See the bibliography for two recent and very helpful works on Colcord by Donald F. Mortland: an essay, "Lincoln Colcord: At Sea and at Home," and a collection of Colcord's writings, *Sea Stories, from Searsport to Singapore*. *Sea Stories* contains two autobiographical pieces about Colcord's boyhood at sea that are particularly memorable, "I Was Born in a Storm at Sea," and "The Bogie Hole."

4. In its entry on Colcord, *The Reader's Encyclopedia of American Literature* supplies this information on *Kicked Out of the Cradle*, but I have been unable to locate a book by that title.

5. In "Rescue at Sea" Colcord also develops a favorite theme that underlies many of his sea stories and that he expressed most explicitly in "American Gallantry at Sea" (1929): that "whenever the opportunity arises, American seamanship still stands ready to seize it, and that the American genius is as clearly in evidence on the sea today, as when our clipper ships brought home the prize of world commerce and oceanic supremacy. It is certainly cheerful news that the ancient traditions of the sea, as strong a heritage of honor as the human race possesses, do not seem to have decayed as industrialism strengthens its hold on our shipping" (157). He commented in this piece on "the remarkable feat of the steamship *America* in picking up the sinking Italian steamer *Florida*, after receiving signals which placed her one hundred and fifty miles from" her actual position (156).

6. Hallet uses the expression "the heavy workers of the world" in his sea story, based on his experience on the *Orvieto*, "The Quest of London" (708).

7. In an excellent biographical and bibliographical essay on Hallet in 1967, Richard Cary noted that "the confrontation of Cagey, the anthropoidal stoker, and Avis Wrenn, an heiress, presages that of Yank and Mildred Douglas in Eugene O'Neill's *The Hairy Ape*, produced six years later" (427); but neither Cary nor any other critic has examined the extensive similarities between the novel and the play.

8. In "The Best Fifty Short Stories of 1916" (563).

9. Two other books by Binns are of interest for his handling of the maritime experience in the Pacific Northwest: *You Rolling River* (1947), a novel set in the Astoria area of the lower Columbia River, and *Sea in the Forest* (1953), nonfiction about the Puget Sound area.

Chapter 9

1. Thoreau quoting Mencius (Meng-Tse): "That in which men differ from brute beasts . . . is a thing very inconsiderable; the common herd lose it very soon; superior men preserve it carefully" ("Higher Laws," *Walden*, 146).

2. Despite Hemingway's claim that he could not "tell" about Thoreau because he had not read him, his complaint about naturalist writing that is shaped by "economic-religion" seems aimed at Thoreau's crucial chapters, "Economy," and "Higher Laws," in which he asserts that "Chastity is the flowering of man; and what are called Genius, Heroism, Holiness, and the like, are but various fruits which succeed it." The idea that chastity could engender heroism seems to have especially galled Hemingway, for his most emphasized complaint about writers like

Thoreau is that "no woman could love . . . them long enough so that they could kill their lonesomeness in that woman, or pool it with hers, or make something with her that makes the rest unimportant" (*Green Hills*, 21–22).

3. West 12. West's essay focuses on Frederick's remark in *A Farewell to Arms*, "you always feel trapped biologically."

4. As Baker notes, "In biology class [in 1914] he made a minor triumph with a six-page paper on the anatomy of grasshoppers, without once mentioning that he had been using them for years as trout bait. The paper was graded 90 and marked 'very good'" (*Life Story*, 18).

5. Hemingway's fascination with the Gulf Stream is also an outgrowth of his boyhood experiences on the Des Plaines and Rapid rivers. After a night's fishing on the Rapid in 1916, he recorded the thrill of "fighting them in the dark in the deep swift river" (Baker, *Life Story*, 24).

6. The story, dated 17 April 1911, is printed in Baker's *Life Story* (12): "I was born in a little white house on the Island of Marthas Vineyard in the State of Massachuset. My mother died when I was four years old and my father, the captain of the three masted schooner 'Elizabeth' took me and my little brother around the 'Horn' with him to Australia.

"Going we had fine weather and we would see the porpoises playing around the ship and the big white albatross winging its way across the ocean or following the brig for scraps of food; the sailors caught one on a huge hook baited with a biscuit but they let him go as soon as they had caught him for they are very superstitious about those big birds.

"One time the sailors went out on a barrel fastened on the bow sprit and speared a porpoise (or sea pig as they call them) and hauled him up on deck and cut out the liver and we had it fried for supper it tasted like pork only it was greesier. We arrived in Sydney Australia after a fine vouge and had just as good a vouge going back."

7. The image of the jumping marlin appears often in Hemingway's work, for example, in "Out in the Stream" (19), "On the Blue Water" (185), and repeatedly in *The Old Man and the Sea*.

Chapter 10

1. It is clear that Hemingway had Melville strongly in mind during the years when he was at work on his sea book; see, for example, his references to Melville and *Moby-Dick* in letters to Charles Scribner in 1949 and Bernard Berenson in 1952 (*Letters*, 673, 780).

2. He had already published the first two Harry Morgan stories and was devising a suitable structure for the novel they would become.

3. Many interpreters have concluded that Harry's famous last words about a man alone having no chance are the book's key meaning and then, in some cases, complain that the novel is not artfully unified around this idea. But the question seems wisely answered in Scott Donaldson's remarks that "to conclude with left-wingers of the 1930s that Harry Morgan's last words signalled Hemingway's political

change of heart would be to distort everything that the novel has to say. If one man alone doesn't have a chance, neither do two men in the *Queen Conch*" (110); nor, we might add, do the four Cuban revolutionaries Harry kills.

4. Although the character Albert remarks that Harry "never had no pity for nobody" (98), Hemingway took care to emphasize Harry's sympathy for the "Conches" who work for him. Of Albert, Harry thinks, "That poor bloody Albert. Christ, he looked hungrier than ever down at the dock" (148). Of the drunk Eddy, he says, "You know you had to feel sorry for him. He certainly looked bad" (62). And of Wesley, Hemingway tells us that "the man [Harry] was still sorry for him" and that Harry speaks "kindly" to him (69, 73). It seems a mistake, however, to elevate Harry to the status of a tragic hero or to attribute to him such high motives as the "desire for justice," as Gerry Brenner does in his discussion of the novel: "Because Harry mentions his former employment as a policeman," it is his "desire for justice" that drives him to kill the Chinese character Sing (14).

5. "When Joseph Conrad died and Ford got together a special Conrad supplement for the *Transatlantic,* Ernest went out of his way to remark in print that if he could bring Conrad back to life 'by grinding Mr. Eliot into a fine dry powder and sprinkling that powder over Conrad's grave in Canterbury,' he would 'leave for London early tomorrow morning with a sausage grinder'" (Baker, *Life Story,* 135).

6. In his chapter on *Islands in the Stream,* Carlos Baker explains how Hudson's "rehabilitation" comes about through the "renewal of contact with the sanative sea"; but this comes, as he imagines, not through loss, suffering, and acceptance but "through his pride in the sea-command" (*Artist,* 408, 393).

7. Similarly, the shark that later threatens David (chap. 7) has come in on the tide.

8. As Edmund Wilson complained, "In 'Islands in the Stream,'" the troubling experiences in Hudson's past "have been pushed down out of sight"; and though they "are continually rising into [his] consciousness . . . we [are not] told exactly what they are" (quoted in Meyers 577). See also Christopher Ricks's remarks: "Devious and secretive, 'Islands in the Stream' is an elaborate refusal to say what is the matter with Thomas Hudson. . . . There are altogether too many things which could have killed [his] spirit" (in Meyers 542–43).

9. There are three suicides in the novel: Mr. Pascin (74), Roger's girlfriend (156), and the character called "old Suicides" (157–58).

10. Hemingway seems to have been enough of a student of biology to get this fact right. The flamingo group "is very old, and existed as early as the Upper Oligocene, about thirty million years ago, before many other avian orders had yet evolved. The flamingos illustrate a phenomenon often observed in the animal kingdom, namely that old forms are often displaced by younger ones and can only continue to exist if they can adapt to certain conditions" (Grzimek 7:250). Also, as amateur naturalists, Hemingway and Hudson might have been attracted to the birds' relatively nonviolent method of feeding: like the great whales, they filter out the "small swimming crustacea, algae, and unicellular organisms" from the water sucked in through their beaks (248–49).

11. This idea is reinforced throughout the novel by Hudson's ironic remarks about the depressing mechanicalness of life, as at the end of "Bimini," when, try-

ing to cope with the deaths of his sons, he tells himself, "I'll ride on one of those bicycles that goes nowhere and on a mechanical horse" (199).

12. Thomas Hudson sees such "prism" light in the water, but, perhaps because he is a far more civilized and complicated man than Santiago is, it cannot guide him (112).

Chapter 11

1. For a brief discussion of how the motive "to get away" is typical of American writers, see Wright Morris's chapter "The High Seas" in *The Territory Ahead.* Writing about Western man's habit since Ulysses of going to sea "in search of some notion of himself," Morris emphasizes how peculiarly American it is to "go to sea just to get away, to get away from it *all*" (69).

Chapter 12

1. A brief discussion of Matthiessen's use of the image and his creation of what James Dickey has called "our new vision" is contained in George Plimpton's interview with Matthiessen (79–80).

2. Raib's feelings for his father and son are usually hidden beneath his hardbitten exterior, but his gentleness toward them does surface, as in the scenes on pages 52 and 292–93.

3. For a version of a similar scene in Matthiessen's own experience, see *Men's Lives* (116).

4. Like the other great works in its tradition, *Far Tortuga* will always resist our efforts to comprehend it fully in mere essays such as this. I have limited myself here to a discussion of the novel's most significant traditional elements. But much more remains to be said of Captain Raib, for example, who is more complex than I have been able to suggest here, particularly in his relationships with his father, son, and half-brother. Nor have I found an opportunity here to discuss the compelling character Speedy, the music and poetry of the men's speech, Matthiessen's powers as a dramatist, or his acute sensitivity to the political unrest in the Caribbean and Central America.

Bibliography

Adams, Bill. "Calm." *Atlantic Monthly* 148 (1931): 791–94.

———. "Consider the Insect." *Outlook* 141 (Aug. 1925): 691.

———. *Fenceless Meadows.* New York: Stokes, 1923.

———. "The Finger of Evolution." *Outlook* 141 (Dec. 1925): 616.

———. "In the Other Fellow's Shoes." *Outlook* 141 (Nov. 1925): 455–56.

———. "The Lubber." *Scholastic,* 5 Jan. 1935, pp. 4f.

———. "Politics vs. Whales." *Outlook* 140 (June 1925): 200.

———. "Singers of the Sea." *Outlook* 140 (May 1925): 168.

———. "Way for a Sailor." In *Great Sea Stories of All Nations and All Times,* edited by H. M. Tomlinson. Garden City, N.Y.: Garden City Publishing, 1937, pp. 585–605.

———. *Wind in the Topsails.* London: Harrap, 1931.

Adams, Henry. *The Education of Henry Adams.* New York: Modern Library, 1946.

Appleman, Philip. "Darwin: On Changing the Mind." In *Darwin,* edited by Philip Appleman. Norton Critical Edition. New York: Norton, 1979.

Arvin, Newton. *Herman Melville.* New York: Sloane, 1950.

Auden, W. H. *The Enchafèd Flood, Or the Romantic Iconography of the Sea.* New York: Random House, 1950.

"Author Rescued at Sea." *New York Times,* 16 Dec. 1903, p. 1.

Baird, James. *Ishmael: A Study of the Symbolic Mode in Primitivism.* Baltimore: Johns Hopkins University Press, 1956.

Baker, Carlos. *Ernest Hemingway: A Life Story.* New York: Scribner's, 1969.

———. *Hemingway: The Writer as Artist.* 4th ed. Princeton: Princeton University Press, 1972.

Baldwin, Charles C. *The Men Who Make Our Novels.* New York: Dodd, Mead, 1924.

Beale, Thomas. *The Natural History of the Sperm Whale.* 1839. London: Holland Press, 1973.

Beer, Thomas. *Stephen Crane.* Garden City, N.Y.: Garden City Publishing, 1923.

Binns, Archie. *Lightship.* New York: Reynal and Hitchcock, 1934.

———. *Sea in the Forest.* Garden City, N.Y.: Doubleday, 1953.

———. *You Rolling River.* New York: Scribner's, 1947.

Bone, David W. Review of *Lightship* by Archie Binns. *Saturday Review of Literature*, 25 Aug. 1934, pp. 65f.

Bonner, Willard H. *Harp on the Shore: Thoreau and the Sea.* Edited by George R. Levine. Albany: State University of New York Press, 1985.

Brennan, Joseph X. "Stephen Crane and the Limits of Irony." *Criticism* 11 (1969): 183–200.

Brenner, Gerry. *Concealments in Hemingway's Works.* Columbus: Ohio State University Press, 1983.

Carlson, Eric T. "Medicine and Degeneration: Theory and Praxis." In J. Edward Chamberlin and Sander Gilman, eds., *Degeneration: The Dark Side of Progress.* New York: Columbia University Press, 1985, pp. 121–44.

Cary, Richard. *Richard Matthews Hallet: Architect of the Dream.* Special issue of *Colby Library Quarterly* 7.10 (1967): 417–65.

Chamberlin, J. Edward. "Images of Degeneration: Turnings and Transformations." In J. Edward Chamberlin and Sander Gilman, eds., *Degeneration: The Dark Side of Progress.* New York: Columbia University Press, 1985.

Chase, Richard, ed. *Melville: A Collection of Critical Essays.* Englewood Cliffs, N.J.: Prentice-Hall, 1962.

Colcord, Lincoln. "American Gallantry at Sea." *Nation* 128 (Feb. 1929): 156–57.

———. "Are Literary Hoaxes Harmful? A Debate." *Bookman* 69 (1929): 347–51.

———. *The Drifting Diamond.* New York: Macmillan, 1912.

———. *The Game of Life and Death.* New York: Macmillan, 1914.

———. *An Instrument of the Gods and Other Stories of the Sea.* New York: Macmillan, 1922.

———. "Notes on 'Moby Dick.'" 1922. Reprinted in Hershel Parker, ed., *Recognition of Herman Melville: Selected Criticism since 1846.* Ann Arbor: University of Michigan Press, 1967, pp. 174–86.

———. Review of *The Cradle of the Deep* by Joan Lowell. *New York Herald Tribune Books*, 17 Mar. 1929, p. 5.

———. Review of *Lightship* by Archie Binns. *New York Herald Tribune Books*, 2 Sept. 1934, pp. 1–2.

———. Review of *Ships and Women* by Bill Adams. *New York Herald Tribune Books*, 11 Apr. 1937, p. 6.

———. *Vision of War.* New York: Macmillan, 1915.

Connolly, James Brendan. *Head Winds.* New York, Scribner's, 1916.

———. *Out of Gloucester.* New York: Scribner's, 1902.

———. *The Port of Gloucester.* New York: Doubleday, 1946.

Review of *The Cook and the Captain Bold* by Arthur Mason. *New York Times*, 13 Apr. 1924, pp. 19f.

Crane, Stephen. *Stephen Crane: Letters.* Edited by R. W. Stallman and Lillian Gilkes. New York: New York University Press, 1960.

———. *Stephen Crane: Tales of Adventure.* Edited by Fredson Bowers. Charlottesville: University Press of Virginia, 1970. Vol. 5 of *The Works of Stephen Crane.* 10 vols. 1969–76.

———. *The War Dispatches of Stephen Crane.* Edited by R. W. Stallman and E. R. Hagemann. New York: New York University Press, 1964.

———. *Wounds in the Rain: War Stories.* New York: Stokes, 1899.

Darwin, Charles. *The Descent of Man, and Selection in Relation to Sex.* 2d ed. International Science Library. New York: Wheeler, n.d.

———. *The Voyage of the Beagle.* Harvard Classics 29. New York: Collier, 1909.

Davis, Merrell R. *Melville's Mardi: A Chartless Voyage.* New Haven: Yale University Press, 1952.

Day, Cyrus. "Stephen Crane and the Ten-Foot Dinghy." *Boston University Studies in English* 3 (1957): 193–213.

DeFalco, Joseph M. "Hemingway's Islands and Streams: Minor Tactics for Heavy Pressure." In *Hemingway in Our Time,* edited by Richard Astro and Jackson J. Benson. Corvallis: Oregon State University Press, 1974, pp. 39–51.

de Hartog, Jan. *The Call of the Sea.* New York: Atheneum, 1966.

DeMott, Robert J. *Steinbeck's Reading: A Catalogue of Books Owned and Borrowed.* New York: Garland, 1984.

Dewey, John. *A Common Faith.* New Haven: Yale University Press, 1934.

Donaldson, Scott. *By Force of Will: The Life and Art of Ernest Hemingway.* New York: Viking, 1977.

Elder, Arthur J. "William McFee—Engineer and Author." *Bookman* 44 (Sept. 1916): 57–62.

Eliot, T. S. *The Complete Poems and Plays.* New York: Harcourt, n.d.

Review of *Endless River* by Felix Riesenberg. *Boston Transcript* 3 (Oct. 1931): 1.

Feidelson, Charles, Jr. *Symbolism and American Literature.* Chicago: University of Chicago Press, 1953.

Foner, Philip, ed. *Jack London: American Rebel.* New York: Citadel, 1947.

Foster, Elizabeth S. "Melville and Geology." *American Literature* 17 (1945): 50–65.

Franklin, H. Bruce. "The Island Worlds of Darwin and Melville." *Centennial Review* 11 (1967): 353–70.

Freud, Sigmund. *Civilization and Its Discontents.* Translated and edited by James Strachey. New York: Norton, 1961.

Fussell, Edwin. *Frontier: American Literature and the American West.* Princeton: Princeton University Press, 1965.

Gell, Arthur, and Barbara Gell. *O'Neill.* New York: Harper, 1960.

Gerstenberger, Donna. "'The Open Boat': Additional Perspective." *Modern Fiction Studies* 17 (1972): 557–60.

Gidmark, Jill B. *Melville Sea Dictionary.* Westport, Conn.: Greenwood, 1982.

Gilkes, Lillian. *Cora Crane: A Biography of Mrs. Stephen Crane.* Bloomington: Indiana University Press, 1960.

Ginsberg, Allen. *Howl and Other Poems.* San Francisco: City Lights Books, 1956.

Goldberg, Joseph P. *The Maritime Story: A Study in Labor-Management Relations.* Cambridge, Mass.: Harvard University Press, 1958.

Greenberg, Robert M. "Cetology: Center of Multiplicity and Discord in *Moby-Dick.*" *Emerson Society Quarterly* 27 (1981): 1–13.

Grzimek, H. C. Bernhard. *Grzimek's Animal Life Encyclopedia.* 13 vols. New York: Van Nostrand, 1968–75.

Hains, Thornton Jenkins. *The Black Barque.* Boston: L. C. Page, 1905.

———. *The Strife of the Sea.* New York: Baker and Taylor, 1903.

———. *Tales of the South Seas.* Portland, Maine: Brown Thurston, 1894.

———. *The Voyage of the Arrow.* Boston: L. C. Page, 1906.

[———.] Captain Mayn Clew Garnett. *The White Ghost of Disaster: The Chief Mate's Yarn.* New York: Dillingham, 1912.

———. *The Wreck of the Conemaugh.* Philadelphia: Lippincott, 1900.

Hallet, Richard Matthews. *The Lady Aft.* Boston: Small, Maynard, 1915.

———. "The Quest of London." *Everybody's Magazine* 35 (1916): 697–708.

———. *The Rolling World.* Boston: Houghton Mifflin, 1938.

———. *Trial by Fire.* Boston: Small, Maynard, 1916.

Hedrick, Joan D. *Solitary Comrade: Jack London and His Work.* Chapel Hill: University of North Carolina Press, 1982.

Heflin, Wilson. "Melville's Celestial Navigation, and Dead Reckoning." *Melville Society Extracts* 29 (1977): 3.

Hemingway, Ernest. *By-Line: Ernest Hemingway.* Edited by William White. New York: Scribner's, 1967.

———. *Ernest Hemingway: Selected Letters, 1917–1961.* Edited by Carlos Baker. New York: Scribner's, 1981.

———. "The Good Lion." *Holiday,* Mar. 1951, pp. 50–51.

———. "The Great Blue River." *Holiday,* July 1949, pp. 60f. Reprinted in Hemingway, *By-Line: Ernest Hemingway.* Edited by William White. New York: Scribner's, 1967, pp. 403–16.

———. *Green Hills of Africa.* New York: Scribner's, 1953.

———. *Islands in the Stream.* New York: Scribner's, 1970.

———. *The Old Man and the Sea.* New York: Scribner's, 1952.

———. "On the Blue Water: A Gulf Stream Letter." *Esquire,* Apr. 1936, pp. 31f. Reprinted in Hemingway, *By-Line: Ernest Hemingway.* Edited by William White. New York: Scribner's, 1967, pp. 236–44.

———. "Out in the Stream: A Cuban Letter." *Esquire,* Aug. 1934, pp. 19f. Reprinted in Hemingway, *By-Line: Ernest Hemingway.* Edited by William White. New York: Scribner's, 1967, pp. 172–78.

———. *The Sun Also Rises.* New York: Scribner's, 1926.

———. "There She Breaches! Or Moby Dick Off the Morro." *Esquire,* May 1936, pp. 35f. Reprinted in Hemingway, *By-Line: Ernest Hemingway.* Edited by William White. New York: Scribner's, 1967, pp. 245–54.

———. *To Have and Have Not.* New York: Scribner's, 1937.

Hillway, Tyrus. "Melville as Amateur Zoologist." *Modern Language Quarterly* 12 (1951): 159–64.

Hofstadter, Richard. *Social Darwinism in America.* New York: Braziller, 1959.

Hunter, Allan. *Joseph Conrad and the Ethics of Darwinism.* London: Croom Helm, 1983.

Hunter, George M. "The Novels of the Sea." *Bookman* 31 (1910): 316–18.

International Seamen's Union of America. *The Red Record: A Brief Resume of Some of the Cruelties Perpetuated upon America at the Present Time.* A Supplement of *The Coast Seamen's Journal.* San Francisco: N.p., [1897?].

James, Henry. *The Notebooks of Henry James.* Edited by F. O. Matthiessen and Kenneth Murdock. New York: Oxford University Press, 1961.

James, William. *The Varieties of Religious Experience.* New York: Longmans, 1902.

———. *The Will to Believe and Other Essays in Popular Philosophy* and *Human Immortality: Two Supposed Objections to the Doctrine.* New York: Dover, 1960.

Jannasch, Holger W. "*Chemosynthesis:* The Nutritional Basis for Life at Deep-Sea Vents." *Oceanus* 27 (1984): 73–78.

Knight, Grant C. *The Strenuous Age in American Literature.* Chapel Hill: University of North Carolina Press, 1954.

Labor, Earle. *Jack London.* New York: Twayne, 1974.

Lawrence, D. H. *Studies in Classic American Literature.* 1923. Reprint. Garden City, N.Y.: Doubleday, 1953.

Levenson, J. C. Introduction. Stephen Crane, *Stephen Crane: Tales of Adventure.* Edited by Fredson Bowers. Charlottesville: University Press of Virginia, 1970. Vol. 5 of *The Works of Stephen Crane.* 10 vols. 1969–76, pp. xv–cxxxii.

Lewis, Charles Lee. *Books of the Sea: An Introduction to Nautical Literature.* Annapolis: Naval Institute Press, 1943.

Leyda, Jay. *The Melville Log: A Documentary Life of Herman Melville.* 2 vols. New York: Harcourt, 1951.

"Literature and Its Rewardings." *New York Times,* 26 Mar. 1915, p. 12.

London, Charmian. *The Book of Jack London.* 2 vols. New York: Century, 1920.

London, Jack. *Great Short Works of Jack London.* Edited by Earle Labor. New York: Harper, 1965.

———. *The Human Drift.* New York: Macmillan, 1917.

———. *John Barleycorn.* London: Bodley Head, 1964. Vol. 2 of *The Bodley Head Jack London.* Edited by Arthur Calder-Marsall. 4 vols. 1964–66.

———. *Martin Eden.* London: Bodley Head, 1965. Vol. 3 of *The Bodley Head Jack London.* 4 vols. 1964–66.

———. *Michael, Brother of Jerry.* New York: Macmillan, 1917.

———. *The Mutiny of the Elsinore.* New York: Collier, 1914.

———. *On the Makaloa Mat.* New York: Macmillan, 1919.

———. *The Sea-Wolf.* 1904. Edited by Matthew J. Bruccoli. Boston: Houghton Mifflin, Riverside Edition, 1964.

Lucid, Robert F. "The Influence of *Two Years Before the Mast* on Herman Melville." *American Literature* 31 (1959): 243–56.

Magner, Lois N. *A History of the Life Sciences.* New York: M. Dekker, 1979.

Mahan, Alfred T. *The Interest of America in Sea Power, Present and Future.* Boston: Little, Brown, 1898.

Martin, Jay. *Harvests of Change: American Literature, 1865–1914.* Englewood Cliffs, N.J.: Prentice-Hall, 1967.

Martin, Robert K. *Hero, Captain, and Stranger: Male Friendship, Social Critique, and Literary Form in the Sea Novels of Herman Melville.* Chapel Hill: University of North Carolina Press, 1986.

Martz, Louis L. "Wallace Stevens: The World as Meditation." In *Literature and Belief: The English Institute Essays for 1957,* edited by M. H. Abrams. New York: Columbia University Press, pp. 139–65. Reprinted in *Wallace Stevens: A Collection of Critical Essays,* edited by Marie Borroff. Englewood Cliffs, N.J.: Prentice-Hall, 1963, pp. 133–50.

Mason, Arthur. *The Cook and the Captain Bold.* Boston: Atlantic Monthly Press, 1924.

———. *The Flying Bo'sun: A Mystery of the Sea.* New York: Holt, 1920.

———. *Ocean Echoes.* New York: Holt, 1922.

Matthiessen, F. O. *American Renaissance*. New York: Oxford University Press, 1941.

Matthiessen, Peter. *At Play in the Fields of the Lord*. New York: Random House, 1965.

————. *Blue Meridian*. New York: Random House, 1971.

————. *Far Tortuga*. New York: Random House, 1975.

————. "Horse Latitudes." *Anteus* 29 (1978): 7–14.

————. *Men's Lives*. New York: Random House, 1986.

————. *Partisans*. New York: Viking, 1955.

————. *Race Rock*. New York: Harper, 1954.

————. *Raditzer*. New York: Viking, 1961.

Mayr, Ernst. *The Growth of Biological Thought: Diversity, Evolution and Inheritance*. Cambridge, Mass.: Belknap Press of Harvard University Press, 1982.

McClintock, James I. *White Logic: Jack London's Short Stories*. Grand Rapids: Wolf House, 1975.

McFee, William. *Aliens*. Garden City, N.Y.: Doubleday, Page, 1918.

————. *Casuals of the Sea: The Voyage of a Soul*. Garden City, N.Y.: Doubleday, Page, 1918.

————. *Derelicts*. London: Faber, 1939.

————. Introduction. *Great Sea Stories of Modern Times*. Edited by William McFee. New York: McBride, 1953.

————. Introduction. *Two Years Before the Mast* by Richard Henry Dana. New York: Limited Editions Club, 1947.

————. *Swallowing the Anchor*. London: William Heinemann, 1925.

————. Review of *Mother Sea* by Felix Riesenberg. *New York Herald Tribune Books*, 12 Feb. 1933, p. 8.

Melville, Herman. *Clarel: A Poem and Pilgrimage in the Holy Land*. Edited by Walter E. Bezanson. New York: Hendricks House, 1960.

————. *Collected Poems of Herman Melville*. Edited by Howard P. Vincent. Chicago: Packard, 1947.

————. *Great Short Works of Herman Melville*. Edited by Warner Berthoff. New York: Harper, 1970.

————. *Israel Potter*. Evanston: Northwestern University Press, 1982.

————. *John Marr and Other Sailors with Some Sea-Pieces*. N.p.: Norwood Editions, 1976.

————. *Mardi*. Evanston: Northwestern University Press, 1970.

————. *Moby-Dick*. Edited by Harrison Hayford and Hershel Parker. Norton Critical Edition. New York: Norton, 1967.

————. *White-Jacket*. Evanston: Northwestern University Press, 1970.

Meyers, Jeffrey, ed. *Hemingway: The Critical Heritage*. London: Routledge & Kegan Paul, 1982.

"Morgan Robertson Dies Standing Up." *New York Times*, 25 Mar. 1915, p. 1.

Morgan Robertson the Man. New York: Metropolitan Magazine, 1915.

Morison, Samuel Eliot. Review of *An Instrument of the Gods* by Lincoln Colcord. *Yale Review* 14 (1924): 195–96.

Morris, Wright. *The Territory Ahead*. New York: Harcourt, Brace, 1958.

Mortland, Donald F. "Lincoln Colcord: At Sea and at Home." *Colby Library Quarterly* 19 (1983): 125–43.

————, ed. *Sea Stories from Searsport to Singapore: Selected Works of Lincoln Colcord.* Thorndike, Maine: North Country Press, 1987.

Nordau, Max. *Degeneration.* New York: Appleton, 1895.

Norris, Frank. *Moran of the Lady Letty.* New York: Doubleday & McClure, 1898.

O'Brien, Edward J. *The Advance of the American Short Story.* New York: Dodd, Mead, 1923.

————. "The Best Fifty Short Stories of 1916." *Bookman* 44 (1917): 563–67.

O'Hanlon, Redmond. *Joseph Conrad and Charles Darwin: The Influence of Scientific Thought on Conrad's Fiction.* Edinburgh: Salamander, 1984.

O'Neill, Eugene. *The Plays of Eugene O'Neill.* 3 vols. New York: Random House, 1951.

Parker, Hershel, ed. *The Recognition of Herman Melville: Selected Criticism since 1846.* Ann Arbor: University of Michigan Press, 1967.

Parker, Hershel, and Harrison Hayford, eds. *Moby-Dick as Doubloon: Essays and Extracts (1851–1970).* New York: Norton, 1970.

Philbrick, Thomas. Introduction. *Two Years Before the Mast* by Richard Henry Dana, Jr. Edited by Thomas Philbrick. New York: Penguin, 1981.

————. *James Fenimore Cooper and the Development of American Sea Fiction.* Cambridge, Mass.: Harvard University Press, 1961.

————. Review of *La mer et le roman américain dans la première moitié du dix-neuvième siècle* by Jeanne-Marie Santraud. *American Literature* 45 (1973): 456.

Plimpton, George. "The Craft of Fiction in *Far Tortuga.*" Interview with Peter Matthiessen. *Paris Review* 60 (1974): 79–82.

Poirier, Richard. *A World Elsewhere: The Place of Style in American Literature.* New York: Oxford University Press, 1966.

Riesenberg, Felix. "'Communists' at Sea." *Nation* 145 (23 Oct. 1937): 432–33.

————. *Living Again: An Autobiography.* Garden City, N.Y.: Doubleday, 1937.

————. *Mother Sea.* New York: Claude Kendall, 1933.

————. *Under Sail.* New York: Macmillan, 1918.

Riesenberg, Felix, and Archie Binns. *The Maiden Voyage.* New York: John Day, 1931.

Robertson, Morgan. *Down to the Sea.* New York: Harper, 1905.

————. *Futility: Or the Wreck of the Titan.* 1898. Republished as *The Wreck of the Titan; Or Futility.* New York: McClure's, n.d.

————. *Land Ho!* New York: Harper, 1905.

————. *Over the Border.* New York: McClure's, n.d.

————. *Shipmates.* New York: Appleton, 1901.

————. *Sinful Peck.* New York: McClure's, n.d.

————. *Three Laws and the Golden Rule.* New York: McKinlay, Stone and Mackenzie, n.d.

————. *Where Angels Fear to Tread.* New York: McClure's, n.d.

————. "Will Battleships Be Obsolete?" *World's Work* 9 (1904): 5515–21.

Romig, Walter. *The Book of Catholic Authors.* 3d ser. Kingsport, Tenn.: Kingsport Press, 1945.

Russell, W. Clark. "Sea Stories." 1884. Excerpted in *The Recognition of Herman Melville: Selected Criticism since 1846,* edited by Hershel Parker. Ann Arbor: University of Michigan Press, 1967, pp. 117–20.

Russett, Cynthia Eagle. *Darwin in America: The Intellectual Response, 1865–1912*. San Francisco: Freeman, 1976.

Ryan, Paul R. "The *Titanic*: Lost and Found (1912–1985)." *Oceanus* 28 (1985–86): 4–14.

Santraud, Jeanne-Marie. *La mer et le roman américain dans la première moitié du dix-neuvième siècle*. Paris: Didier, 1972.

Sinclair, Andrew. *Jack: A Biography of Jack London*. New York: Harper, 1977.

Slocum, Joshua. *Sailing Alone Around the World and Voyage of the Liberdade*. Edited by Walter Magnes Teller. New York: Colliers, 1958.

Slotkin, Richard. *Regeneration through Violence: The Mythology of the American Frontier, 1600–1860*. Middletown, Conn.: Wesleyan University Press, 1973.

Smith, Henry Nash. *Virgin Land: The American West as Symbol and Myth*. 1950. Reprint. New York: Vintage, 1957.

Smith, Myron J., Jr., and Robert C. Weller. *Sea Fiction Guide*. Metuchen, N.J.: Scarecrow, 1976.

Springer, Haskell. "The Nautical *Walden*." *New England Quarterly* 57 (1984): 84–97.

Stallman, Robert W. *Stephen Crane*. New York: Braziller, 1968.

Tanner, Tony. *The Reign of Wonder: Naivety and Reality in American Literature*. Cambridge: Cambridge University Press, 1965.

Taylor, Paul S. *The Sailors' Union of the Pacific*. 1923. Reprint. New York: Arno, 1971.

Thoreau, Henry David. *Walden and Civil Disobedience*. Edited by Owen Thomas. Norton Critical Edition. New York: Norton, 1966.

Tomlinson, H. M., ed. *Great Sea Stories of All Nations*. Garden City, N.Y.: Garden City Publishing, 1937.

Traven, B. *The Death Ship: The Story of an American Sailor*. New York: Knopf, 1934.

Turner, Frederick Jackson. *The Frontier in American History*. 1920. Reprint. New York: Holt, 1967.

Vincent, Howard P. *The Trying-Out of Moby-Dick*. Boston: Houghton Mifflin, 1949.

Walker, Dale L., and James G. Sisson III. *The Fiction of Jack London: A Chronological Bibliography*. El Paso: Texas Western Press, 1972.

Walker, Franklin. *Jack London and the Klondike: The Genesis of an American Writer*. San Marino, Calif.: Huntington Library, 1966.

Ward, J. A. "The Function of the Cetological Chapters in *Moby-Dick*." *American Literature* 28 (1956): 164–83.

Watson, Charles N., Jr. *The Novels of Jack London: A Reappraisal*. Madison: University of Wisconsin Press, 1983.

West, Ray B. "The Biological Trap." *Sewanee Review* 55 (1945): 120–35. Reprinted in *Hemingway: A Collection of Critical Essays*, edited by Robert P. Weeks. Englewood Cliffs, N.J.: Prentice-Hall, 1962.

Wharton, Donald P., ed. *In the Trough of the Sea: Selected Sea-Deliverance Narratives, 1610–1766*. Westport, Conn.: Greenwood, 1979.

Whitman, Walt. *Leaves of Grass*. Edited by Sculley Bradley and Harold W. Blodgett. Norton Critical Edition. New York: Norton, 1973.

Williams, Blanche Colton. *Our Short Story Writers*. New York: Dodd, Mead, 1929.

Woodbridge, Hensley C., et al. *Jack London: A Bibliography.* Georgetown, Calif.: Talisman, 1966.

Young, Philip. *Ernest Hemingway: A Reconsideration.* University Park: Pennsylvania State University Press, 1966.

Ziff, Larzer. *Literary Democracy: The Declaration of Cultural Independence in America.* New York: Viking, 1981.

Chronology

1851	*Moby-Dick* (Melville); *Flying Cloud* sails for Cape Horn and San Francisco
1855	*Israel Potter* (Melville); Panama Railway opened
1856	*The Piazza Tales* (Melville)
1857	Joseph Conrad born
1859	The *Origin of Species* (Darwin)
1860	Melville sails around Cape Horn on the *Meteor,* captained by his brother Thomas
1861	Morgan Robertson born (1861–1915)
1866	Thornton Jenkins Hains born (1866–?)
1868	James Brendan Connolly born (1868–1957)
1869	*Glory of the Seas* launched; transcontinental railway opened
1871	Stephen Crane born (1871–1900); *The Descent of Man, and Selection in Relation to Sex* (Darwin)
1876	Jack London born (1876–1916); Arthur Mason born (1876–?)
1879	Felix Riesenberg born (1879–1939); Bill Adams born (1879–?)
1881	William McFee born (1881–1966)
1883	Lincoln Colcord born at sea, off Cape Horn (1883–1947)

1887	Richard Matthews Hallet born (1887–1967)
1888	Eugene O'Neill born (1888–1953); *John Marr and Other Sailors* (Melville)
1890	*The Influence of Sea Power upon History* (Alfred T. Mahan)
1891	*Billy Budd, Sailor* finished; Melville dies
1897	*Commodore* sinks; *The Red Record* (1897?)
1898	"The Open Boat"; *Futility* (Robertson)
1899	Hemingway born (1899–1961); Archie Binns born (1899–1971)
1900	*Sailing Alone Around the World* (Joshua Slocum)
1903	*The Strife of the Sea* (Hains)
1904	*The Sea-Wolf* (London)
1906	*The Voyage of the Arrow* (Hains)
1909	Joshua Slocum disappears at sea; *Martin Eden* (London)
1912	*Titanic* sinks; *The Drifting Diamond* (Colcord)
1912–13	Jack London sails around Cape Horn on *Dirigo*; Richard Matthews Hallet sails around Cape of Good Hope on *Juteopolis*
1914	*Mutiny of the Elsinore* (London); *Game of Life and Death* (Colcord); Panama Canal opened
1915	*The Lady Aft* (Hallet); *Lusitania* sunk
1916	*Trial by Fire* (Hallet)
1918	*Casuals of the Sea* (McFee)
1920	*The Flying Bo'sun* (Mason)
1922	*An Instrument of the Gods* (Colcord); *The Hairy Ape* (O'Neill); *Glory of the Seas* burned for salvage
1923	*Fenceless Meadows* (Adams)
1924	*The Cook and the Captain Bold* (Mason); *Billy Budd, Sailor* published

1927   Peter Matthiessen born

1933   *Mother Sea* (Riesenberg)

1934   *Lightship* (Binns)

1937   *To Have and Have Not* (Hemingway)

1945–47   Hemingway writes "Bimini"

1950   Hemingway writes "Cuba"

1951   Hemingway writes "The Sea Chase"

1952   *The Old Man and the Sea* (Hemingway)

1954   *Race Rock* (Matthiessen)

1961   *Raditzer* (Matthiessen)

1970   *Islands in the Stream* (Hemingway)

1975   *Far Tortuga* (Matthiessen)

Index